He Mele O Hawaii

A Song of Hawaii

Produced in cooperation with the
Chamber of Commerce of Hawaii

He Mele O Hawaii

A Song of Hawaii

A Celebration
of Life and Work
in the Aloha State

BY SCOTT C.S. STONE WITH PHOTOGRAPHS BY BOB ABRAHAM

Jostens Publishing Group, Inc.
Book Division
Jack C. Cherbo, President

He Mele O Hawaii: A Song of Hawaii
Merlyn Holmes, Editorial and Design
Lee Cline, Editorial and Layout
Roger Coryell, Editorial
Abby Weltman, Layout
Guava Graphics, Layout

All photos, other than those appearing in the *Partners in Hawaii* profiles, are by Bob Abraham.

Library of Congress Catalog Card Number: 93-78514
ISBN: 1-882933-01-X

In Dedication to
Robert B. Robinson

*E*ven before he assumed the helm of the Chamber of Commerce of Hawaii, Bob Robinson was a dynamo in the local business community. He served as Chairman of Pacific Concrete and Rock Company, Ltd., and as deputy director of the Hawaii State Department of Economic Development; he held several industrial relations positions, and was partner in a management consulting firm. His leadership roles in the community range widely, from chairman of the Hawaii Tourism Conference to president of Junior Achievement.

But it is his 15-year tenure as president and chief executive officer of the Chamber that thrust Robinson into the very heart of the business community; he became a champion of logical growth, a man whose acumen and ethics set standards, a man whose personal commitment to Hawaii never wavered. Bob Robinson is due a large measure of gratitude from his community, and as at least a partial tribute we who are involved in this book are proud and pleased to dedicate it to him.

And to wish him a fair wind and following sea as he returns to private life.

CONTENTS

Foreword & Acknowledgements 10

PART I

A Song of Hawaii

1

Prelude 14

2

Ka Moana: *The Ocean* 24

3

Ka Aina: *The Land* 44

4

Na Po'e: *The People* 62

5

Holo I Mua: *To Go Forward* 88

6

Reprise 106

PART II

Partners in Hawaii

7

Networks, Professions & Services *112*

8

Business & Finance *130*

9

Building Hawaii *142*

10

The Marketplace *154*

11

Quality of Life *172*

Bibliography 188

Index 189

Foreword & Acknowledgements

No business enterprise operates in a vacuum but in context with the larger community. This is true particularly in Hawaii, where businesses function not only as a part of the present community but as outgrowths of the political and social dynamics of the past. This book deals with the economics of Hawaii today but attempts to show how local firms evolved and how a progression of events has led to the islands' development. A part of the book points to some possible futures. *He Mele o Hawaii* thus becomes a song of Hawaii with far-reaching lyrics.

The book, inevitably, is subjective and reflects the author's own viewpoints based on information gathered and a life spent mostly in the islands. No writer operates in a vacuum either, and I dare say that the reader will find some things to agree with, and some to argue with. When one writes a book, the strengths and weaknesses become public and subject to challenge, and what goes with the territory is the necessity for the writer to take responsibility for the book's contents. I do so take such responsibility, while at the same time acknowledging the contributions of many other people. No blame must accrue to them for any errors.

This book would never have materialized without the enthusiasm of the former president of the Chamber of Commerce of Hawaii, Bob Robinson, who is acknowledged properly elsewhere in these pages. Also at the Chamber, we received invaluable help from Lois Faison, a shrewd and dynamic lady, and Iris Lactawen Laa. A very special thanks goes to Tatsuko "Tats" Honjo, Vice President and Secretary at the Chamber, who provided splendid assistance and advice. For outstanding support, we are happy to acknowledge Gerald M. Czarnecki, Chairman, President, and Chief Executive Officer of Bank of America. Most enthusiastic were the editor and production staff, where uncommon expertise was the commonality, and they have my thanks. During the writing of this book I enjoyed both the help and the humor of multifaceted Roger Coryell, whose research assistance was of considerable value. To work with Bob Abraham and his staff at Pacific Rim Productions, particularly the talented Mary Van de Ven, was a pleasure. My wife, Walelu, lent her usual strong support.

I am pleased also to offer a heartfelt *mahalo nui loa* to the distinguished men who contributed short articles for inclusion in this book, and these articles enhance the book because of their insight and

opinions. My gratitude, then, to Dr. John P. Craven, Director of the Law of the Sea Institute; J.W.A. Buyers, Chairman and President of C. Brewer and Company, Limited; Stanley Hong, President of the Hawaii Visitors Bureau; Myron Thompson, Member of the Board of Trustees of the Kamehameha Schools/ Bishop Estate; Dr. David L. Ramsour, Senior Vice President and Chief Economist of the Bank of Hawaii; and Dr. Michel Oksenberg, President of the East-West Center.

Others too numerous to mention were helpful in offering data and background, but the following individuals must be acknowledged and thanked:

Gordon Sakamoto of the Department of Business, Economics & Tourism, for his guidance and knowledge, and other state officials, notably Linda McCreary, Jack Wiers, Dr. Craig D. MacDonald, W. Ross Smith, Marilyn E. Kali, Sukil Suh, Janet Zakahi, Jennifer Styer, C. Richard Fassler, Barbara A. Hastings, Rich Budnick, Ilima A. Piianaia, Letitia N. Uyehara, Ester Ueda, Leo Asuncion, Patrick Demerath, Gregory Barbour, Allen Choy, Stephen R. Lee, and the University of Hawaii's Merle Kanemori.

Also, Robert H. Hughes, former president of the Hawaii Sugar Planters Association, Dole Foods' Carol Aramaki, Robert L. Dawdy of Matson, Elisa Yadao of Kamehameha Schools/Bishop Estate, Bill Bass of the High Technology Development Corporation, Paul S. O'Leary of the Economic Development Corporation of Honolulu, AT&T's William H. Martin, and Carrie Hyun and Patrick K.S. Mau of GTE Hawaiian Tel.

Scott C.S. Stone

PART I

A Song of Hawaii

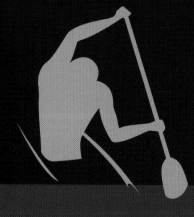

By Scott C.S. Stone
Photographs by Bob Abraham

1
Prelude

↑ From wind-hewn cliffs to the tops of grand mountains to varicolored beaches to deep valleys — the land pleases the eye and calms the heart.

A cold wind rising far to the northeast and moving unchecked across entire latitudes of ocean arrives finally at the most remote landfall on earth; in its passing the wind has become gentled, so in touching the islands that lie some 20° north of the equator the wind becomes a benediction, a cool and welcome blessing. Transiting the archipelago the wind moves along the ramparts of the mountains and dips into deep valleys and sweeps across fields of sugarcane and pineapple and macadamia nuts, across acres of fruit and flowers and coffee. It sets up harmonics in the crowns of the trees with their euphonious names: ohia and kamani and lauhala. When it is parted by the soaring and majestic volcanoes, the wind meets again out to sea in the lee of the mountains.

Palpable but ethereal, the wind is one of the forces that lie deep in the psyche of the people who live in the islands. Another force is the mightiest ocean on earth, surrounding the islands and washing up on the coast of California and the coast of China. Still another force is the islands themselves, dramatic and beautiful, land which gives the islanders their strong sense of place. Aloha aina, they say, love the land.

And what a land.

One hundred and thirty-two islands, reefs and shoals stretching a little more than fifteen hundred miles northwest to southeast. Seamounts, the tops of volcanoes. Eight major islands, seven of them populated, one of them forbidden. On the largest of the islands are two of the tallest mountains in the Pacific, on another an awesome canyon striped with the striations of age. All the islands have their wonders and their individual histories and legends, and here the legends are as important as the history.

The islands share a commonality of grandeur, lands born in fire and upheaval, lands that lay for millennia awaiting the coming of plants and insects and birds. And one day an odd-shaped sail appeared on the horizon south of the largest island, and the long isolation was shattered like the breaking of glass, a sound that resonates through history. The first men who came brought their gods and their morals, their society, views of death, concerns with everyday life. Because they were the first they earned the right to give the islands a name, and they named them for an ancient homeland, the culmination of a dream.

Other men followed, populating the main islands of the archipelago. Geography and circumstances and the clash of human natures and the immutable laws of nature produced a turbulent history and haunting stories of courage and love and treachery. As relentless as the tides, change came with the passing years. The islands were initially a scattering of petty

↑ Makani Hoʻolapa, Hawaii's 3.2 megawatt wind turbine.

chiefdoms, then a kingdom, a republic, a territory of a parent power, and finally a state of a powerful republic of states.

The people changed as well, merging their identities while still celebrating them, becoming islanders. An ideal emerged, and the people clung to it in a climate of acceptance as real in its way as the trade winds or the sea or the green islands. It was an ideal of tolerance. The islanders worked this out for themselves, but it stood as a model to the world, and as the island people lived their lives and played out their destinies the very name of their place began to stand for the flowering of the ideal. On the islands *they talked of aloha, meaning love and acceptance. The islands themselves they called Hawaii.*

Hawaii.

Today men climb to the tops of the island mountains and stare over an empty ocean to the southeast, toward the Marquesas and Society Islands, homelands of the discoverers. Then it is easy to be awed by the enormity of the Polynesian voyages, epic sea-treks that were taking place at a time when few, if any, Europeans would leave the sight of their own coasts.

The Polynesians accomplished more than a one-way voyage. In a series of crossings between Kahiki (Tahiti) and Hawaii, they became colonists and turned the new islands into something profound. During some 1,500 years of isolation the Polynesians underwent a subtle evolution of language, customs, forms of government; they became Hawaiians. And it was as Hawaiians that they stood on their shore one fateful day and watched two tall ships appear offshore, ships with square sails, ships bearing men with white faces.

The end of their isolation had direct and immediate consequences for the Hawaiians; it killed many of them with diseases for which they had no immunity so that their numbers dropped from 300,000 before those square sails appeared to about 50,000. The new ideas and customs changed their spiritual lives as well as their daily lives, sometimes for the better but sometimes violently.

Others came because of the fecundity of the land, which produced pineapple and sugar and other crops and demanded more workers than were available. From thousands of miles and from exotic lands those men and women came to harvest, and stayed to build lives among others who spoke and dressed differently and often thought differently. Love, color-blind and unfettered, resulted in intermarriages that created a people who enjoyed their differences as much as their similarities.

In part because of the ideal of tolerance, partly because of the immensely enjoyable quality of life, partly because of the geographic position of the islands, and partly because the islands held all the allure of the storied old South Seas, men and women found their way to this distant landfall. Preachers came, and plunderers, scholars and beachcombers, traders and planters and farmers. In time came the stockbrokers and computer programmers and people who worked in fiber optics and superconductors. The islands which once slept in a splendid and indolent isolation moved at an increasing tempo toward an inevitable conjunction with the era.

The economies that sustained the people sprang from the same elemental forces that influenced their emotions and outlooks. Ka moana, the ocean, remained a source of food and a pathway to other places. Hawaiians were at home on the sea,

↑ Waikiki Beach, Oahu.

comfortable in it, their hearts attuned to its moods and pulsating to the rhythm of its tides. In old Hawaii they farmed the seas, setting up aquaculture systems that were sophisticated and workable and became the inspiration for a modern industry.

Other industries grew around whaling, fishing, and the movement of goods. One of the earliest and most respectable citizens of the islands was the trader, and often he had to double as a sea captain. The trader who found himself in a shop along Fort Street in Honolulu this year might find himself in Canton next year, or Mazatlan. Industries grew from the sea and modernized as the years passed, so that the ocean was the foundation for sports and recreation even as it provided for commercial fish harvesting.

The land, ka aina, also was a source of food, and of medicinal plants, building material, clothing, flowers for adornment. If in Polynesian lore the sky was father, then the earth was the nurturing mother, a dependable resource to be cherished, imbued with a mystical quality. The Hawaiians understood the value of land in the middle of an ocean, knowing it was the basis for their very lives. They understood how to husband the land's bounty. They knew that to provide for all their needs, a family must have land that stretched from the mountains to the sea, to give them the variety of plants and trees and soil as well as access to the ocean; they called this an ahupuaa, and many land divisions in Hawaii today conform to the wedge-shaped strips of land reaching from upland to the ocean. The fertile fields produced diversified agriculture for local consumption and vast tonnage of products which could be exported to bring new revenue to the islands.

A magnificent resource was the pooled skills of na po'e, the people. Each immigrant group brought talents and trends that were woven into the social and economic fabric of the islands, and gave that tapestry its distinctive hues. The Chinese brought their attachment to land as well as foods and herbs; the Japanese came with a strong drive for education and civic service; the Filipinos came with music and dance and an affinity for growing things; the Portuguese added a penchant for colorful customs and a deep religiosity that greatly enhanced island society; the Caucasians brought their drive and their business sense; and the myriad other arrivals contributed individually and collectively.

To all this, the Hawaiians added their own ability to take any segment of another culture and make it uniquely Hawaiian. It was a propensity that kept their own culture alive and gave the islands their distinctive flavor.

A historian today can look back and note milestones in the annals of the islands that were dictated in large part by the economies. One powerful, wily, and tough — some say treacherous — Hawaiian united all the islands under his command by 1810, and the era of Kamehameha I was a time when commoners practiced subsistence economics and Kamehameha traded in sandalwood to America and China. Kamehameha I's death in 1819 coincided with the advent of the whaling era, which lasted until 1870 and provided a variety of jobs on the islands. The end of whaling helped usher in the era of the planters, and sugar barons were among the more

→ Hula dancer,
Waimea Falls Park,
North Shore, Oahu.

↑ **Wailua Falls with rainbow, Kauai.**

affluent and powerful islanders for decades. Wafting across the years was the aromatic smell of coffee and the earthy odor of diversified agriculture.

Recently, the islands have become vigorous in the exporting of fruits and flowers and lead the world in the planting, harvesting, and marketing of macadamia nuts. A U.S. military presence on the islands has been a strong — in many years the strongest — contributor to island economies. There is a new impetus toward research and development, oceanographic studies, the positioning of the most powerful telescopes in the world on top of a Hawaiian volcanic mountain; there has been a concomitant movement to position Hawaii as a link between East and West, as a hub of the Pacific.

What is considered today the islands' most powerful industry is driven by people who come to the islands with no intention of staying. Statehood in 1959 and the introduction of the jet engine brought about incredible increases in the number of visitors. They come to enjoy a lifestyle still as romantic as any on earth, swimming and surfing under a great yellow Hawaiian sun, dancing on lanais under a soft Hawaiian moon to melodies that are familiar throughout much of the world. They continue to bring new ideas to the islands and take back with them a sense of the ideal, an awareness that tolerance is possible.

The islands have moved from the age of sail to the age of satellites, from a time when the Polynesian discoverers crossed thousands of miles of open ocean without charts to a time when movements of stars and planets can be predicted. The political history spanned years of petty chieftains and monarchs and elected officials. The history also includes a bloody Sunday in December when the islands came under an attack that launched America — to which Hawaii was attached but still did not belong — into world-wide conflict.

While the common denominator was change, still there were constants. The islands continued an old tradition of welcoming strangers and turning them into friends. There was a willingness to contribute to the United States, which had made Hawaii a territory, and an eagerness to be accepted as full citizens via statehood. As the population grew there were increasing intermarriages, so that no racial group seemed dominant; the people were clever

↑ Orchid plant farm.

enough to preserve ancestral traits because they had value, but also to merge them with others.

Other important constants remain: the sky is still a vaulting blueness, the air unpolluted and fresh as it moves beneath the trade winds. The old, trackless ocean still washes the beaches and whispers of distant shores. The deep and verdant valleys remain enchanting places

↑ Ho'olaule'a, Iolani Palace.

replete with hidden bowers and romantic stories. In the morning freshness the mountains are green and glorious, and then the sun comes out of the sea and splinters on the rim of the massifs and sends light dancing across the wavelets of the harbors.

Not the least striking feature of the Hawaiian Islands is the intensity of the love for the land shared by all its people. Whether born here as na keiki o ka aina, children of the land, or ventured here like the wind from some distant and colder place, the people of Hawaii today treasure their heritage, but in their deep heart's core they are all islanders.

Each generation has added a grace note to the harmony of the islands, part of a melody that echoes the primitive rhythms of the past and blends with today's lilting sounds. The lyrics tell of an incandescent future, a song of Hawaii that will be heard across the seas and down the years.

2
Ka Moana

The Ocean

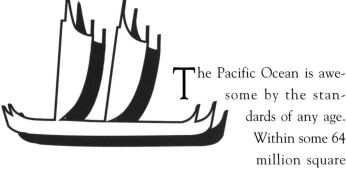

The Pacific Ocean is awesome by the standards of any age. Within some 64 million square miles is 46 percent of the earth's water. At one point, in the Marianas, its floor is more than six miles deep, and to cross it by air from, say, San Francisco to Singapore, is a flight of more than 8,000 miles. In its far reaches, islets are born and die, sometimes unobserved and unrecorded, and storms can whip across it for days before blowing themselves out. From either pole to the equator, the winds reverse themselves, and along the equator itself there are often no winds at all, and seamen still dependent on sail look at the sky and the horizon and the dead calm of the sea and shake their heads.

The Polynesians were on intimate terms with this mighty force. They did not know that 70 percent of the human body is water as is 70 percent of the earth, but they may have sensed it, sensed the correlation between the pull of the tides and the flowing of their blood. Surely their eyes gladdened when looking on the sea in all its moods and its subtle, shifting colors. And if death sometimes lay beneath its surface, more often it was life in the form of food and joy in the thrill of the hunt.

In double-hulled canoes carrying basic provisions, the Polynesians sailed from the southeast about 500 A.D., very likely from the Marquesas Islands. They observed the flight of birds going northward, the set of waves, drifting wood and its direction, the rise and setting of stars. The astonishing thing was that they never turned back, and on one glorious morning they sighted land, more than two thousand miles from their point of departure. They came ashore on the island they named Hawaii, near what is now the southernmost point of the United States, *Ka Lae* (The Cape), known locally as South Point. They had reached the apex of what we call

← **Indisputably, the Polynesians had more than a thousand years on the islands. Their own evolution from wandering Polynesians into Hawaiians was subtle but profound, and involved nuances of language and custom as well as new folklore involving volcanoes and snow.**

today the Polynesian Triangle, made up of New Zealand, Easter Island, and Hawaii. They also had reached the apex of their discoveries, and afterward there would be few if any major discoveries in eastern Polynesia. Hawaii was the realization of a dream.

Always, there was the relationship to the sea, and in Hawaii there sprang up a type of fish harvesting process that was unique to these islands, found nowhere else in Polynesia: the building of enclosures to trap fish. In today's terminology, it is known as aquaculture.

The enclosures were not flimsy affairs, but rock-walled and containing gates where fish could get in but not out, and one estimate is that it took some 8,000 men to build a fishpond. The fishponds varied in size, but an average pond covered some 18 acres. Before the arrival in 1778 of Captain James Cook, the English explorer-navigator who discovered Hawaii for the West, there were close to 400 fishponds on the islands, and protein from fish was a staple of the Hawaiian diet. The fish supplemented bananas and taro, sweet potatoes and coconut, dogs and chicken and, to a lesser degree, pigs.

In 1819–1820 the *kapu* system was broken, and the fishponds began to fall into disuse. By 1901, 104 ponds produced a harvest of 680,000 pounds of fish. The industry languished until the 1960s, when research began on oyster cultivation and mullet farming, along with hatching studies on fresh-water prawns from Malaysia. By 1978 there were 20 farmers raising prawns, and Hawaii led the world in prawn culture. This success led to the culture of other species such as oysters, mullet, milkfish, and Chinese catfish.

With its warm waters and its mid-Pacific location – allowing access to markets in Asia and the U.S. mainland – aquaculture has grown into a promising source of revenue. It is limited only by the cost of land and the denial of entry to the islands of some exotic fish which may damage Hawaii's fragile environment.

However, by 1989, Hawaii's 47 aqua-farmers were

↑ **Pokai Bay.**

raising 35 different products in fresh, brackish, and salt water with a variety of systems. More then a million pounds were produced, with a value of more than $6 million. Adding the $14 million in research, training, and technology activities, the value of the industry came to more than $21 million. Two years later there was a significant increase: commercial production soared to $9.2 million, a 35 percent gain, and research and technology activities stabilized at $13.9 million.

Aquaculture's future in Hawaii is promising in terms of harvesting new species, and the industry is expected to continue to attract federal funds for research. Additionally, expertise from Hawaii will continue to be exported to Asia and Central and South America, as funds for research into global aquaculture development continue to pour from the World Bank, the Asian Development Bank, and the United Nations. Simultaneously, there has been

HAWAII AT A GLANCE

Hawaii was discovered by Polynesian voyagers about 500 A.D., and for the West by British explorer-navigator Captain James Cook in 1778.

There are eight major islands — Kauai, Oahu (where Honolulu is located), Niihau (privately owned and generally off-limits), Molokai, Lanai, Maui, Kahoolawe (an uninhabited target complex), and the Big Island.

Hawaii's de facto population in 1992 was approximately 1.2 million, with a statewide population density of about 194 people per square mile. The median age is 32.6, and life expectancy is 77.03 years for males, 80.92 for females.

Ethnic groups according to a recent survey: Caucasians, 24 percent; Japanese, 22 percent; mixed races primarily part-Hawaiian, 33 percent. Other major groups include Chinese, Filipinos, Koreans, Puerto Ricans, other Pacific Islanders, Southeast Asians.

There are two levels of government: state and county. A governor and lieutenant governor are joined by a bicameral legislature, 41 members in the House and 25 in the Senate, which meets annually. There are four counties, each with an elected mayor and council.

There are six English and three foreign language (or bilingual) newspapers, 52 radio stations, 21 television stations, and eight cable television companies. Hawaii currently accesses 22 communications satellites and expects to reach 35 by 1995. The islands link the U.S. mainland and Asia through an undersea fiber-optic cable capable of 40,000 simultaneous conversations or transactions.

Hawaii's unemployment rate is 2.8 percent, with a range by island from 2.4 to 10.3 percent. The civilian labor force totals approximately 580,000. The average annual earnings of wage and salary workers is $23,156.

There are 7l unions, the principal ones being the AFL-CIO, Teamsters, and the International Longshoremen's and Warehousemen's Union (ILWU). Membership is more than 160,000.

Hawaii's major source of income is from the visitor industry. Almost 7 million people visited Hawaii in 1991 and spent more than $9 billion. Daily expenditures averaged $137 for westbound visitors, $294 for Japanese visitors. Some 4.4 million visitors came from the U.S. mainland, 1.4 million from Japan, and 318,000 from Canada, the three leading sources of visitors.

The visitors had access to seven national parks, 77 state parks, 582 county parks, 65 golf courses, 279 public tennis courts, 1,600 recognized surfing sites and about 25 miles of sandy beaches.

The second-ranking source of income in Hawaii's economy is federal expenditures at about $6 billion, with defense expenditures alone at $3.2 billion. There are more than 110,000 military personnel and dependents on the islands.

Agriculture is Hawaii's third-highest source of income. Sugar produced $214 million in sales, pineapple $99 million. Flowers and nursery products totalled $70 million. The value of crop and livestock sales reached $275 million (not counting sugar and pineapple). There are 710 farms in Hawaii.

Hawaii has 10 banks with 199 locations, six savings and loan associations with 146 locations, and four trust companies with seven branches. There are 47,000 corporations and partnerships registered in Hawaii. Hawaii's Gross State Product is about $32 billion.

Imports from foreign nations are about $2.3 billion; exports from the islands to foreign countries reach $512 million. (Figures refer to merchandise through the Honolulu Customs District.) Hawaii's leading trade partner is Japan. Its Foreign Trade Zone and five subzones housed 395 companies in one recent year.

Hawaii has seven commercial airports, 15 airports that are general aviation, military, or semi-private, and 13 civilian heliports. Airlines and air taxis carry about 10 million passengers inter-island, and some 75,000 tons of cargo in a given year. In 1990, more than 7 million overseas passengers arrived by air, while overseas air cargo was 169,000 tons.

There were 1,700 documented vessels in the state in 1990, and about 14,000 undocumented. Overseas vessels brought 17,500 passengers to Hawaii last year. Received cargo was more than 11 million tons from overseas and 6 million inter-island.

In a recent year, 28,000 building permits were issued in the state with an estimated value of $2.4 billion. The median selling price of a single-family home on Oahu during 1990 was $352,000 (based on Multiple Listing Service data). For condominium units the figure was $187,000.

Hawaii spends upwards of $2 billion a year for fuel and electricity. Ninety percent of energy needs are met by imported petroleum. The state has become one of the nation's leaders in the development, use, and continuing search for alternate energy. There are both gas and electric utilities.

Hawaii became the 50th state of the union in 1959.

↑ The "people of many islands," the Polynesians, worked their way down the Asian land mass, and at a propitious moment some 40,000 years ago stood facing a new element, the sea. In a feat unequalled by any other seafaring people, they crossed the Pacific and discovered major land areas — Samoa and Tonga and the Marquesas, Tahiti and the Cook Islands and New Zealand. Their crowning achievement was Hawaii. In a 1987 recreation of the Polynesians' first voyage, pictured above, thousands of people volunteered to man the *Hokule'a*.

increasing interest in preserving the remaining 60-odd Hawaiian fishponds as a cultural asset.

The financial climate for aquaculture development is favorable, with strong government support; Hawaii is the only state to sponsor a major aquaculture development program, an active loan program for aquaculture, and campaigns to strengthen exports. The U.S. Department of Agriculture operates one of five national aquaculture research centers in Hawaii, the Center for Tropical and Subtropical Aquaculture.

The per capita consumption of seafood in Hawaii is more then twice the national average, cause enough for a vigorous aquaculture industry and for a strong fishing industry as well. Fishing has been important to islanders from their first arrival, with some 700 species of fish in island waters. Commercial fishing has been a part of the economic life of Hawaii for decades and in recent years has shown new signs of life. In the past four years at least 75 fishing vessels have relocated to Hawaii from the U.S. mainland. Fishing boats operate out of more than 70 landing ports across the state, but most of the catch goes through the ports of Kewalo Basin on Oahu, Maalaea on Maui, and Kailua-Honokahau on the Big Island. Fishing is done by hand-line, long-line and trolling, and in 1990 fishermen landed 21 million pounds of fish and generated revenues of $50 million.

For potential investors, commercial fishing looms strong and advantageous, not the least of which is a state-supported marketing and advertising program. Additionally, Hawaii's commercial fishing methods

↑ A *mahi mahi* catch, Kailua-Kona, Big Island.

are environmentally sound; tuna fisheries continue to be open access, fishing grounds are free from pollution, and Hawaii fish markets are accessible — giving buyers ready access to products. The fish most sought are the *aku* (skipjack tuna) and the *ahi* (yellowfin tuna), followed by sea-creatures whose names are as musical on the tongue as the fish are delicious: *opelu, ono, akule, mahi mahi, ulua, opakapaka.*

Recent surveys show the U.S. mainland market for Hawaiian fish is increasing, and export sales to Japan climb 10 to 15 percent per year. Seafood marketing is a dynamic industry with high growth rates predicted in all areas. In a recent five-year period, retail sales of Hawaii seafood rose an estimated 50 percent to an estimated $176 million.

The Hawaiians left the whales in peace. After all, ancestors of these giants were swimming in Hawaiian waters before the islands themselves were born. But if the Hawaiians did not hunt *kohola*, there were others who did — hard, brawling, bawdy men in many instances, men from the U.S. mainland who were on voyages of two to four years at a time, men a long way from Salem and New Bedford and Boston. Such men on two ships took a whale south of the Big Island in 1819, and from 1820 through the next half-century the whalingmen were a fact of life in Hawaii, and not everyone was pleased. In numbers that kept growing, the whaling ships put into Hawaii ports in spring and autumn to re-provision, sometimes to transship goods, to let the crews have a bit of recreation after the long days and nights at sea.

At one time there were more than 400 ships in Lahaina Roads in a single year. The presence of the ships and men left an indelible mark on Lahaina's society then and now; the whaling theme continues to be a leitmotif that is simply too pervasive to disappear. Throughout the decades from 1820 to 1870 the whalingmen significantly impacted Hawaii's economy as well. An earlier industry — sandalwood trading to China — had failed because of unwise stripping of the forests by royalty, who held a monopoly, and whaling eased in to become perhaps the single most important business of the times. A whaling ship arriving at Lahaina would re-provision there, men would spend their wages along Front Street, and traders would deal in transshipping if necessary. Ships might be repaired with materials purchased in port.

Lahaina became the whaling capital of the Pacific, but as suddenly as the whale ships appeared, they were gone. In 1871 a whaling fleet in the Arctic was trapped by encroaching and relentless Arctic ice, and 33 ships were crushed in the icy maws. The death of the fleet and the discovery of petroleum, which made whale oil largely obsolete, brought the whaling era to a turbulent and sudden end. There were those who were not sorry.

The era had focused attention on Hawaii's harbors. The one that would grow into the principal port of Hawaii was more or less stumbled upon by an Englishman, William Brown, who sold furs and guns. Brown's crew gathered pelts in the Pacific Northwest and sold them in Canton for as much as $100 each, and because Hawaii was convenient, the fur traders made frequent calls to the islands. One day Brown found what others had missed: a passage through the reef into a fine harbor adjacent to the barren and dusty village of Honolulu. Unwisely, Brown soon became embroiled in a local war between chieftains, which ended by his being killed and hung on a pole on the first day of the new year of 1795.

In his wildest imaginings Brown could not have envisioned the importance of the harbor he had found. It became central to a network of harbors in Hawaii which grew to include transshipping, warehousing, processing, and marketing cargo in the Pacific trade. The opening of the Panama Canal in 1914 sent even more ships to the islands, and in 1955 was built the Diamond Head Terminal (today's Piers 1 and 2), then considered state-of-the-art and now simply part of a vast and sophisticated harbor system. Called "Fair Haven" in the 1790s, the Honolulu Harbor has lived up to that now-unused name, a natural harbor protected by wind and surge action, straddling the time zones between Asia and the U.S. mainland, providing repairs and bunkering. (Ships refuel in Honolulu to provide more cargo space crossing the Pacific.)

As the centerpiece of Hawaii's 11 harbors on six islands, Honolulu's harbor continues to grow in importance to Pacific traders. State officials now refer to the entire ports system as Port Hawaii and tend to combine statistics, including the significant one that 80 percent of the goods consumed in Hawaii are imported from overseas, and 98 percent of these goods enter the state through Port Hawaii. Honolulu Harbor alone handles more than 12 million tons of cargo a year and serves as Hawaii's primary distribution center. As noted by a former director of the Department of Transportation, "When it comes to passengers, transportation is by air. When it comes to cargo, transportation is by sea." In 1991, Hawaii's airports handled 468,308 tons of cargo, while Hawaii's harbors handled 17,123,023 tons.

Port Hawaii is administered by the state's Transportation Department, which integrates the harbors into an entity that includes highway and airport systems. The harbors are among the busiest places in the Hawaiian Islands, filled with the movement of tugs, the arrival and departure of cruise liners, the loading and unloading of cargo vessels. Construction and maintenance goes on unabated: an $11.7 million extension of Oahu's Sand Island container complex; a master plan for the newest harbor at Barber's Point, 19 miles west of Honolulu; a $9 million expansion contract at Kawaihae on the Big Island; a $25.5 million pier project at Nawiliwili on Kauai; and much more. Improvements are the result of Master Plan 2010.

↑ Start of the Hawaii International Billfish Tournament, Kailua-Kona, Big Island.

Today there is more trade transacted along the Pacific Rim than in any other region of the world, a trend expected to continue. The resurgent dynamism of the Pacific Basin makes Hawaii's ports important to the efficient movement of trade, and a constant upgrading goes on so that demand can be met. As an indicator of how the maritime industry must look ahead, a master plan for the Barber's Point Harbor was completed recently, and even as potential users met with government agencies and interested citizens, the Transportation Department was looking at re-designating another 140 acres of land to allow for expansion of the harbor.

Since statehood in 1959, Hawaii's foreign trade has grown by about 4,000 percent to more than $2 billion. Trading partners are, in order of volume, Japan, Indonesia, Australia, Singapore, and Taiwan, underscoring an Asia-Pacific orientation. More than half the state's international trade is in petroleum products. There are two major oil refineries in West Oahu, and Hawaii sends refined petroleum products to Japan, while bringing in crude oil from Indonesia and Australia.

An advantage that Hawaii offers is its Foreign Trade Zone and various sub-zones. Clients of the zones — more than 350 and expected to grow — enjoy a special legal status. They are able to move goods into the zone without paying dues or excise taxes and must pay duties and applicable taxes only when finished merchandise is imported for sale, and never when goods are exported. There are 270 such zones in the United States, and Hawaii's is one of the largest and most diversified. It features acres of modern warehouse, office, and exhibition space, and almost 200 different kinds of products, from autos to clothing, are handled and distributed from the zone and sub-zones.

The harbors also allow for the berthing of cruise ships.

Standing on a pier and staring at one of these white giants, an observer feels an odd sense of déjà vu, and suddenly it is an earlier and more gracious era, and a mammoth vessel rounds Diamond Head. On the dock the band prepares to play, and the lithe young boys already are in the water, awaiting the coins that will be thrown from the decks to test their diving skills. Then the ship is docking, and paper streamers connect the decks and the dock. The band launches into a medley. Reporters stream up the gangplank to interview arriving celebrities — and there are always some — while the harbor pilot

↑ West Hawaii beach at sunset.

↑ Born in violent volcanic eruptions, battling the erosion of winds and waves, the islands lay barren until wind-borne spores crossed leagues of ocean, to drop into the basaltic soil. Trees with life in their roots washed ashore on the beaches. Birds found their way to the islands and evolved into a startling array of species. Bearing seeds on their bodies and in their bellies, the islands blossomed.

returns control of the ship to its captain, and the crew says goodbye to favorite passengers.

It was a Swedish-born entrepreneur and sea captain, William Matson, who sent many of these great ships to Hawaii, and for decades the words Matson, tourism, hotels and Waikiki were synonymous on the U.S. mainland. Matson himself first appeared on the islands in 1882 aboard the 113-foot schooner *Emma Claudina,* carrying 300 tons of goods to Hilo. This Big Island port became Matson's principal port in Hawaii for a time, and by 1900 the sea captain had four ships plying in and out of historic old Hilo Bay. On the ships, primarily cargo vessels, there were a few rooms for passengers, and Matson was never slow to pick up on an idea. Ten years later the 146-passenger S.S. *Wilhelmina* entered service; some people date modern tourism in Hawaii from that inaugural voyage.

Three more liners entered service as Matson teamed with Castle & Cooke, *a kamaaina* firm, and began to serve Honolulu. Captain Matson died in 1917 after a distinguished career, but his company lived on. In 1926 Matson bought and rebuilt the Moana Hotel, the first one on Waikiki Beach, and a year later the company built the hotel that came to stand for Waikiki itself, the Royal Hawaiian.

In both world wars the Matson vessels also went to war, and afterward Matson spent millions refurbishing the ships. The hotels were refurbished as well, having been used as rest and recreation sites by the U.S. military. The company never forgot its origin as a cargo line, however, and in 1956 Matson introduced cargo handling by freight containerization, revolutionizing cargo operations in the Pacific. Concurrently, the company sold off its hotels and all other non-shipping assets.

Matson's most famous vessels were the *Lurline* and the *Matsonia.* The *Lurline* stayed in service until 1970, finally bowing out in the face of growing jet air service to the islands. In that year the company began a $300 million shipbuilding and terminals program and in a dozen years had totally modernized the fleet and made costly but necessary improvements at its

U.S. mainland headquarters and ports. There were management changes as well: in 1901 Matson's shares were in the hands of various major Hawaii corporations to assure continued shipping services, and by 1909 a major Hawaii sugar company, Alexander & Baldwin, Inc., became part owner. In 1969, Matson became a wholly-owned subsidiary of Alexander & Baldwin.

If Matson was synonymous with tourism, it also was synonymous with romance. Boat Day in Hawaii was justly famous for color and charm, coming as it did at the end of a voyage across the world's mightiest ocean to arrive in sun-washed islands. Most passengers saw Hawaii on the horizon at daybreak, coming out of the sea like a scattering of emeralds, fulfilling every dream of the old South Seas.

For a few lucky voyagers, it still happens. At least eight cruise lines send their vessels into Port Hawaii, and tens of thousands of visitors experience that old-style Boat Day.

Additionally, two 30,090-ton cruise liners operate inter-island on seven-day cruises that allow passengers to experience the best of cruise life while being able to go ashore on different islands. The sister ships S.S. *Constitution* and S.S. *Independence* have been familiar sights in Hawaiian waters since 1980 and are currently the only American-flagged vessels in ocean-going operations. Built in the 1950s by Bethlehem Shipyards in Quincy, Massachusetts, the ships were refurbished and accommodate 798 guests in spacious cabins. They have added a new, yet familiar, touch of romance to island waters.

Six miles west of Honolulu Harbor is another and much more famous harbor. Although closed to commercial vessel traffic, Pearl Harbor has been a factor in Hawaiian lives for almost a century by modern reckoning, and for much longer than that when measured in Hawaiian time. The old Hawaiians knew that oysters lived in the sheltered harbor and called it *Wai Momi*, the water of pearls, and in 1840 the U.S. Navy got a look at the site when Lt. Charles Wilkes explored it; Wilkes concluded that removal of a dead reef blocking the harbor entrance would open

← ↓ Dredging of Pearl Harbor began in 1900. In 1908 the Pearl Harbor Navy Yard was formally established, and the U.S. provided $3 million for development. By the end of 1940, a total of $32 million had been appropriated to improve the site, and Pearl Harbor was humming with activity. Even shipyard workers normally got weekends off, and so it was that few of them were around on a balmy Sunday morning in December 1941 before the Japanese bombers struck. Below is the Arizona Memorial. To the left is the crew of the *USS Birmingham*.

up the area as a splendid anchorage.

The U.S. Navy was not alone in that estimation, and a few other nations began what proved to be a spirited bidding for the site. The Americans had more to offer: a treaty of reciprocity that allowed Hawaiian sugar to enter the U.S. duty-free. In 1887 Hawaii's King Kalakaua granted the United States the right to use the site for a coaling and repair station, and from that moment the base was to grow into a vital Pacific outpost.

↑ Late afternoon light at Honolulu Harbor.

December 7, 1941 was a typical Sunday morning, a day of high, fleecy clouds and a soft breeze. Sailors on the ships in harbor could hear church bells faintly across the calm waters of the harbor. Perhaps most of the sailors were aware of the tensions between the U.S. and Japan, the mis-reading of each other's will and capability, the inexorable drawing toward a point of conflict. But none of the sailors knew the point of conflict was here, and now.

Thirty-one Japanese vessels had sailed undetected across the North Pacific, and 220 miles north of Oahu the Japanese aircraft carriers launched their planes. Just before 8 a.m., 49 bombers, 40 torpedo bombers, and 42 Zero fighters flung themselves at Oahu, the first of 350 aircraft that

would savage the island's military bases. At the end of that bloody morning, 18 ships were sunk or damaged, 347 American airplanes destroyed or damaged, and 2,404 people were dead, with another 1,178 wounded. Japanese losses were light. It appeared to be an appalling disaster for America.

In reality, it was a blunder by the Japanese. The raid on Pearl Harbor solidified the American people as nothing else had. Instead of bringing America to the negotiating table as the raid's planners had hoped, it united America in a total war effort. Further, the raid failed to destroy the submarine pens, the fuel tanks, and — most importantly — the Pearl Harbor Naval Shipyard.

Of the 18 ships sunk or damaged, 14 were repaired and saw action, and the earliest was back with the Fleet in less than three months. Thousands of ship repairs took place at Pearl Harbor as the war progressed, allowing the United States to carry the war at sea to an enemy whose fortunes began to fall. Within six months, the American Navy pounded the Japanese at the Battle of Midway, from which the Imperial Navy never recovered. Ships repaired at the Pearl Harbor Naval Shipyard took part in that action, demonstrating the Shipyard's motto, "We keep them fit to fight." With the end of hostilities, the Shipyard turned to overhauling and repairing the nuclear submarines and the surface ships that transited Hawaiian waters as well as the 40-odd ships home-ported there.

From the air today Pearl Harbor looks much as it did on December 6, 1941 — 12,000 acres of land and water, the harbor itself shaped like the palm of a hand with fingers outstretched and called West, Middle, East, and Southeast Lochs. In the center is Ford Island, a mile and a quarter long, slightly more than a half-mile wide. Within the boundaries are 70 Navy commands and working/housing space for more than 20,000 sailors and Marines. The Shipyard occupies about 700 of the 12,000 acres and employs some 6,000 civilians; the direct economic benefit to the state is close to $300 million in civilian payroll and about $20 million in local purchases of supplies and services.

The Pearl Harbor complex is valued in the multiple billions of dollars, and its strategic value remains incalculable.

↑ **Sunset adds ethereal beauty to Waikiki.**

If man has learned to work on the sea and fight on the sea, he also has learned of its finite possibilities and the need to protect the ocean environment. What once was the wild and untamed sea came to be the fragile ocean, not because of sweeping changes but because of man's growing understanding of its complex ecosystems and the dependency of marine life on factors that man could change for better or worse.

Hawaii has a special interest in the health and vitality of its surrounding sea. The archipelago extends 1,523 miles across a pristine ocean with vast natural resources, both far at sea and along island coastlines. With the establishment of the Exclusive Economic Zones in 1983, Hawaii became the second largest state in the Union with an area of 922,967 square miles, and it became obvious that some sort of coordinated plan was necessary to identify and manage the ocean resources. The 200-mile zone added tantalizing possibilities for uses of the ocean, but it also added complications between Hawaii and the U.S. government as to control of, and benefits from, those resources.

Traditionally, and legally, the old territorial sea was a line drawn three miles offshore; in 1988 a Presidential proclamation extended the U.S. territorial sea from three to 12 miles but specified this did not mean the concomitant extension of jurisdiction and left open to debate where that jurisdiction lay. Having set up the 200-mile EEZ in 1983 and subsequently extending the territorial sea, the federal government brought about a situation in which state and federal governments would have to share concerns regarding use and care of the ocean around Hawaii.

In 1988 the Hawaii Legislature moved to bring some clarity to the situation by enacting Act 235, the Ocean Resources Management Act. The Legislature noted that there were many government agencies

THE FUTURE OF HAWAII AND

By Dr. John P. Craven
Director, Law of the Sea Institute

Some say Hawaii is a crystal ball set in an emerald sea with a rainbow of futures from multiple reflections of sunlight from the multifacets of its diverse cultures and professions — others say its future is dim and cannot be seen because the crystal ball is clouded.

The latter are, in general, folk who see no further than the edge of the land, who do not see the potential of the ocean to provide an environmentally sustainable, economically viable self-sufficiency that extends the life-sustaining functions of the land into a boundless, endless, seamless sea.

These land-oriented creatures do indeed correctly see the world problem as it relates to the continents and can conjure up a realistic, pessimistic future that extends these problems to the islands. These knowledgeable folk are well aware that 50 percent of the developing world's population is under the age of 19. They are aware that nutritional and resource requirements double at the age of 18, and they watch helplessly as these young, parent-less populations migrate to the coastal zone. They realize that resource need projections for the next decade of 20 to 30 percent are now far too low, and

without productivity increases in the vicinity of 100 percent or more in the next decade, the Four Horsemen of the Apocalypse will be galloping across the world's land mass even as they galloped over Iraq, and are galloping over the former Soviet Union, over many countries of Africa, South America, and Southeast Asia.

At the same time they recognize the developing pall of a greenhouse, an ozoneless environment where the energy of the sun is not impeded until it is trapped in the lower atmosphere, changing climate and ice cap and transposing regions of drought and flood. Even the most optimistic must see a world crisis of major dimensions that cannot be resolved in a decade, or two or three or more.

Both optimist and pessimist can now see a migration to the islands of the brightest, the best, the rich and the famous. Their insularity will guarantee protection from invading populations; immigration or cost of living or other social barriers will tend to limit population otherwise. Their accessibility to cargoes from so many sources around the world guarantees goods for import across the spectrum of needs and desires. Their tropical sunshine guarantees a richness and beauty of foliage even though it may be confined in pots and boxes.

Conference centers, business centers, mass transit, stadiums, golf courses, universities, concert halls, art galleries, shopping malls, restaurants — you shall find them all. All well and good, say the pessimists, but projections of growth require one new Honolulu every year, mass transit in quantities faster than can be built; geothermal energy and cables between the islands faster than the culture will allow; low cost, middle-income and affluent housing faster than can be built on lands which resist rezoning; energy needs that cannot be met; highways inadequate for the traffic load; concert halls and stadiums

THE SEA

with three-month ticket lines, etc.

But optimists will turn to the sea and to resources and projects that have already been developed and proven. Cold, deep ocean water will be the major environmental resource. Quickly, so quickly, all of the air conditioners will be replaced by simple heat exchangers, cooled by fresh water which is, in turn, cooled by deep ocean water. The electrical energy bill for air conditioning and cooling will be reduced by a factor of ten. Overnight, the urban energy supply will exceed the demand.

Other heat exchangers will collect condensate for a steady and renewable supply of fresh water for the Kona coasts. Other uses for the cold include cold-water agriculture in which microclimates are established, simulating the mountains in spring for the growth of strawberries and lettuces and spring flowers. The excess ocean water will be immediately available for the aquaculture of salmon and trout, lobster, sea vegetables, and health foods. All of these will grace the tables of home and hotel.

Less soon, the major source of electrical power will be derived from deep ocean water in the form of ocean thermal energy. This, in turn, will be employed for the manufacture of transportable fuels such as methanol and ammonia. Each home will have its own fuel cell and thus its own "clean signal" electrical generating capability. Gone the unsightly poles and transmission lines that bring blackout with every major storm.

What of the clogged highways? Some citizen will surely find Hawaii's detailed plan for marine mass transit that was generated in the early '70s. They will realize that the designers did not lie when they said that ships such as the swath ship *Navatek* could provide smooth, low-cost, high-volume rides to every location served or possibly served by the fixed guideway (except for Diamond

Head and Kaimuki). On weekends and holidays the system is easily diverted to the neighbor islands, relieving the congestion in airports. Swath car ferries such as designed for Hawaii by Mitsui Corporation in the early '70s will carry cars and families between the islands.

What of the overcrowded, congested Waikikis? Some entrepreneur will recall the floating city project and its realization in Japan, and at long last a conference center, conference ships, floating condominiums, and hotels will replace the aging structures along the beach.

New structures on land need not be allowed and, over time, all of the beach-front and coastal zone will be set aside for human enjoyment. The *aina* will be restored as every high-density system moves out to sea. The ultimate goal will be a land reserved for land users, for houses and government centers, recreational fields, agriculture and aquaculture, and parks and preserves. The land will be connected by marine mass transit to stable, attractive floating complexes on the horizon, yet nearby in travel time.

Will this island chain and other island chains be able to limit population growth? Can we not imagine that such will be a criteria for immigration? Will these islands be able to resist onslaught from the sea, or will huge floating cities be constructed in the vast tropic zone? Will these cities act as land masses about which marine transit systems, ocean thermal energy plants, high-density population complexes will orbit?

Will there be many Hawaiis? The answer is, surely, yes. When will they appear? Many moons from now? Yes, many moons from now.

involved with ocean activities but no coordinated ocean policy. To implement its act, the Legislature created the Hawaii Ocean and Marine Resources Council and charged it to develop a plan encompassing the sea from Hawaii's shoreline out to the limits of the 200-mile EEZ. Already identified were major problems: there was a diffusion of management, with the responsibilities spread over a number of agencies; the means of resolving regulatory problems were inadequate; enforcement systems for ocean use laws were inadequate; there was a marked lack of public participation in ocean use and resources planning; and, finally, there was an air of crisis management coupled with a failure to anticipate needs.

There was a precedent for writing a comprehensive ocean resources plan. In 1961 the state had developed and adopted the most complete land use management system in the United States, and now set its sights on a similar plan involving the sea. In mid-1990 a variety of people with a diversity of interests began the process and ultimately took recommendations and ideas to a series of public meetings throughout the state.

What emerged was a series of recommendations to carry Hawaii — with the federal government as a partner where necessary — into a future where respect and care for the sea is inherent. The first recommendation was establishment of an Office of Marine and Coastal Affairs to be the central authority for planning and policy and conflict resolution.

Going into this ambitious plan there were a number of advantages: the Hawaiian Islands were a natural laboratory for ocean research second to none, with an abundance of research sites and educational opportunities and programs. Research and education were under way in virtually every field from aquaculture to energy. The ocean and shoreline area provided opportunities for recreation. The fishing industry, if managed properly, could continue to

↓ Hawaiian Green Sea Turtle, *Chelonia mydas,* off the Kailua-Kona coast.

provide both sustenance and recreation — annual sustainable yields of fish could be as high as 43 million pounds a year if the ocean environment could be maintained properly. In one recent year recreational shore fishermen made an estimated 1.4 million trips to fish, a figure twice that of private boats and charter vessels, and ample evidence that Hawaii's residents appreciate the proximity of the sea.

With Hawaii's heavy dependency on imported oil, the uses of the sea as an energy source stir the imagination. During the decade of the 1980s, Hawaii became a premiere site for various energy research projects, including solar, biomass, wind power, geothermal, and none of them more exciting than hydro power. At Keahole Point, on the Big Island, is the Natural Energy Laboratory of Hawaii Authority, teamed with the state's Department of Business,

Economic Development and Tourism. Here are 870 acres of research resource, where there is warm surface water and near-shore deep, cold water that is pathogen-free, affording research into commercial harvesting of salmon, lobster, abalone, vegetables, and pearls.

Importantly for energy, it is the site of the world's foremost laboratory and test facility for ocean thermal energy conversion (OTEC). No one expects the energy derived from OTEC to supplant the use of fossil fuels in Hawaii in the near future, but OTEC is considered so important to the future energy needs of the islands that there is a strong recommendation for the establishment of a commercial-scale OTEC plant at the earliest possible date.

One of the more exotic resources in the ocean around Hawaii has attracted the attention of the federal government, state planners, environmentalists, and fishermen, and while it presents great opportunities, it also offers great obstacles that must

↓ **Large spotted flounder, _Bothus poantherinus._**

be resolved. The rewards are appealing — an estimated annual $540 million or more to Hawaii, and probably more than 3,000 new jobs. The resource has its variations but can be summed up in a word: cobalt.

Cobalt is vital in a number of significant ways. It goes into alloys that withstand extremely high temperatures; it is useful in tool bits, jet engines, industrial turbines, magnets, and various kinds of drilling equipment. It is used as a catalyst for petroleum de-sulfurization, an important preventative measure against acid rain.

The United States uses a third of the world's cobalt, but produces none of it. In the past decade there have been extensive efforts to find substitutes for cobalt, with little success. With the nation's supply of cobalt in the hands of foreign sources, the U.S. has gone searching for domestic cobalt — and found it.

The cobalt that could meet most of the nation's needs lies along the ocean floor in the 200-mile Exclusive Economic Zone drawn around the Hawaiian archipelago and Johnston Island, 850 miles to the southwest. Manganese nodules containing cobalt, platinum, nickel, and other metals have attracted the attention of the U.S. Department of the Interior's Minerals Management Service, now charged with the possible leasing of seabed areas to mine these minerals commercially.

Hawaii's interest in the progress of these efforts is obvious; a long-term and significant mining operation in these waters must be done in an environmentally sensitive way to protect Hawaii's surrounding waters and the land areas, plus the state wants to share in the economic benefits of seabed mining in Hawaiian waters. In 1984 a task force of state officials supervised the production of an Environmental Impact Statement that was published in 1987. It had three major findings: seabed mining was not viewed as harmful to Hawaii's environment; any major impacts would be associated with any Hawaii-based processing plants; and any commercial mining could be done successfully only after development of new mining technology.

Fishermen got the reassurance they needed when the EIS showed mining operations would be well away from the majority of fishing areas, and in any case

← ↑ The land and the marvelous climate and the clean air and the old, restless ocean all blend in a special sort of allure, the kind of enchantment that has made possible the leading industry in Hawaii — welcoming visitors.

↑ **A golden sunset on Waikoloa, Big Island.**

would have a low impact on commercial fishing. Mining would not be permitted within 50 miles of any Hawaiian shore, with the closest mining site some 300 miles from Hawaii. The most promising sites, in fact, are around Johnston Island, more than 800 miles away.

The first people of Hawaii brought with them a consciousness of the ocean that has persevered in the minds and hearts of Hawaii's people. For all its modernity, Hawaii still is bounded by seas of unimaginable scope and power, and those magnificent Polynesian crossings echo in Hawaii's heart today as islanders lay a justifiable claim to a kinship with the sea matched by few others on earth.

Joseph Conrad could write from the viewpoint of a Western sea captain that "the sea never changes, and its works, for all the talk of men, are wrapped in mystery." Islanders acknowledge the mystery, but also the poetry. There is a symmetry in the waves that is at once profound and satisfying, and an eye-pleasing joining where the sky meets the sea. And if there is poetry there is respect; in that marvelous Hawaiian creation chant, the *Kumulipo*, the respect and poetry combine as the majesty and power of the sea reaches beyond all things:

Born was rough weather, born the current
Born the booming of the sea, the breaking of foam
Born the roaring, advancing, and receding of waves, the
Rumbling sound, the earthquake
The sea rages, rises over the beach
Rises silently to the inhabited places
Rises gradually up over the land....

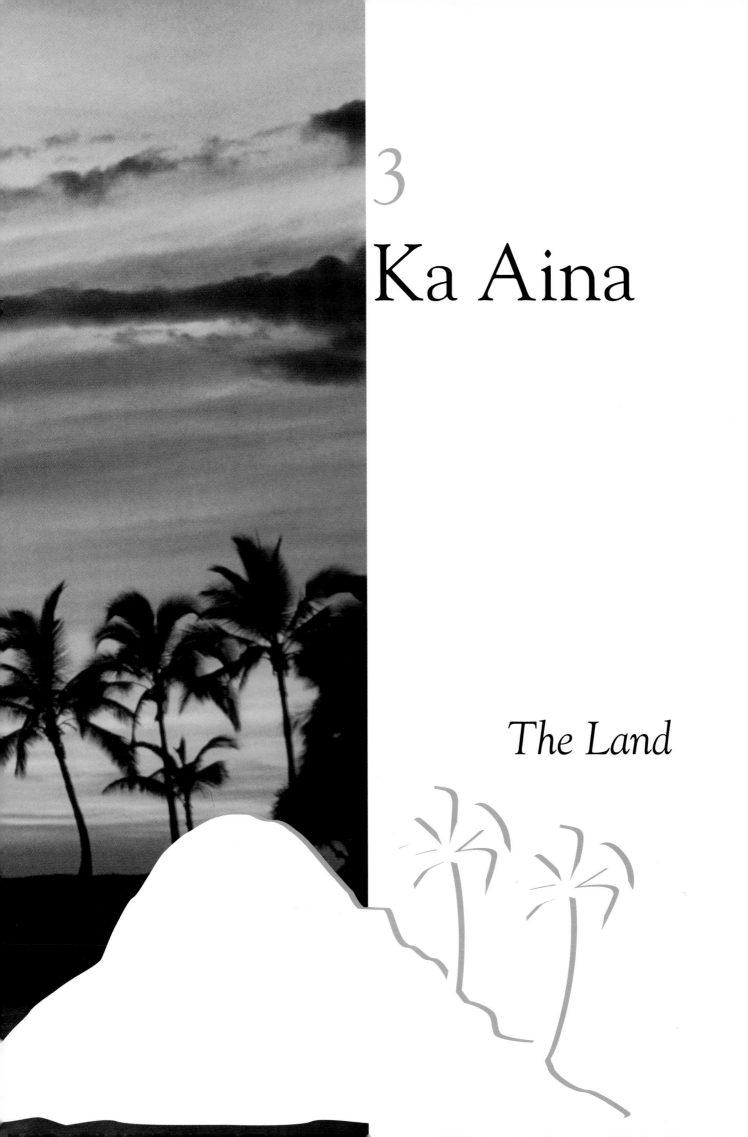

3

Ka Aina

The Land

The land was born in a time hard for human minds to grasp, for in writing its natural history the scientist or historian must begin, "Seventy million years ago...." It was then that seamounts were rising from the Pacific floor, setting the stage for the creation of the Hawaiian Islands. In that antique time the Pacific lithospheric plate moved over a stationary volcanic hot spot, creeping northward and giving rise to the Emperor Seamount, now totally submerged and eroding. About 43 million years ago the plate took a turn and created a bend where upheavals began to form the Hawaiian Ridge. Hawaii's eight major islands were born in successive upheavals of volcanic fury, each island having to battle the erosion of wind and wave for survival. Kauai, to the northwest, came out of the sea and survived some 5.1 million years ago, and the other islands followed. Maui is 1.3 million years old, the Big Island only about 800,000 with two of its five volcanoes still active.

There is a variation on this theme, and it begins with the legendary Haumea giving birth to Pele in an ancient place. Long after other gods came to Hawaii,

↗ Often there is the "curtain of fire" as a volcanic eruption begins along a crack in the earth, and within hours the eruption has concentrated in one spot, producing a fountain of fire that throws magma, molten rock, hundreds of feet into the air. Along with the lava comes ash and pumice, and a roaring sound punctuated by the crash of falling lava, and then the rivers of lava begin to creep downslope as the flow winds its way to the sea where it adds new acreage along the shoreline, continuing the island-building process.

Pele left her dwelling-place on Bora Bora, on the islands of Tahiti, and came in a great canoe northward to Hawaii, guided by her elder brother Kamohoalii, who was also a shark. Pele, beautiful and tempestuous, sought a home for the sacred fires she alone could create. But she was pursued by her sister, and enemy, Namakaokahai, the goddess of water. One version of the tale is that Namakaokahai caught up with Pele near Hana, on Maui, and killed her. (There is a hill on the site called *Ka-iwi-o-Pele*, the bones of Pele). Pele's death freed her spirit, and she became one of the immortals, the goddess of fire. Her restless spirit moved among the island chain and finally settled on the Big Island, sometimes living on Mauna Kea or Mauna Loa, sometimes moving about Kilauea. With her magic spade Pele strikes the earth, and sends the fires of creation across the land.

If the legends occasionally are flawed, Pele rises above them, to move in grandeur about the misty

world of the high volcanoes. She may be heard, or glimpsed, in that cool, clean upland area or among the scree and pumice of the barren places. A visitor may catch an image of her in the firelight. Older people still offer her the sacred *ohelo* berries in homage. A bemused hiker may hear a fleeting sound of the musical Hawaiian language high on a slope where there are no others in sight, for her presence is everywhere in the fires and the lava. She can take human form, the legends say, and become a beautiful young Hawaiian woman, or in another mood assume the looks of a wrinkled old crone, hitchhiking across the island. Her appetites are boundless, her seductions are wild tales of love and treachery, and her detractors somehow curtail their doubts when moving about the fantastic landscape of volcano country. A temptress then and a temptress now, she continues to inspire legend and dance and song, and men who come under her spell pay the price for it — to be forever haunted by her memory.

The ohelo berry, a delicate fruit of this rugged shrub, is a traditional offering to the goddess Pele. ↗

↑ Haleakala vista, Island of Maui, Hawaii.

Like the people who would inhabit the land, each island is separate but similar. Erosion by wind and water hewed the islands into their distinctive shapes, and climate gave them diversity. At elevations near 6,000 feet the annual rainfall can be more than 400 inches, but only 30 inches along the beaches. There are boggy plateaus, steep canyons, rivers, a lava desert, deep coves. Forests on the dry side of the islands differ greatly from the rain forests of the wet side, generally the northeast. The diverse habitats can support a variety of life forms, and early on the life began to arrive — drifting, windblown, carried by birds, and a very few insects and birds under their own power.

When the Polynesians arrived, the islands already were blossoming, and there was abundant food in the shellfish beds, the fishing grounds, and among the numerous turtle populations. There were few edible plants, however, and the Polynesians transported crop plants such as yams, taro, breadfruit, and bananas. They also brought pigs, dogs, and fowl, and the first alteration of the island environment by man took place as the colonists cleared ground for gardens. Stowing away in the canoes of the voyagers were rats, geckos, and skinks.

Everything in the canoes, from people to plants, underwent a population explosion in the new home, and while the first settlement might have been fewer than 100 people, by 1778 when Captain Cook arrived and the written chronicles began, there probably were 300,000. By the year 1200, the people had settled the leeward coasts of the main islands, and by 1400 they were clearing large tracts to plant sweet potatoes and taro.

With the introduction of pigs, goats, cattle, and deer, the native plants suffered anew. Having grown in isolation, the plants did not develop poisons or spines or other protection, and the feral animal population began to devastate whole ranges. Additionally, mistaken practices by governments and large landowners saw the replacement of native Hawaiian forests with exotic species, and in many if not most instances the substitution was not sound economically and merely added to the destruction of the native forests. As the islands moved into step with the times, demands on the land continued unabated, frequently to its detriment.

In time, conservationists and environmentalists and the landowners themselves came to appreciate the intrinsic value of land in the middle of an ocean; then the clock was turned back and a deep concern for the land surfaced from where it had lain dormant, and once again was heard words that rose from the very soul of Hawaii's people: *aloha aina,* love the land.

On July 31, 1843, Hawaii regained its independence, having lost it briefly to Great Britain, and King Kamehameha III read a new proclamation of independence to his people that included the words that became the motto of Hawaii: *ua main ke ea o ka aina i ka pono,* the life of the land is preserved in righteousness. Land was linked to prestige and power, and Hawaiian chiefs were large landholders. The land divisions often were pie-shaped, with the point in the mountains and the base on or beyond the offshore reef. This configuration allowed the chief to enjoy all the variety the land and sea offered. Under the *konohiki* system the chief had an agent to manage his land, and people to work it. The people were not slaves and could move from chief to chief, but while they had their own plots to cultivate, their *kuleana,* they did not own the land.

The complexities of the system made it unsatisfactory to almost everyone except the chiefs, and in counterpoint came the cry of the foreigners on the islands to be allowed to lease land. There was diplomatic maneuvering as the king finally regained control of his islands — and everyone began to focus on the status of the chiefs and foreigners and the division of the land itself. The idea surfaced that commoners might be allowed to own land which, in the constitution of 1840, was affirmed. In 1846 a Board of Land Commissioners was appointed (the somewhat amorphous forerunner of a Land Use Commission a century later), and the Board set about registering claims.

The resulting land division was mired in controversy. Essentially, the king gave up rights to all lands except certain estates to be known as Crown Lands. The chiefs were required to take out titles on land they held, but so many of them were dilatory about doing so that the titles became lost or challenged. Foreigners were given the right to lease land for 50 years, and eventually a new law allowed them to buy property. The Caucasians in Hawaii, having come from backgrounds in which title to land often was a passage to power, set about reaching for as much land as they could acquire. Commoners looking to buy a *kuleana* learned that surveys of land were imprecise; a *kuleana* could be an acre or 40 acres.

The land division was known as the Great Mahele, and commoners found it gave them rights they had never enjoyed — rights to buy, lease, or

⬂ **Among the splendid flora that color Hawaii's hillsides, valleys, and gardens are the Bird of Paradise, the Toyama Red, and over 160 types of orchids.**

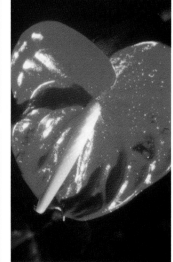

cultivate, rights to let the land lie fallow, rights to sell if they wanted to, and many did sell. By the end of the 19th century foreigners owned four acres for every acre owned by a Hawaiian. The movement that began with the idea of keeping the Hawaiian on Hawaiian land ended with many of them losing it.

In 1893, with the overthrow of the Hawaiian monarchy by a group of foreign revolutionaries, the land became a prize, and the revolutionaries vowed they would offer the islands to the United States. One consequence of the revolution was the seizure of Crown Lands and their addition to the acreage owned by the government. This meant some 43 percent of land in Hawaii was in government hands.

Much of the rest of the land came under the control of a class that wielded most of the business, political, and social power on the islands from the turn of the century forward. They were Caucasians (*haoles*, the Hawaiians called them, a word that initially meant stranger and through usage came to mean white foreigner). They were mostly Republicans, often related to each other through marriage, had a tendency to attend the same Ivy League schools, occasionally took Hawaiian wives, and sat on each other's Boards of Directors. Leaders among them were the "Big Five" companies — Castle & Cooke, Alexander & Baldwin, American Factors, Theo H. Davies, and C. Brewer and Co., Ltd. Added to this lineup was the powerful Dillingham firm, involved in construction and transportation.

The ties between the businessmen and politicians were strong and constant; from 1900 to 1940 eight out of every 10 legislators elected were Republicans — and the property holdings of the businessmen grew to enormous sizes. Prior to World War II, Hawaii became mostly a plantation society, and while the government still held nearly half the

↑ **Workers in a macadamia nut orchard pause for a break.**

total land area, almost all of the rest was in the hands of just 80 private owners.

The post-war years brought changes. A strong labor union, the International Longshoremen's & Warehousemen's Union (ILWU), organized the plantations and became a factor in local politics. Additionally, in a "revolution" of 1954, the sons and daughters of immigrants who had come to work on the plantations could vote, and did so to the point of turning out most of the entrenched legislators. The immigrants themselves, allowed to become citizens by the McCarran-Walter Act of 1952, also voted, adding to the landslide. A new regime of the Democratic Party took power, and kept it. There would be a new focus on uses of the land.

The land — basaltic, fertile and rain-swept (or irrigated, where necessary) — proved to be as fecund and reliable as a farmer could wish. Out of it sprang coffee, rice, pineapple, and sugar. Also proliferating were herds of wild cattle; by the 1830s the mountains and plains were filled with them because of the king's *kapu*. The cattle were owned jointly by the king and the government and had proliferated beyond belief. Already there were goats,

THE GOOD EARTH OF HAWAII

By J.W.A. Buyers
Chairman and Chief Executive Officer,
C. Brewer and Company, Limited

The story of agriculture in Hawaii is a story of hard work, experimentation, and taking to heart that Hawaiian saying, *aloha aina,* love the land. We who are close to the good earth of Hawaii know how vital it is to nurture the soil and to cultivate it with care.

Land is the most precious commodity on an island, and its uses are not to be considered lightly. There has been an effort by the major growers and farmers over the years to get the greatest yields from the land, both for consumption on the islands and for export. Only the highest and best use of the land is justified, for the land is finite.

And the land has, not inexplicably, been a power base in Hawaii for decades. Large landholders have long been aware of the need to make the land produce for the good of all islanders; to provide food and jobs connected with growing and farming; to continue to search for ways to make the land productive without depleting its precious resources. People who have owned and worked the land in Hawaii over the years often have become influential in developing housing and the infrastructure for the community.

C. Brewer and Company, Limited, is the oldest business firm in terms of continuity on the islands, indeed, west of the Rocky Mountains. Every chief executive from its founder, James Hunnewell in 1826, to the present day, has been conscious of the debt the company owes the larger Hawaii community, and of the responsibilities this multifaceted conglomerate bears in the growth and development of the islands.

Like other growers, our company could not have prospered without the infusion of new blood and new ideas from Asia and the Portuguese islands. Our greatest inventory was, and is, the people who coaxed the soil, people whose strong hands and steady hearts help produce the pineapple and sugar and fruits, the flowers and macadamia nuts that helped make Hawaii justly famous. Throughout all the changes and all the new technology, it has been the people with a love for the land and a feel for the soil's capabilities that have made possible the acres of Hawaii products.

To reach a high level of productivity in Hawaii has required experimentation, a certain amount of trial and error. To create and maintain a market niche for Hawaii products has meant no little effort in Washington, where Hawaii's Congressional delegation has fought for the sugar subsidies and the farm bills that give the islands at least an equal opportunity to grow and market products in the face of fierce international competition. From the days of the Treaty of Reciprocity, which gave sugar a fighting chance to be marketed in the United States, to the present day, Hawaii's growers have helped make agricultural products a vital industry, and beneficial to all our people.

Hawaii's growers continue to experiment, and continue to seek markets. The crops that grace our fields are so important they cannot be considered separately from the future of the islands. No matter what new and innovative technologies portend for Hawaii, the land will always be there, rich and productive, necessary for our very survival.

sheep, turkeys, ducks, donkeys, mules, and other animals brought by settlers. The cattle, however, were a menace, and by 1846 there were an estimated 25,000 of them. In time, hunted for their hides, wild cattle became scarce but not before ranching had taken hold.

Farming techniques improved. Missionaries taught the Hawaiians how to fertilize crops and how to use oxen to plow. Chinese immigrants brought rice cultivation to a fine art, and the government imposed a protective tariff of one cent per pound of rice in the husk, 1.5 cents for clean rice. The Reciprocity Treaty of 1876 let rice tariff-free into the United States, and by the turn of the century, rice production in Hawaii was up to more than 33 million pounds. The industry remained strong for decades, but eventually declined in the face of mechanized rice-growing in California.

Coffee was first grown in Hawaii in 1817, the first plants having been nurtured in Manoa on Oahu in 1825. There were plantings in Kona, on the Big Island, in 1828 and on a much larger scale at Hanalei, on Kauai, in 1842. The crops went boom and bust for decades, rising significantly after World War II only to drop again. Kona developed into the prime growing area, and the recent rise of the gourmet coffee market has given the Hawaiian crops new value. New processing and harvesting techniques have made the crop cost-effective, and after years of uncertainty Kona coffee today appears strong on the world market. Acreage in production is expected to increase.

Hawaii produces other major crops in addition to sugar and pineapple, including flowers and nursery products, milk, vegetables and melons, taro, macadamia nuts — which has grown into a giant industry — and fruits, poultry, and livestock.

Because of the growing importance and the need for quality controls, the Board of Commissioners of Agriculture was organized in 1903, evolving into the Board of Agriculture and Conservation in 1960 and the Department of Agriculture in 1961, with greatly expanded responsibilities. The mandate to the Department is nothing less than the development, conservation, and utilization of agricultural resources of the state.

Despite increased urbanization, Hawaii's farmers have persevered and had the satisfaction of watching agriculture prosper and grow as an industry. There are some 4,600 farms in Hawaii with a total area of 1.7 million acres, and at least 14,000 persons deriving a

↓ Patterns, macadamia nut orchard, the Big Island of Hawaii.

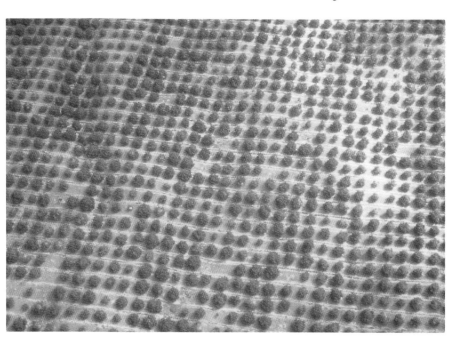

living from farming. The major crops are flourishing: flowers and nursery products, worth $70 million; macadamia nuts, $41 million; livestock, $88 million. Diversified crops — defined as all crops other than sugar and pineapple — climbed from $91 million in sales in 1980 to $187 million in 1990, a jump of 105.5 percent. Untabulated are statistics on the growth of marijuana and other illicit plants.

Through all the uses of the land and the long years of cultivation, two crops stand out as inseparable from any story of Hawaii, for sugar and pineapple impacted heavily, not only on the land itself, but on the society of the islands.

↑ In 1851 the sugar industry got a boost, for David M. Weston arrived on the islands with ideas in his head and some new sugar machinery. Weston had invented the method of applying centrifugal force to sugar manufacturing, a separator that pared molasses from sugar crystals, thereby increasing the quality of the sugar and making higher prices possible. Because of these advances, it was possible to attract more capital to sugar. The industry advanced on all fronts but one: there was still a shortage of labor, and for this the industry had to turn to the East.

Sugarcane is a grass, but a very special one. All green plants produce sugar, but none as efficiently as this large grass which has become specialized in combining carbon dioxide from the air with water in its leaves and using the sun's radiation and the plant's own chlorophyll to make sugar. After the sugar is formed, some is used for the plant's growth, the rest stored in its stalk.

Polynesians brought sugarcane with them to Hawaii but never made sugar from it. Instead, they chewed the stalk for its sweetness. When Captain Cook reached Hawaii in 1778, he saw "several plantations of plantains and sugar-canes."

In 1802 a hopeful Chinese man stumbled down the gangway of a vessel in the place the Chinese thought of as *Tan Heung Shan*, the Sandalwood Mountains. He was carrying a collection of boiling pans and a village-type sugar mill, and Wong Tze-Chun also carried two ideas in his head, one good, one bad: he would produce sugar, but he chose the wrong island. Lanai was essentially dry and did not

lend itself to sugar production, and after a year the disappointed Wong packed up and left. But others still considered Hawaii-grown sugar as potentially profitable, so much so that *tong see*, sugar masters, came from China to work for their countrymen in the Sandalwood Mountains.

To a lot of people, sugar seemed to be a good idea. The missionaries, who arrived in 1820, thought sugar was potentially one of the finest crops the islands could produce. The Chinese had such faith in it that they simply kept working at it all through the 1830s. Some Chinese entrepreneurs made it pay, notably Samsing & Co., with operations at Lahaina, on Maui, and on the Big Island at Waimea, Kohala, and Hilo. It did not come easily, however, and the Chinese often were frustrated by simple needs, such as cattle to pull a plow, or better quality seeds to improve the crops. There were droughts, pests, and a lack of labor, but the early planters shared problems that created a spirit of cooperation among them.

In 1835 Ladd & Company started a successful plantation at Koloa, Kauai, and two years later had a 50-acre harvest that yielded two tons of raw sugar, which was sold for $200. Within 15 years there were other plantations on Kauai, and on Maui, Oahu, and the Big Island. In 1850 the sugar planters teamed up with other farmers to form the Royal Hawaiian Agricultural Society as a way of swapping ideas and information, and in 1882 the sugar planters organized the Planters' Labor & Supply Company. Three years later the company's activities were expanded and its name changed to Hawaiian Sugar Planter's Association, the name under which it is active today.

Many sugar plantations failed, but many held on as the technology improved. In 1837 the islands were able to export 4,000 pounds of sugar, but even then the crop faced competition from the Philippines and Central America, so early on the Hawaii sugar growers realized that sugar from the islands had to be better than any other or simply sink under the weight of foreign competition.

Politics helped. In 1876 the Treaty of Reciprocity allowed Hawaiian sugar to enter the United States duty free, and in exchange the islands allowed America to acquire Pearl Harbor, as a coaling station and then as a full-blown Navy Yard. A dozen years later the Spanish-American War made the U.S. acquisition look like a very good deal indeed for the United States, and America then moved to annex Hawaii. At the time of the 1876 treaty, the islands were producing 13,000 tons of sugar a year, and by the time of annexation the figure had climbed to 225,000 tons. Ten years later that figure doubled, and then doubled again.

Sugar entered its boom years. Valuable by-products came about — molasses, used worldwide as a livestock feed supplement, and power, the latter coming from sugar factory boilers burning bagasse (crushed fiber of sugarcane stalks left after milling). The steam from burned bagasse is used in factory operations, and the electricity is sold to electric utilities. Marketing has kept pace with the technology, and Hawaii's cane sugar is sold in more than 100 types and grades. Early on the sugar planters cooperatively bought into a sugar refinery in Crockett, California, 30 miles northeast of San Francisco, where sugar is transformed into products sold throughout the western United States.

Through a century of sugar growing, there have been frustrations that kept many sugar planters up at night, going over their books. Weathering the early growing pains, developing the technology, perfecting the seeds, bringing in the requisite labor — these are tangible situations that a planter must handle. More frustrating has been the up-and-down relationship with the U.S. government, which alternately offers a sugar subsidy that gives Hawaii a competitive edge, and then takes it away — or tries to.

Captain Cook's botanists, who noted and recorded the sugarcane in Hawaii on their arrival in 1778, saw no pineapple, and it is not known how pineapples first reached Hawaii, or when. What is known is that a colorful gentleman named Don Francisco de Paula y Marin planted a pineapple on January 21, 1813 — but probably not the first one to be planted on the islands. Don Francisco jotted the date down in his diary, taking a break from his busy duties as interpreter for the king, manager of trade, and father of numerous children from the several female chiefs he lived with. While Don

← Recently, local sales of pineapple have increased, but there has been a drop in out-of-state shipments. Local acreage has shrunk because of resort development on the land, notably Lanai, and there has been a nagging labor shortage. Nevertheless, pineapple sales in 1990 were at $99 million, and that represented a 26.6 percent increase over the 1980 total. Some 2,000 employees keep the industry humming, augmented seasonally by part-time workers.

Francisco called it a pine-apple, the Hawaiians called it *halakahiki*, meaning roughly a foreign plant. In the early 1800s, no one foresaw the enormous crop it would become.

However and whenever the pineapple reached Hawaii, it found ideal growing conditions. The plant

↑ **Picking coffee beans, Holualoa, Kona, Big Island.**

demands an environment about 1,500 miles north or south of the equator, free from frost, temperatures between 70°F and 90°F, and plenty of sunshine. Hawaii is ideal, and the plant was growing well by the mid-1800s. A "Wild Kailua" variety of pineapple was planted in Oahu's Manoa Valley in 1882 by Captain John Kidwell, an English horticulturist who went on to import 1,000 Smooth Cayenne plants from Jamaica in 1886, and it was the Jamaican variety that became the foundation for the vast Hawaii plantings. Kidwell himself failed economically, but he had introduced a plant that would reign on the islands.

The same Treaty of Reciprocity that allowed sugar to enter U.S. markets tariff-free, let rice in as well, and also cleared the way for Hawaiian pineapples. Coincidentally, it was the year a group of California farmers came to Hawaii and took property in Wahiawa, in central Oahu, and became known as the "Wahiawa Homesteaders." One of them was Alfred W. Eames, who believed in pineapple and began to expand his fields. A year after Eames arrived, James D. Dole, fresh from Harvard, also turned up on the islands with an eye to pineapple harvesting. By 1900, D.D. Baldwin's pineapple crop was thriving on Maui, and these early pioneers made the industry not only possible but profitable.

It was Dole in 1901 who organized the first of the

modern pineapple companies, building a cannery near his Wahiawa fields and, in 1903, packing 1,800 cases of pineapple. His company would flourish as Dole Company and later be a subsidiary of the *kamaaina* firm of Castle & Cooke. Eames built his Wahiawa cannery in 1906 as part of the Hawaiian Island Packing Company, which also went through an evolutionary process and become Del Monte Corporation. On Maui, the Baldwin family was operating efficiently as early as 1903 and in 1912 organized the Baldwin Packers, to merge with another firm in 1962 and remain in business today as Maui Pineapple Company, or as they say on Maui, Maui Pine.

Today, Del Monte, Dole, and Maui Pine continue to grow pineapple. The plant is grown on Oahu, Maui, and Molokai — Dole having dedicated its former large pineapple holdings on the island of Lanai to other uses — and some 30,000 acres of Hawaiian land is planted in pineapple. The industry produces upwards of 600,000 tons a year.

For years Hawaii had longed for statehood. Territorial status implied that the people of the islands were somehow second-class citizens, a term that was heard often in the 1950s. After all, Hawaii had been under the U.S. flag since 1898; it was paying taxes; it contributed to the national economy and sent its young men off to America's wars. There was a feeling that the bloc of Southern senators who previously checked the impulse toward statehood had done so simply out of prejudice. And there was the fact that the bombing of Pearl Harbor was enough to send the U.S. into World War II, implying close ties.

So the impetus was strong and growing, and then Alaska entered the picture also asking for statehood. Hawaii's strategy became one of watchful waiting, letting Alaska go first to become the 49th state, for then in all fairness Hawaii could not be denied. Alaska was to destroy the argument against non-contiguous states, and in June 1958, was admitted to statehood. There was jubilation in Honolulu.

In February 1959, the House Committee on Interior and Insular Affairs voted favorably for statehood for Hawaii, and then in March a similar bill emerged from the Senate's committee. On March 11, 1959, the U.S. Senate passed the Hawaii Statehood Bill, and the following morning the House did the same. Later that day the word was flashed to Honolulu, and the impromptu parties began, for now there were no second-class citizens.

Changes came in the wake of statehood — new industries, new entrepreneurs, men like Henry J. Kaiser who built new hotels and thousands of homes, investors who brought prosperity and made demands on the economy at the same time. Hawaii's lawmakers

Statutes recognized the limitations on Hawaii's lands and acknowledged the responsibility of the state to set up a system of land use management, the Legislature having determined that a lack of adequate controls had resulted in land abuse for short-term gains.

The state Land Use Law that emerged from the Legislature (and subsequent amendments) created four districts — Urban, Rural, Agricultural, and Conservation. The lawmakers also created the Land Use Commission, a body that today is composed of nine members appointed by the governor and confirmed by the State Senate. All are non-paid volunteers, five appointed at-large and one from each of the four counties.

The commission's responsibilities are profound, considering the importance of land in Hawaii. The commission establishes district boundaries, acts on petitions for boundary changes, and acts on requests for special use permits within the Agricultural and Rural Districts. Today about 5 percent of the state's 4.1 million acres is classified Urban, with a little more than half of it in the city and county of Honolulu. Included in this figure are vacant lands for future development, and jurisdiction of the district lies primarily with the counties. The Rural District is made up of mostly residential lots and small farms and represents 0.25 percent of the state's acreage. A majority of the

↑ A giant replica of the 48-star flag that flew over Pearl Harbor 50 years ago. That Hawaii had not yet gained statehood, despite the fact that the bombing of the harbor had become a national call to arms, is an irony that was not lost on the people living in Hawaii.

were challenged to encourage the economy, while at the same time protect the land.

In 1961 the first State Legislature adopted a measure that was hailed throughout the United States as one of the most comprehensive and far-reaching land use laws extant. Chapter 205 of the Hawaii Revised

lands, almost 48 percent, is classified Agricultural and is broad enough to include not only cultivation of crops, but also raising livestock, aquaculture, forestry, wind farms — even golf courses.

Uses here are sometimes governed by statute, sometimes established by the Land Use Commission. The Conservation District is more than 47 percent of the state, and 66 percent of that amount is on the Big Island. Conservation lands are primarily lands in existing forest and water reserve zones and include areas for protecting watersheds, parks, wilderness, recreational sites, habitats of endemic fish, plants, and wildlife — and all submerged land seaward of the shoreline.

To oversee the portion of the land under the state's jurisdiction, there is a Board of Land and Natural Resources and a powerful Department of Land and Natural Resources whose mission is to manage and conserve state lands and water resources. The department handles problems from endangered species protection to historic preservation, a job which grows yearly more complex, especially as environmental concerns bump up against the need for housing, or the need to find alternate energy sources.

If statehood brought political and social changes, it also created a "boom" that made new demands on the land. As a state the islands afforded the protection of U.S. rules and regulations and opened Hawaii up to investments, and speculation, and each arriving aircraft brought its share of people who had bought one-way tickets. On the eve of statehood there were some 620,000 people in Hawaii, increasing to 769,913 in 1970, to 964,691 in 1980 and to 1,134,800 in 1991. There has been a parallel rise in the demand for housing, for office space, for schools and shopping centers and freeways and all the things attendant to population growth.

While Honolulu grew vertically beginning in the 1960s, it also began to spread out in the 1980s. The neighbor islands felt some of the pressure for expansion of urban areas, but it was Honolulu, with its concentration of jobs, that generated more demands for housing and related facilities and infrastructure. In 1986 there began a serious effort to inaugurate a "second city" to the west of Honolulu toward the Ewa area, and a state-assisted housing project at Kapolei got under way; private developers began planning thousands of homes. There were conflicts as the need for subdivisions often broke on the reefs of environmental concerns. Such problems are not likely to disappear as population increases and puts accelerating demands on Hawaii's fragile ecology.

In spite of delays, Kapolei is stirring and taking shape. On 890 acres some 5,000 homes are coming into being as the state's Housing Finance and Development Corporation, the master developer, inaugurates a community of homes, parks, schools, apartments, commercial areas, and a golf course.

State-planned communities that include homes of varying prices are one kind of real estate activity, but more common is a market that has been influenced both by local conditions and money from foreign investors. Housing prices are among the

↑ A recent four-year span of dramatic increases in real estate prices was precipitated by swift economic growth which in turn stemmed in part from investments from Japan which hit $2.1 billion in 1989. In the wake of that boom came lower interest rates and a greater affordability of houses. Still, Oahu median single-family home prices almost doubled from $185,000 in 1987 to $352,000 in 1990, and there was a corresponding rise in the cost of condominium units.

↑ **Mauna Kea seen from Kamuela. The islands' highest mountain invites the most daring of skiers.**

highest in the nation, in part because of the high cost of land itself, a situation sometimes worsened by its lack of availability. Prices have climbed more or less steadily since the "boom" atmosphere of the 1960s, but there have been up and down periods when home prices reflected availability, or a recession, or some inflationary situation that caused home mortgage interest rates to fluctuate.

Home-building is only one facet of a construction industry in Hawaii that has rebounded from a low point of $1.23 billion in 1984 to $4.4 billion in 1991. Private building permits rose steadily over the past few years, then leveled off in late 1991, suggesting a turning point in the private construction cycle, according to the Bank of Hawaii's annual economic report in 1991. Similarly, government construction contracts reached a peak of $1.49 billion in 1990 but declined to $1.2 billion through most of 1991. Economists expect that public infrastructure projects will keep government construction at levels high

enough to counter any slowdown in private construction.

In addition to growers and all the ancillary jobs that are connected with agriculture and real estate and construction, other occupations rely on land use. Sometimes this may be nothing more — or less — than locating a business on a particular site, that most fundamental use of the land. For example, there are close to a thousand establishments on the islands devoted to manufacturing, and while many of them are concerned with turning out small products, all are important in the business ecology of Hawaii.

Manufacturing falls easily into four categories: sugar-connected, pineapple canning, petroleum, and diversified manufacturing, the latter including food processing, garment making, printing and publishing, and stone, clay, and glass products. Diversified manufacturing leaped almost 15 percent to $754.4

↑ Downtown Honolulu bustles with an eclectic and exciting energy common to cosmopolitan cities everywhere.

million recently, and accounted for more than 16,000 jobs across the state. In the busy shops are fabricated metal products, furniture, electronic equipment, miscellaneous plastic products, clothing, lumber, and wood products.

Because of businesses that flourish on the land, retail and wholesale sales continue to grow. The growth rate in retail sales holds steady at between four and five percent, and the impact of the Gulf War on retail sales in Hawaii was less severe than expected. Labor productivity has increased, and the retail job count has been growing. In wholesale sales, the average yearly growth rate in recent years has been almost 15 percent; the statewide job count in the wholesale sector has been increasing, especially on the neighbor islands (Kauai, Maui County, and the Big Island).

A sizeable amount of land in Hawaii is owned or controlled by the military; in 1991 the figure was more than 265,000 acres. The Army owns or controls most of the acreage, most of which is on Oahu. Some 29,000 acres comprise the island of Kahoolawe, which has been a bone of contention between the Navy, the military caretakers of the islands, and a group of Hawaiian activists who claim the island has religious and historical significance. The military has been using Kahoolawe as a target complex since the early days of World War II, but has agreed to turn the island over to the state of Hawaii when the military no longer has a need for it. Meanwhile, through a memorandum of understanding with the state, the Navy is helping to rehabilitate the island. Other acreage has other uses — air bases, combined arms training areas, storage, barracks and classrooms, docks.

The military pays its way on the islands, as shown by the statistics; in a recent year total expenditures were $3.2 billion, military prime contract awards were $512 million, civilian employment was 19,857, and by any yardstick the military was the second-ranking (after tourism) source of income to the state. There are some 54,000 military personnel and 63,000 dependents in Hawaii, and more than 10,000 Hawaii residents in uniform around the world. Even the retired military personnel in Hawaii contribute to the state's income; more than 11,000 of them are receiving a total of $15 million monthly.

In any discussion of the myriad uses of the land in Hawaii, there is a single dominant reality: the land is beautiful.

The islands are similar, but different.

Kauai comes to you softly, yielding, a lover wearing flowers and looking best in the bright sunlight; Kauai hides its rugged side on the north, where deep valleys spill into the sea and the sea itself surges into hidden grottos. It is the sun-kissed and gentle land that beckons and invites comparison with the old, indolent South Seas.

Offshore, the island of Niihau lies on the horizon but beyond reach, a privately-owned land populated by people who still speak Hawaiian more often than not, and who exist on the periphery of the state, aware of changes that pass them by and accepting only what they want to accept.

Oahu glitters and hums and vibrates with 80 percent of the state's population and the majority of most other things — jobs, buildings, cars, traffic, the performing arts, the seat

of power. The capital shifted here from Lahaina, on Maui, in the 1850s, and the fine harbor has made it the power hub of the state. It is en route to becoming a true Pacific center as well, for many Pacific nations do their banking in Hawaii and have representatives here.

Topographically, Oahu is one of the prettier islands, a fact easily missed by those who see only its sprawling power and its kinetic pace. The Koolau and Waianae mountain ranges divide the island into sections even as freeways link them, and looking past the man-made structures an observer notes the magnificent *pali*, the cliffs of the Koolaus that separate Windward and Leeward Oahu, and the serrated coastline that affords fine views up the windward coast.

Storied old Maui is two islands linked by a large isthmus. The entire eastern end is a 10,023-foot quiescent volcano, Haleakala, with probably the world's largest volcanic crater and a spectacular view from any angle. Across the connecting isthmus the West Maui mountains rise to almost 6,000 feet, craggy and with valleys sheer through them like the slash of a

↓ **Kauai's incomparable Na Pali Coast. Its famous trail invites hikers through guava forests to towering water cascades and hidden beaches.**

↑ Ulupalakua Ranch, upcountry Maui.

knife. Around the shore, the brilliant white-sand beaches glisten in the reliable daily sunlight.

From the shore can be seen the islands of Kahoolawe, Lanai, and Molokai. Kahoolawe is a military target complex, perhaps the single most bombed place in the world. Lanai's vast pineapple fields cover most of the island, flowing away from the rising center to a rugged shoreline and a couple of hidden beaches, but the pineapple fields are giving way to other uses. Molokai is an elongated stretch of island, rising on the eastern end, green and pretty.

On the northwest coast of Molokai is the peninsula where unfortunates with Hansen's Disease — and some only suspected of it — were isolated starting in 1865. There were some 8,000 of them, suffering lifetime banishment at the hands of a fearful populace seeking to protect itself. The city of Kalaupapa has an intrinsic beauty and was, and is, a place that has known love and heartbreak in epic proportions. It was here that Father Damien de

Veuster, a Catholic missionary priest from Belgium, spent his last 16 years among the afflicted before dying of the disease himself, a martyr, and today a candidate for beatification.

At the extreme southern end of the island chain is the island of Hawaii, which has lent its name to the entire archipelago. Residents call it the Big Island and with reason; its 4,038 square miles easily make it the largest of the islands, a land so large it has at least five distinct regions, and almost as many localized weather patterns. It was built by five volcanoes, two of which are still active. Towering Mauna Kea and Mauna Loa, both close to 14,000 feet, are among the Pacific's tallest peaks, and Hualalai is more than 8,000 feet. The island serves up its diversity in style, with a lava desert, frequent snowfalls on the mountains, a rain forest, a tropical shore, one of the largest privately-owned cattle ranches in the U.S., and a score of other ranches, and the high, clean, bracing Volcano area with all its legends and mystery. The crucible of

Hawaiian civilization, the Big Island melds its history with its grandeur.

Many have fallen in love with the islands, and some were famous enough, and talented enough, to leave tributes that outlasted the writers themselves. Mark Twain penned what is probably the most-quoted line, that Hawaii was "the loveliest fleet of islands anchored in any ocean," an observation worn smooth with use. Herman Melville, who was to write *Moby Dick*, jumped ship in Hawaii in 1843 and wrote searchingly about the white man's domination. Robert Louis Stevenson came in 1888 and took a cottage in Waikiki, where he wrote "The Bottle Imp" and completed work on *The Master of Ballantrae* and wrote a gentle and memorable poem to Scottish-Hawaiian Princess Kaiulanl ("Light of heart and bright of face: the daughter of a double race...").

Somerset Maugham came in 1916 and wrote his most famous story, "Rain." Isabella Bird visited in 1873 and wrote a fine account of her travels in the Sandwich Islands. Jack London and his wife visited, and London was fascinated by Kalaupapa and its victims. James Jones, Kathryn Hulme, James A. Michener — all viewed the islands in their distinctive way, and wrote well about them. The English poet Rupert Brooke, soon to die young and mourned, was enthralled by Hawaii and wrote of the islands' spell: "And new stars burn into the ancient skies, over the murmurous soft Hawaiian sea...."

For those lacking the ability to articulate that intense love of the islands that grips and holds, perhaps a borrowed verse can serve. Again it is Mark Twain, in a reflective, a nostalgic, perhaps a bittersweet mood, remembering the islands he knew as a young man:

> *No alien land in all the world has any deep strong charm for me but that one, no other land could so longingly and so beseechingly haunt me, sleeping and waking, through half a lifetime, as that one has done. Other things leave me, but it abides; other things change, but it remains the same. For me its balmy airs are always blowing, its summer seas flashing in the sun; the pulsing of its surf-beat is in my ear; I can see its garlanded crags, its leaping cascades, its plumy palms drowsing by the shore, its remote summits floating like islands above the cloud rack; I can feel the spirit of its woodland solitudes, I can hear the splash of its brooks; in my nostrils still lives the breath of flowers that died twenty years ago.*

4
Na Po'e

The People

One of the richest women in the world lives in Hawaii, and counts her dollars in the billions; here also are families below the poverty line.

• The people of Hawaii live longer on the average than people in the rest of America — 77.03 years.

• They also enjoy a cleaner environment but spend more for groceries, have more dentists per capita — 80 for every 100,000 population — and spend more for housing.

• Hawaii ranks 38th in the nation in the rate of violent crime per 100,000 population, but sixth in the property crime rate.

• Hawaii also spends more for art than other states.

• In national rankings, the Hawaiian Islands are 41st among the states in population, with just over a million people; 80 percent of them live on the island of Oahu.

• There are 103 men for every 100 women. Families average 3.48 members per family, and there are some 260,000 single people throughout the islands.

• People in Hawaii tend to marry and divorce with greater frequency than elsewhere in the U.S.

• The median age is 32.

• Hawaii ranks 10th in the nation in terms of per capita disposable personal income.

• In a recent year there were 6,687 deaths in the state; 2,054 of them were attributed to heart disease, by far the leading killer.

• In the same year, 5,802 immigrants raised their hands before a U.S. official and swore to be loyal to the American laws and Constitution, and thus became U.S. citizens; it was a typical year for numbers of new citizens settling in Hawaii.

• And the people are peripatetic; in one year 444,000 of them went traveling outside the state.

• There may well be more passports issued per capita in Hawaii than anywhere else in the United States, attributable to both Hawaii's geographic proximity to Asia, and to the multiracial makeup of island people and their tendency to visit their ancestral homelands.

• Islanders rank high in the number of college graduates, low in the number of legal abortions, and fare much better in terms of employment, with an unemployment rate of less than three percent.

• Hawaii compares favorably with other states in energy consumption per capita, but almost all of that consumption comes from petroleum, and the state is heavily dependent on foreign oil.

• Hawaii ranks second in the nation in the number of people employed by foreign-owned businesses.

• About 40 percent of the civilian labor force — that totals more than a half-million — belongs to a union.

Statistics tell only some of the story. Anyone who spends time in Hawaii soon discovers a people as diverse and interesting as any on earth. In addition to being a multiethnic populace, the people of Hawaii tend to be individualistic, sports-mad, supporters of the arts, proud of their multiracial bloodlines, rather more inclined to gamble (on a football game or a new business venture), tolerant of each other's proclivities and — not the least of their traits — ambitious and hard-working.

Often, it seems, they also face in two directions.

↑ **Eager participants at the Aloha Festival, Iolani Palace, Honolulu, Hawaii.**

Islanders look back on a Hawaii that seems slower-paced and more charming than today, islands that once moved to the ticking of a more leisurely clock. At the same time, the people pride themselves on being up-to-date, and any businessman will stop and talk about the new communications assets, the satellites and fiber-optic cables. Business calls from Hawaii to the financial capitals of the world run into the uncounted millions, and the latest computers and other electronic devices grace the desks of local business establishments. And if a businessman sits in traffic and fumes about it, he is apt to complain to his secretary via a cellular telephone.

The varied cultural aspects of Hawaii are taken as a matter of course. A businessman whose workday may be spent contracting for services in California, watching the Hang Seng Index in Hong Kong and looking at sales figures in Australia, may then turn out in the late afternoon to visit an art show of ancient Chinese jades, have a drink with a colleague at a modern chrome-and-glass bar, and go on with friends to a Thai restaurant for *kaeng jued* and *yum-nuer* and *pad prig* and find nothing remarkable about his day.

If islanders guard their money, they also give it generously for a good cause. Aloha United Way revenues, for example, have climbed steadily, and in the decade 1979 through 1989, contributions climbed from $8.8 million to $14.1 million. Islanders are quick to spend money on ethnic festivals, on attendance at any sporting event and, as noted, on travel. This is as true for taro farmers in Waipio Valley as it is for Bishop Street businessmen. It is unusual, but by no means rare, for islanders to bump into each other on the Via Veneto or the Rue St. Honoré or Rama IV Road.

And while visitors may talk of "rock fever," the true islander never feels confined. To him the ocean is a means of escape, to swim or snorkel or sail; it is a vast, unoccupied and thus uncrowded area where there are no roads or buildings or traffic, and far from being restrictive, it means freedom. The welcome seas surround his land of great beauty, and it is the rare islander who does not pause now and then and thank his fate that he or his ancestors made their way to this distant landfall.

Cook's arrival threw cultures into conflict. Within a half-century the *haole* presence was settled on the islands, never to depart. White men were traders, sea captains, whalingmen, missionaries, entrepreneurs, drifters. From the earliest days onward there was never a time when Caucasians were not on the islands and impacting events, and dimly through the mists of history, the flash of tartan, and the skirl of bagpipes comes softly on the air, for of all the *haoles* to find their way to the islands, the Scots were the most tenacious and had the greatest influence. That presence was so hardy, in fact, that Hawaii today may have more people of Scots ancestry, per capita, than any other state.

Young Scots found a home on the sugar plantations of Hawaii. At one time there were 26 plantations along the Hamakua Coast of the Big Island, and Scots were represented at various levels on each of them. (Today the area is still called by old-timers, "The Scots Coast.") Most Scottish immigrants came between 1880 and 1930, but

↑ Descendants of Hawaii's Scottish pioneers spread throughout the islands during the 19th century, many of them gaining prominence, but because of the nature of the Scots they never flaunted this prominence. Only in recent years has there been a renewed interest in Scottish heritage and the Scots' influence on islands far from the crags and misty valleys of their homeland.

there were two Scots aboard Cook's ships. Later Archibald Scott Cleghorn from Edinburgh married Hawaiian royalty and became father of the beautiful and tragic Princess Kaiulani, for whom another Scot, Robert Louis Stevenson, wrote poetry. Glasgow-born Archibald Campbell was a sailmaker to King Kamehameha I; another close friend of the king was Alexander Adams. Robert C. Wyllie, from Ayeshire, was Minister of Foreign Affairs under Kamehameha IV and V. Scottish entrepreneurs Robert Catton and John Neill founded Honolulu Iron Works, and Donald Macintyre came from Scotland to develop the Moanalua Gardens. Scottish bachelors on Oahu settled in at the Macdonald Hotel on the site of what is now Maryknoll High School. Scotswoman Janet Macintyre was the first woman vice president of a Hawaiian company, Bishop Bank & Co.

For the first half of the 19th century the white population of Hawaii was never more than a few hundred permanent residents, although *haoles* manned many of the ships that called in island ports. After the Treaty of Reciprocity in 1876 the white population increased to more than 15,000. By far the greatest number of whites to come en masse came from Portuguese islands in the Atlantic, from Madeira, the Azores, Cape Verde, and they came to escape poor economic conditions in those islands, fleeing to what they hoped would be much improved situations in the Pacific Islands, seeking the elusive *Terra Nova*.

There were Portuguese on the islands at an earlier date, coming as crewmen or castaways or paid passengers on sailing vessels, but in 1878 the migrations began in earnest as the German bark *Priscilla* arrived after 116 days at sea bringing about 120 Portuguese as contract workers on the sugar

→ Portuguese *malasadas* have been a popular contribution to Hawaii's cuisine.

plantations. From 1878 to 1913 there were 29 voyages bringing almost 26,000 people. The Portuguese were steady, sober people, welcomed because of their work ethic, their deep religiosity and their stable family lives. The Portuguese also had no aversion to intermarriages; by 1980 there were at least 55,000 persons in Hawaii of Portuguese ancestry.

While the Portuguese were considered sober and industrious, Hawaii without them would have been *uma mesa sem vinho*, a table without wine. They brought the instrument that became the famous *ukulele*. They brought dances, especially the *chamaritta*, and interesting foods such as *pao doce*, sweetbreads, sausages, *bulo de mel*, honey cake with almonds, and the doughnut-like *malassadas*, which would become an island tradition. With their work ethic and their incredible zest for life, the Portuguese struck a vibrant note in the music of Hawaii.

Other Europeans came — 600 Scandinavians arrived, but most preferred other climes and other lifestyles, and few stayed. Some 1,400 Germans came, some Russians, and more than 5,000 Puerto Ricans along with a smattering of Italians, blacks, and a few Greeks. In 1853 there were some 1,600 whites in Hawaii, but a century later there were almost 300,000 or nearly 40 percent of the population. Today the whites in Hawaii are 24 percent of the population.

↑ In response to a labor shortage on the islands, the Chinese population jumped from less than 2,000 in 1866 to more than 18,000 two decades later. Eventually, the importing of Chinese contract workers was adjusted to more or less coincide with the departure of other Chinese. The later arriving Chinese were not all field workers, however, and included merchants, priests, teachers, doctors, and bankers.

As the 19th century dawned there was a handful of Chinese among the more than 300 foreigners in Hawaii, and Chinese ships' crews were familiar with landfalls in what they came to term *Tan Heung Shan*, the Sandalwood Mountains, because of the sandalwood trade between Hawaii and Canton. But beginning in 1852 a stronger whiff of joss sticks drifted across the islands as Chinese were brought in to work on the plantations. The Chinese came primarily from Guangdong and Fujian, and came willingly, for their homeland was in a state of unrest because of the T'ai P'ing rebellion under the leadership of Hung Hsiu-ch'uan, a mystic who believed himself to be the younger brother of Christ.

The Chinese were hard workers, but lonely; the government of Hawaii brought in no Chinese females. The Chinese men tended to work out five-year contracts (at $3 per month, plus food, clothing, room and board) and then move into the city to try their hands as entrepreneurs. With the Treaty of Reciprocity in 1876, even more Chinese arrived, wages increased, and the Chinese began to intermarry.

Over the past 200 years more than 40,000 Chinese have arrived in Hawaii and left an imprint as indelible as a brush stroke of calligraphy. In the new century, more than 60 percent of them married into another race. In practically all fields of endeavor in

TOURISM: AN INDUSTRY WITH A MISSION

By Stanley Hong
President, Hawaii Visitors Bureau

n 1950 the visitor industry ranked third in Hawaii, behind the giants of sugar and pineapple; today it is the primary industry on the islands and probably will remain so into the foreseeable future.

Growth has not been an accident — nor has it been easy, nor without purpose. A combination of public sector and private sector contributions in both talent and funding has built the visitor industry into the primary source of revenue in the state.

Elsewhere in this book there is a brief history of the industry, but it is important to point out here the tremendous growth as one gauge of how successful promotional efforts have been over the years. From the first available visitor figures in 1927 — 17,451 — we have seen an increase to more than 6.8 million in 1991.

If this were the only measurement of an industry, it would be impressive enough. And if the Hawaii Visitors Bureau wanted to rest on its laurels, we could point to visitor spending of $9.92 billion in 1991, and the fact that the industry provides 35 percent of the Gross State Product, the fact that 40 percent of the jobs in the work force are related to tourism.

These are impressive enough, and make for interesting projections.

But that isn't all.

In the infancy of the visitor industry, everyone played the numbers game to the fullest: how many visitors, how much money. As we have gotten more sophisticated in the business we now focus on the deeper responsibility the industry has to the public, to the islands at large.

We have, in fact, become an industry with a mission: we are striving to be the keepers of the culture, the industry preserving not only the physical but the psychic environment.

Candidly, part of this outlook is self-serving; the realization has taken place that on islands depending on a pristine environment as part of their attraction, the environment must be preserved. It is quite clear that every local businessman with any dependency, however remote, on the visitor industry must, per se, be concerned with protecting the physical environment.

Similarly, we know that the many fortunate facets of our local culture must be nourished, not only because these cultural observances are visitor attractions, but also because it is the right thing to do. As the leading source of revenue in Hawaii, it falls on the visitor industry to take a major share of the responsibility.

Thus, we are sensitive not only to the numbers but with the quality of the visitor experience here and how it relates to the experiences and the environment of our local people. We are interested in the visitor-local interaction. We are concerned, ultimately, that the visitor industry be positive and desirable for our local residents, for whose benefit we have built this industry.

The physical plants that have been erected here are beneficial to the local resident as well as the visitor. Without this industry there probably would not be the quantity and quality of facilities and attractions — the restaurants, parks, hotels, golf courses, and tennis courts. Visitors continue to be at least a part of the impetus toward better-quality facilities, and we know from experience that these generally are more affordable in Hawaii than many places in Europe, Asia, and the Caribbean.

For reasons of culture and the environment, we must maintain a strong visitor industry, one that is reliable and productive year in and year out. Other destination areas have the same view, and thus we compete with them for the visitor in a market that grows ever more demanding. Our battle cry remains "marketing, marketing," and we have to promote our islands for what they truly are — a place unique in culture and arts as well as providing the old standbys of sun, surf, and sand.

The industry must continue to diversify, as, for example, in the meetings and conventions market. That sector alone brought more than a billion dollars to Hawaii in 1991.

The future is bright for the industry, but only as long as we remain flexible, innovative, and vigilant for opportunities. And a bright future for the industry is linked with the bright future of our people — for the industry belongs to the people of Hawaii.

Hawaii there is a Chinese representation, a strong and colorful presence. In restaurants and herbal shops, in acupuncture clinics and across drafting tables, in bank and real estate offices and hospital corridors, the Chinese penchant for hard work and achievement is notable and noted. They were the first of the Asian immigrants to be brought to Hawaii, and their accomplishments and those of their descendants is remarkable. Today some five percent of Hawaii's population is Chinese.

The second group of Asians came from a civilization famous for its pride, its long isolation, and its impressive traditions. From under the shadow of Mount Fuji came the first immigrant workers from Japan, via the British ship *HMS Scioto* in 1868. They were "first-year persons," denoting it was the first year of the Meiji Restoration, marking the end of the Tokugawa shoguns' power and the opening up of a Japan that had been restricted since 1633. Like the

← A young Islander of Japanese ancestry.

initial group of Chinese workers, the Japanese had problems and were happy to return to Japan.

In 1881, King Kalakaua and a handful of Hawaiian officials visited Japan during a world tour, and in that visit the king cemented relations with the Emperor Meiji. The result was that on February 8, 1885, the *City of Tokio* brought 943 Japanese to Hawaii in the role of *Kanyaku Imin*, contract workers, and the king himself went down to meet them. Seventy-five percent of them would go back to Japan or on to the U.S. mainland, but the others would demonstrate the drive to better themselves that became characteristic of Japanese in Hawaii, and many of them began to move into town or into other industries.

In the ensuing years the Japanese watched as the United States closed the door on additional immigration from Japan and limited their passports; it was a move to block foreign labor from entering the United States, and it made Orientals ineligible for citizenship in the land to which they were contributing so much. The Japanese males were not much inclined to intermarry, and 1908 to 1920 was the era of the "picture brides," when young women in Japan and Okinawa were selected by photos to marry the Japanese men in Hawaii. The Japanese population increased to the point that in 1920 more than 40 percent of Hawaii's population was Japanese.

The first generation, the *issei*, were Japanese citizens and were forced to remain so until the U.S. made citizenship possible for them in 1952. Their next generation, born in Hawaii, were *nisei* and automatically U.S. citizens. This dichotomy within the home proved painful in World War II, as the older Japanese citizens saw their sons march off willingly to fight for America, while they themselves were forced to watch their adopted home and their ancestral homeland locked in combat.

(The *nisei* also had to fight American bureaucracy and prejudice. Finally allowed to form a combat unit, the *nisei* were organized into the 100th Battalion and then formed the backbone of the 442nd Regimental Combat Team. Sent to Europe, the *nisei* took incredible casualties but became one of the most decorated units in the American Army).

In a century in Hawaii the Japanese population soared to more than 250,000, and the individual Japanese began to climb into positions of power and influence. Japanese and part-Japanese rose to prominence in government and politics. In time, an American of Japanese ancestry would be the first non-*haole* governor of Hawaii. But even before that, the Japanese had proven a point and no longer had to fight for acceptance in islands where their ancestors had come as contract laborers. The next generations of the *Kanyaku Imin* were at home in Hawaii, and Japan was another time and place. On the islands today the Japanese represent 23 percent of the population.

In 1882, a treaty action by the United States cleared the way for another immigrant group. In that year America was the first Western nation to make a treaty with an ancient, proud land, the Land of the Morning Freshness: Korea. A beautiful, rugged peninsula that produced strong-willed and energetic people, Korea was suffering political unrest, and the Korean Emperor anticipated better opportunities for the Koreans in Hawaii. In 1902 there was active recruiting in Seoul

cities and adapted readily because of a high degree of literacy and an apparent willingness to abandon values they considered outworn for new values that worked well for them. They also had no hesitancy about intermarriage.

In the second half of the 20th century the Koreans became one of the larger immigrant groups to settle in Hawaii, moving to the islands at a rate of more than 1,000 a year from 1969 to 1985. They are upwardly mobile, and only recently have shown a strong inclination toward ethnic values. Like some others in Hawaii, the Koreans have been searching for their roots and finding them in that ancient land of great charm and historical fascination — but then hurrying home to the islands they have taken to their strong hearts.

↑ The ancient traditions of teamwork and cooperation take on new meaning among Hawaiians.

The Filipinos came to Hawaii bringing a musical language and an ebullient air; the men were among the hardest workers anyone had seen and the women among the

and other large cities, and on January 13, 1903, some 100 Koreans arrived and looked for their opportunities. Not confined to plantation work, they spread throughout the islands to seek their destiny.

Only three years later, with now more than 7,000 Koreans on the islands, the gates were closed on this group as well. Reports of mistreatment of Koreans in Mexico were cited, but the Japanese government — now in command in Korea — saw the Koreans as competition for the Japanese workers in Hawaii. The Korean workers already in Hawaii moved into the

most beautiful. They started coming in 1906, and like others they came both because of opportunities in Hawaii and unsettled conditions in their homeland. Hawaii's door opened because of political realities; the passage of the Organic Act of 1900 automatically made U.S. citizens of Hawaii's residents, and it also made Hawaii subject to American labor laws, laws that at the time prohibited Chinese immigration and limited recruitment in Japan and Korea. Additionally, the Spanish-American War had just ended and the U.S. was left in charge of the Philippines. There seemed no reason why Filipino laborers could not be recruited, and every reason why they should.

The Filipinos found work in Hawaii, but it was hard work, and the pay averaged $16 a month for men, $12 for boys, and $10 for women. But by 1930 there were more than 100,000 Filipinos

↑ People of a surprising range of heritages call Hawaii their home.

in Hawaii. At least a third of them were illiterate, making advancement difficult, so many returned to the Philippines, and many went on to the U.S. mainland. Interestingly, there was a renewed interest in Filipino workers after World War II, when more than 7,000 Filipinos made the journey an earlier generation had made. Subsequently, U.S. immigration laws have been generous to the Filipinos, and they are one of the fastest-growing ethnic groups on the islands; today they make up 11 percent of the population.

Much of the credit for successful pineapple and sugar production over the decades must go to the Filipinos, but they have not confined themselves to farming. A new, young, progressive spirit moves today throughout the Filipino community, and no one will be surprised when, in the future, the Americans of Filipino ancestry have a deeper and more lasting impact on the political and social events taking place on the islands.

Other Pacific Islanders came to Hawaii, especially from Samoa; these people have strongly identified with the Mormon Church. Samoans have had their problems in Hawaii as have the other immigrant groups, but the passing years bring promise. The Samoans tend to intermarry easily, but generally with *haoles* or Hawaiians.

Of the other groups in Hawaii — the blacks, the American Indians, the newly-arrived peoples of Southeast Asia — their experiences reflect those of the earlier immigrants, if on a smaller scale. Extant on the islands are Fijians, Lao, Pakistanis, Tahitians, Indonesians, Vietnamese, and others. Their presence may not be overwhelming but gently adds exotic touches to an already exciting social and cultural life.

All of these wonderfully diverse people play out their lives against a backdrop painted earlier in the vivid colors of Hawaiiana, for the Hawaiians were first on the land, the sons and daughters of that energetic and enterprising Polynesian civilization. In post-contact Hawaii, the Hawaiians fell victim to the outsiders' diseases, first the physical ones, then the psychological ones. At the heart of the developing problems was low self-esteem in areas where modern progress was being measured: in the classrooms. Academically, the Hawaiians often were bright but lacked confidence, and tended to drop out. They suffered from a high mortality rate brought on in part by worsening diets and abandonment of the splendid general health practices enjoyed in isolation by the pure Hawaiians. And the pure Hawaiians, by almost every measurement, ultimately suffered more than the part-Hawaiians.

The considerable intermarriages of the Hawaiian people have accomplished at least one thing: they have disseminated throughout various communities some of the atti-tudes and practices of old Hawaii, and thus kept alive aspects of the Hawaiian culture that might have disappeared. The most intermarried and intermingled of all the races in Hawaii, the Ha-waiians may have diffused their blood lines from a strictly biological standpoint, but it has increased the awareness of Ha-waiiana on the

↑ The striking thing about the people of Hawaii is, and has been, their open hearts, that willingness to take in others and comfort them, to extend their *aloha* to strangers.

cultural front. In a survey taken a few years ago, approximately 207,000 people in Hawaii reported they had some Hawaiian blood, while the same survey showed 9,417 pure Hawaiians. It is many of the mixed-bloods who have sparked the maturing cultural renaissance, the new focus on Hawaiian history, dance, music, language, social and religious practices, and general lifestyles. It is a genuine renaissance within the confines of that definition, and it reaches across all age groups.

These are the people of Hawaii.

There is something else that must be said about them, something that is mirrored in their productivity, their social consciousness. It is the fact that in the sun-washed islands they put aside their prejudices to create an atmosphere of tolerance, a sense of focus on the important things of life. They accomplish this in a variety of ways involving academics and religion and simple propinquity, but mostly they have done it by marrying each other.

The people came together in a way that was miraculous, and not a collective miracle but one that took place individually, in each untrammeled heart. They reached across barriers of color and custom, leaped across the barricades of intolerance to embrace each other in a kind of acceptance that did not seem to be occurring anywhere else. No attempt was made to disguise their differences; rather, each of them found something in those dissimilarities to admire and enjoy. It was as if each decided that the other was exotic rather than eccentric, and in surrendering their xenophobia, each found a freedom to associate, to encompass, to love.

This was the miracle: that it happened one-on-one, not by *ukase* and not en masse but in the tentative turning of one soul toward another, individuals free to abandon false pride while keeping the best of their heritage. The people of these fortunate islands were blessed with a clarity of vision that permitted them to appreciate individualism. The islands themselves linked the people in a commonality of beauty and gave them the rich loam of tolerance in which to plant the seeds of their futures. And while the islands gave them freedom, their own histories gave them perseverance, and their own genes gave them strength, and their own spirits gave them an acceptance of their time and place and circumstances, so that in the end there were no strangers in paradise but only others superficially unlike themselves, but very much alike in the ways that mattered.

In a recent year, 46.5 percent of all marriages in Hawaii were inter-racial, and 60 percent of all children born that same year were of mixed blood, and so the miracle continues. Overall, about 33 percent of Hawaii's people are of mixed races.

Realizing that the people of Hawaii must be educated, King Kamehameha III established Hawaii's first public school system in 1840; 150 years later the state's Department of Education looked back on the decades of struggle and forward to the challenges — some foreseen, some yet to be determined — of the year 2000. The Department cited eight ambitious goals that ranged from "children entering kindergarten eager and ready to learn" to a "lifelong learning" plan that shows all segments of society valuing lifelong learning, and collaborating to make that possible.

After 150-plus years, the goals of educating people have not all been met, but the drive to do so seems to be gaining momentum. When Hawaii became a state it entered the comparison sweepstakes, where ranking with other states became possible, and it was apparent that the islands were lagging behind in terms of money spent for education. Recently, Hawaii ranked 35th of all the states in terms of per public school pupil expenditure, and 47th in per capita direct school expenditures. The islands also ranked 45th in class size ratio.

To staff the programs, the state employs 10,724 teachers plus 5,881 various staff professionals and 23,177 temporary, substitute and summer teachers, and others.

To oversee the system, the state funds a Superintendent of Education, and a 13-member elected Board of Education to make policy (a 14th member is a student elected by the Hawaii State Student Council). The system they oversee includes 232 regular schools, five special schools and 11 adult community schools, serving more than 170,000 students from kindergarten through the 12th grade, and almost 100,000 of what the Department calls adult "lifelong learners."

And while the state continues to be frustrated by a shortage of teachers that is likely to continue for the next few years, there is consolation in the fact that the existing corps of teachers has shown remarkable interest in furthering their personal qualifications. There are intern programs, leadership courses, a

← Despite ups and downs in the education budget, the trend has been toward providing a better education system for Hawaii's youth through more and improved facilities, teachers, and opportunities.

framework of staff development; these are effective enough to draw state support in the form of a $1.1 million appropriation for direct support for professional growth. In addition, educators wisely have developed partnership programs with the community which bring in outside professionals to deal directly with students for their practical and intellectual development. Particularly successful is the business-education partnership. There are more than 200 of them in operation.

In the past two years there has been a more intense focus on mathematics, science, languages, and social skills, and schools have been given more flexibility to work out after-hours learning programs, tutorial services, and credit make-up. Education in Hawaii has taken on a decidedly more practical bent at just about every level. One innovative program looks both to the future and back into history: at five school sites, 240 students in 13 classes are studying both Hawaiian and English languages with the same intensity. Hawaii is the only state with two official languages, Hawaiian and English, and this experimental program is designed to make participating students fluent in both languages by the end of grade six. By 1999, seven elementary school sites throughout the state will be involved with the language immersion project.

↑ A new generation of computer users in Honolulu.

For those who prefer private schools, there are 134 in the state, with 2,485 teachers and 35,765 students. For those going on to college, the islands offer a range of possibilities. The best-known college in the state began in 1907 as the College of Agriculture, with five regular students and 12 faculty, operating out of a building in downtown Honolulu. Today it is the University of Hawaii at Manoa, with 18,810 students and 8,014 faculty on a lush 300-acre campus in Manoa Valley.

Reflecting the changing times, the College of Agriculture added a College of Arts and Sciences in 1920, thus becoming the University of Hawaii, and in 1972 it added the "at Manoa," for other campuses were being established. The University of Hawaii at Hilo has 4,449 students, and 652 students attend the University of Hawaii West Oahu. A community college system has grown both in numbers and popularity, with six campuses serving a total of 21,831 students. Equally popular are Brigham Young University, Hawaii Campus in Laie; Chaminade University of Honolulu; and Hawaii Pacific University.

Almost 57,000 students attend Hawaii's colleges, and nearly a quarter of all state residents 25 years old or older have completed four or more years of college. But among adults almost 19 percent were functionally illiterate as of a few years ago, so the last three years have seen a strong push for literacy spearheaded by a committee of prominent residents.

Statistics show no lack of resource material for inquiring minds: the University of Hawaii libraries alone count three million volumes, and the Hawaii State Library System, with its 49 locations on six islands, has 2.4 million books, 9,500 periodical subscriptions, and 84,000 phonodisks and phonotapes with an annual circulation of 6.2 million.

As an educational institution, the University of Hawaii has, pragmatically, turned its attention to Hawaii's particular geography and climate. While medicine, law, and other disciplines get their proper attention, there is a decided focus on problems and resources that deal with a tropical environment, and this focus crosses various disciplines. Marine sciences encompass a great variety of studies, as do Asia and Pacific studies. There is significant *tsunami* research, as studies continue into the arcana of these seismic sea waves.

↑ **Several observatories take advantage of the clear skies at the summit of Mauna Kea, one of the most valuable space viewing areas in the world.**

Additionally, there is a strong concentration on astronomy and astrophysics, logical enough in a state where 13 telescopes will dot the summit of Mauna Kea by the end of the century; as the "landlord" of the summit viewing site, the University can and does demand sufficient time on the telescopes to complement classroom work as an exciting and practical adjunct. The Keck I and Keck II telescopes, both operational by 1996, will help maintain Mauna Kea as the world's premier viewing site, and students will continue to benefit from this pace-setting asset in their backyard.

On 21 acres adjacent to the University of Hawaii, another educational institution got its start in 1960, but this was to be an institution unlike others. It began in an uneasy, shifting year: 1960 saw France explode a nuclear bomb, Gary Powers get shot down in his U–2 spy plane, OPEC hold its first meeting, the U.S. launch the first communications satellite (Echo I), and blacks hold a sit-in at lunch counters in the South. The East-West Center was the product of several minds and one dominant voice — Senator and President-to-be Lyndon Baines Johnson. Johnson posed the question at a Women's Press Club dinner in Washington: "Why do we not establish in Hawaii an international university as a meeting place for the intellectuals of the East and West?"

More than 30 years later, the East-West Center has proven itself to be exactly what was envisioned and more — a place where East and West not only swap concepts and methods, but also exchange subtle social ideals and outlooks. The center continues to contribute significantly to the cause of East-West understanding at many functioning levels. Center graduates have gone on to powerful leadership positions in their home countries and take with them a better understanding of what makes the rest of the world tick.

Often the East-West Center cuts across traditional lines in its impetus toward international interaction, and it remains a unique institution which inspires thousands of research fellows and others to come for a time, however brief, to breathe the heady air of a truly international resource. The center's administrators today face the task of taking the institution, with its valuable linkage, into rapidly changing regions of the world.

↓ Economists look at trends and make reasonable projections, only to find them sometimes skewed by events beyond Hawaii's control. For example, a construction industry that endured hard times in the early- to mid-1980s recovered nicely in the latter part of the decade, spurred by demand and by favorable interest rates. But then growth rates dropped because of a recession, and a simultaneous dip took place in architecture and engineering. In addition, military spending dropped when troops from Hawaii went off to the Gulf War in 1991. The war caused a similar impact on tourism. When a recession in Japan followed, it cut the rate of investments on the islands, but here the picture turned hopeful: in stressful economic times, Japanese travelers tend to come to Hawaii because it is affordable and, as a Pacific destination, closer to home.

In 1989 the state's Department of Labor and Industrial Relations produced an outlook of the five-year-period 1988–1993, with a few projections beyond 1993.

A picture emerged of a state with a growing population, but growing at a slower rate in the 1990s. From 1970 to 1980 the population grew at 2.6 percent, from 1980 to 1990 at 1.7 percent, and through the rest of this decade it is projected at 1.3 percent. This means a parallel slowdown in the rate of growth of the labor force, but does not mean fewer jobs. From 1970 to 1980, the labor force grew by 3.7 percent and from 1980 to 1990 by 2.4 percent; it is expected to average 1.9 percent for the rest of this decade.

In the five-year study period, the results showed a total of almost 72,000 new jobs created on the islands, a growth rate of 3.1 percent. The job total rose from 469,030 in 1988 to a projected 540,810 in 1993.

In the professional, para-professional, and technical occupations, an estimated 25,110 jobs will be available in the life of the study period, with nurses in high demand and at least 400 new openings each year waiting for them. Physicians and surgeons will increase by some 250 a year. About 22,000 jobs will open for clerical and administrative types. In sales, some 21,000 jobs will open, or more than 4,000 over the five years.

Overall, the state looked at a pattern and produced these figures for job openings: managerial and management related occupations, 17,140 in 1988 and 19,730 in 1993; professional, paraprofessional and technical, 84,370 in 1988 and 97,810 in 1993; sales and related occupations, 59,120 in 1988 and 69,130 in 1993; clerical and administrative support occupations, 91,600 in 1988 and 103,030 in 1993; service occupations, 115,210 in 1988 and 136,350 in 1993; agriculture, forestry and fishing, 5,090 in 1988 and 5,850 in 1993; and production, operating and maintenance occupations, 96,510 in 1988 and 108,920 in 1993.

The fastest-growing occupations can be identified, and leading the statistics are travel agents, with a five-year growth rate of 57.1 percent, from 1,770 in 1988 to 2,780 in 1993. Right behind them are civil engineering technicians, from 210 in 1988 to 320 in 1993, a growth rate of 52.4 percent. Others growing rapidly are tax preparers, architects, paralegals, guides, drafters, bus drivers, surveyors, dental hygienists, and travel clerks.

In mid-1992 it was possible to draw an overview of Hawaii's economic situation that showed no extreme rates, either dropping or gaining, but an overall slower performance that was still healthy enough. The population increased by a modest 1 percent, the Gross State Product was some $32 billion, a gain of more than 6 percent, and per capita income was more than $23,000, up by 6 percent. One economic report noted that a drop in some growth rates from very high levels of the past few years was not actually a negative overall drop, as occurred on the U.S. mainland over the same period. The report talked of stability.

The outlook is encouraging.

Tourism will continue to play its dominant role, with visitors totaling more than 7 million a year (an increasing number of them coming from Europe) and spending more than $10 billion a year in Hawaii.

Agriculture, which reached a record level in farm value of $588.8 million in 1990, is expected to

↑ Day's first light in Honolulu's business district.

maintain a steady growth. Construction has presented often confusing statistics because government construction contracts tend to rise and fall, reflecting the odd-year decrease in government contracts tied to the state's biennium budgets. Ongoing are infrastructure projects that include freeways and airport improvement; lagging behind are housing projects, which are expected to catch up in the mid-1990s.

Diversified manufacturing sales continue to increase overall, though experiencing upturns and downturns, and show gains in productivity. Highways and harbors improvements will mean funding for both construction and transportation jobs. In the energy field, gas and water sales are forecast to continue their climb with a concomitant rise in jobs. In communications in one recent year there were more than 100 employers paying an average annual wage of $33,844, almost one and a half times the state average wage, and the job count is rising. Retail sales were slow, but strong by comparison with the U.S. mainland, and in 1990 had increased to $13.7 billion, up 12.3 percent over the previous year; adjusted for the local inflation rate it was a gain of 4.7 percent. Wholesale sales figures dropped in 1991, then rose again.

Hawaii's 47,000 businesses have a choice of financial services on the islands; 10 banks with 199 locations are joined by six savings and loan associations with 146 branches, and four trust companies with seven branches and 46 industrial or small loan licensees with 186 branch offices. And they are healthy; deposits in those institutions are at least $28 billion, and there is another $2.5 billion in the 130 credit unions across the state. Some of the $28 billion on deposit undoubtedly comes from the shares held by 260,000 people in U.S public corporations or investment companies. Some Hawaii banks reach on across the Pacific, to other islands such as Guam and Saipan, as far afield as Grand Cayman, and in Asia capitals such as Singapore and Tokyo and Hong Kong. The Asia/Pacific market will account for much of the banks' growth in the next few years, experts say. The banks' conservative lending policies have made them safe and earned the plaudits of international bankers.

By early 1992 there were more than 47,000 partnerships and corporations registered on the islands. More than 800 of those firms were insurance companies collecting premiums of close to $2 billion a year. In a state that has pioneered various medical insurance programs, more than 90 percent of islanders are covered by some type of insurance plan.

Small businesses are the backbone of Hawaii's industries, for more than half of the 47,000 corporations across the state employ five people or fewer. Business enterprise remains consistently upbeat, and in a recent year in which 3,600 new companies were formed, less than 200 failed. Interestingly, 36 percent of the businesses in Hawaii are owned by women — perhaps not too surprising in a state that always had a high percentage of working women, some of

whom have been able to break out of the clerical and administrative ranks and rise to ownership positions.

The high percentage of labor union membership also is logical in the context of Hawaii's history. The early field workers, especially the Japanese, were inclined to band together to protest conditions in the fields that seemed inhumane or unfair, and the tradition of unionism took hold in such a labor-intensive society. Unionism showed its muscle in 1938 when the International Longshoremen's and Warehousemen's Union (ILWU) took on the Inter-Island Steamship Company, a battle in which the company was the nominal winner but the union showed its strength. In 1941 the union organized the docks and by 1946 had organized pineapple and sugar workers. In 1946 more than 20,000 sugar workers took part in a 79-day strike that ended in a union victory. Another strike in 1949 lasted 177 days and had political fallout that included some union leaders being indicted the following year on various charges that failed to stick — charges that many islanders felt were brought in retaliation for the strikes.

In any event, the unions were in Hawaii to stay. Today there are more than 70 of them, from airline pilots to asbestos workers, glaziers to government employees, mechanics to musicians. Union leadership represents some of the people most involved in community activities, and union executives sit on boards and commissions alongside business executives.

← ↑ No matter what the sport, recreation in Hawaii is always enhanced by the tropical climate and lush surroundings.

↑ **A fresh start to the IronMan Triathlon: the Rough Water Swim.**

If islanders work hard, they also know how to play.

A quick count of sporting events on the islands in 1992 showed 204 events scheduled, from golf matches to tennis contests to bodybuilding competition to canoeing, kite-flying and more. Some of the events receive worldwide attention, such as the Ironman Triathlon held each October, and the Hawaii International Billfish Tournament held annually in August. In any given year there may be a ski tournament atop Mauna Kea, snow permitting, and other contests include windsurfing, archery, volleyball, motorcycle races, sailing, surfing, polo, and

enough marathons to leave one breathless. The annual Jeep Eagle Aloha Bowl takes place on Christmas Day, and the widely-televised Hula Bowl football contest is a treat for players as well as fans.

On islands that have an annual average temperature of 77°F and generally clear and sunny weather, it is not surprising to find 65 golf courses and 282 public tennis courts. Nor is it surprising to find 1,100 miles of hiking trails.

For the outdoor-minded, the state has seven national parks, 77 state parks, 582 county parks and a number of designated scenic points. There are at least 75 museums.

What may be surprising to some visitors is the concentration on art and cultural activities. The Honolulu Symphony has grown experienced and highly professional; it performs not only in the heart

THE FUTURE OF HAWAIIANS

By Myron Thompson
Member, Board of Trustees
Kamehameha Schools/Bishop Estate

I have been asked to share my views on where Hawaiians will be from this year on — the prospects for the future of our people. I am not one who is comfortable predicting what might happen, but rather someone who prefers to deal with the realities of today. It is my strong belief that unless we take a hard look at our current realities, there is no point in talking about the future. Unless we take full advantage of the opportunities here today, we may not survive to face tomorrow.

A look at statistics on native Hawaiians is sobering. We suffer from poor health, low incomes, over-representation in the prisons, and under-representation in the professions.

We have the highest percentage of teenage mothers in the state, and of all the low birthweight babies born, 31 percent are Hawaiian. More than 34 percent of the expectant Hawaiian mothers receive little or no prenatal care, far more than the state average. And studies estimate that 44 percent of our Hawaiian children under the age of 18 are living in a broken home.

Hawaiian children begin their educational careers behind national and state norms for vocabulary. They rank first among the major ethnic groups for alcohol and drug abuse, and they enroll in and complete higher education at rates below their peers.

Given this picture, how can we Hawaiians hope to improve our well-being, become more productive, and have a strong hand in shaping our destinies? I have dedicated my professional life to this work, and I continue to approach this effort with a strong sense of hope and optimism, for despite the gloomy facts and figures, we are making progress. And the effort truly is a collaborative one, as people and organizations throughout the state are hard at work.

Kamehameha Schools/Bishop Estate has made early childhood education a strong priority. We have programs which begin before the child is born, teaching the expectant mother and her family about effective parenting, child development and family health. Once children reach two years of age, they and their care-givers can participate in our Traveling Preschools. In partnership with the Federal Department of Education, these preschool sessions are held outdoors, and introduce children to organized group activities. Families are taught how to provide their children with a stimulating learning environment.

Once children reach the age of four, they can enroll in center-based preschools, to learn the skills which will help them later in their educational careers. In brief, our philosophy is that by giving children the best possible start, we can have a positive and lasting impact.

We've begun to see some remarkable progress. Hawaiian children

IN HAWAII

entering kindergarten score in the 10th to 12th percentile on the Peabody Picture Vocabulary Test. The state average of all children is around the 18th percentile. Children who have graduated from Kamehameha's early education programs, however, score in the 28th to the 30th percentile, and these gains stay with them as they go through their early elementary school years.

Programs intended to improve Hawaiian representation in higher education are having much success. While in 1981 Hawaiians made up only 7.5 percent of the regular University of Hawaii enrollment, today that figure has risen to 10.5 percent. If present growth rates continue, 20 percent of Hawaiian enrollment in the state's higher education programs is projected shortly after the turn of the century.

Recognizing that without good health, educational and all other reforms are meaningless, the federal government passed the Native Hawaiian Health Act. This multi-million dollar piece of legislation is enabling Hawaiians to approach the issue of medical care in a culturally sensitive and appropriate context. We are renewing traditional care-giving methods, and we are teaching our people to heal themselves.

While we address the needs of the body, we are also attending to the needs of the spirit. The Native Hawaiian Culture and Arts Program, also federally funded, is dedicated to cultural renewal and to making that critical connection between our ways of the past and our needs in the present. By illuminating that rich heritage of the Hawaiians and sharing this knowledge with all the people of Hawaii and the world, we assist our people to take their rightful place in this multiethnic society.

Given *this* total picture then, what do I see for the Hawaiian people as we go forward?

If we continue the work we are involved with today, if we accept our challenges *now* and take advantage of our opportunities, if we face the future with optimism tempered by reality, I see bright and productive times ahead, with our people as contributing members of contemporary society. It is often said that the hope for the future lies with the children, and I agree with this wholeheartedly. While we need to take an integrated approach to solving our problems, if we lose the children then we lose everything. If, on the other hand, our children begin their lives with inquiring minds, healthy bodies and positive self images, then there is absolutely no limit to what they, and we as a people, can achieve.

of the city but takes its talents across the state to perform in small towns, and always to a delighted audience. In a recent season the Symphony performed 101 concerts to audiences that totalled almost 170,000. Throughout the islands — in school auditoriums, in theaters, in college and university halls — 377 performing arts productions drew more than 960,000 to operas, rock concerts, ballets and other dramatic and musical productions.

The spry and shrewd Don Francisco de Paula y Marin — he of the plethora of wives and children, the diarist who noted his planting of a pineapple — was not slow to note that a considerable number of sea captains were footloose in Honolulu as the 19th century rolled on. He also observed that they were forced to live in typical grass shacks, and as men of substance they probably would be happier in something more comfortable. Don Francisco looked at his own house, made of coral and only a half-block from the waterfront where the sea captains landed, and decided his many children could double up in their rooms even more than they already did. By 1811, the intrepid Don Francisco had become what probably was Hawaii's first innkeeper, renting rooms in his house to the sea captains. He called it the Oahu Hotel.

He was soon followed by Navarro's Inn, by Allen's Place — reportedly built and operated by a black ex-slave — and the Warren House, the latter bought some years later by three Chinese who promptly changed the name to the Canton Hotel in a burst of patriotism. Or homesickness.

With the advent of the whaling era, the hotel operators on Oahu and Maui enjoyed what hotelmen

today still long for: the long-term guest. Whalingmen tended to be in town for two or three weeks at a time, and they liked to hang their hats in places where rum was plentiful, women were willing, and there was,

↑ A celebration of natural riches and an invitation of peace between peoples — Hawaii's flower wreaths are a symbol that has lost none of its resonance through the centuries.

incidentally, a place to stay. Up went the Blonde Hotel, the National, the French, the Royal, the Commercial, the Globe, the White Swan, and others. While the residents of Lahaina and Honolulu may not have cared overmuch for this fledgling "visitor industry," the hotel proprietors and ancillary activities simply took the whalingmen's money and ignored any complaints. When the whaling industry went out of existence, the hotels followed suit, except for a handful that became restaurants and saloons.

As 1870 neared, it became obvious that Honolulu needed a good hotel for an increasing number of business visitors, particularly the wealthy from San Francisco. King Kamehameha V persuaded his cabinet to appropriate $50,000 in government money to build a new hotel and immediately ran into objections from some residents who did not want Hawaii to be overrun by tourists. The hotel went up nevertheless, but considerably over budget — $116,528 — and was named the Hawaiian Hotel. It had gaslights, doors that would lock, and indoor plumbing. In the first two years of the hotel's existence the visitor count decreased instead of increasing, the number dropping about 20 percent to the great satisfaction of those who had argued against building the hotel. Throughout the quarter-century leading up to 1900, the number of visitors staying overnight or longer averaged a little more than 2,000 per year.

The islands entered a period of growing political unrest. King Kalakaua was on the throne and in 1887 had been forced to grant a new and more liberal constitution to the islands. His successor, Queen Liliuokalani, feuded with the establishment to the

↑ At the King Kalakaua Jubilee, participants recreate the Hula, circa 1886. Iolani Palace, Honolulu.

point where rebellion broke out and the Queen was forced to abdicate, leading to Hawaii's becoming a republic, then a territory and, ultimately, a state. These events had a curious effect on tourism in Hawaii: carried in U.S. mainland newspapers, the dramatic accounts of Hawaii's trials brought the islands to the attention of millions of readers, and in 1899, just a year after Hawaii had been annexed to the United States as a territory, there were more visitors to the islands than there had been previously.

A new century seemed to mean a new life for the fledgling industry. Kalakaua had spent some time in

the old Hawaiian Hotel and so it was re-named the Royal Hawaiian. Its thriving business underscored the need for more hotels, and an enterprising Scot named Alexander Young spent $2 million building a 300-room hotel in downtown Honolulu that he named after himself; it opened in 1903. Already extant were the Hamilton, the Queen, the Majestic, the Occidental, the Blaisdell. The Alexander Young Hotel was to be a model of its kind, structurally sound, modern, and with first-class accommodations, but would be the last large hotel of its kind to open downtown — for now the visitors had signalled their preference for the very things Hawaii was becoming known for: the sea, the surf, the beach. And the move was on toward a scruffy part of Oahu that had, nevertheless, a fine beach and plenty of palm trees. Waikiki was a coconut grove surrounded by fish ponds and taro patches and a legion of mosquitoes. The Royal Hawaiian Hotel had opened a day-annex there, and some modestly-scaled overnight establishments had sprung up, among them the Park Shore and the Sans Souci, both destined to close after a few years.

But in 1901, things changed. The Moana Hotel opened and proved to be exactly what visitors wanted, a charming and comfortable hotel on a good, sandy beach. The Royal Hawaiian Hotel's annex was improved and became the Seaside Hotel. Robert Lewers' former home became the Halekulani, and the visitor industry began to thrive in spite of the taro patches and mosquitoes. (Finally, in the mid-1920s, the Ala Wai Canal was dug as a rather splendid drainage ditch which helped rid the area of mosquitoes.) In 1918 more than 8,000 visitors had found their way to Hawaii, and most of them to Waikiki. In 1922 the visitor count was 9,676; in 1929 it was 22,190. In 1927, a $4 million Royal Hawaiian

Hotel opened in Waikiki, a grand, romantic establishment that in itself was a visitor lure. But with the decade of the 1930s, the Depression that rocked America also rocked the small, remote islands, and visitor travel to Hawaii dropped to a low of 10,111.

Still, it was the era of the Beautiful People.

They came from the political ranks, from Hollywood, from the establishment East and the enterprising West. They brought their classy automobiles with them, and their chauffeurs, their pets, often their hairdressers. They danced on the *lanais* of the splendid hotels to the languorous soft

→ A Paniolo, or Hawaiian cowboy, rides in the Kamehameha Day Parade.

worth living.

Between 1936 and 1940, some 20,000 to 25,000 such visitors a year kept the image of blue Hawaii alive across a nation struggling with an economic malaise that really ended only with a deeper tragedy beginning with the bombing of Pearl Harbor.

↑ A pa'u rider in the Aloha week Parade, Waikiki.

Hawaiian music. They wore flower *leis* and made daring motor trips to other parts of Oahu, accompanied by hampers of food and fine champagne. A certain number of them, with certain proclivities, made close friends among the Waikiki beachboys who taught them a variety of lessons, including how to swim, or handle an outrigger canoe, or to surf. In the glory of Hawaiian sunsets they walked the sandy beach of Waikiki and admired the distinctive profile of Diamond Head and thought that life was, indeed,

On the islands, meanwhile, the economic potential of the visitors was not unnoticed or unappreciated. On May 14, 1902, members of the Chamber of Commerce and the Merchants Association met to decide on a proposal by W.C. Weedon to advertise the territory on the U.S. mainland via a series of illustrated lectures. The group knew there was a precedent for such an action. In 1892, Lorrin Andrews Thurston started the Hawaii Bureau of Information to spread the word about Hawaii's charms; the organization became moribund, and it was not until the Chamber of Commerce meeting in 1902 that the visitor industry started to get organized. The Chamber and the Merchant's Association agreed to Weedon's proposal and gave him $100 a month for six months, and two local firms gave Weedon free passage to San Francisco and back — an early example of in-kind contributions from segments of the industry.

Weedon's series of lectures on the West Coast were well attended, and he brought along the now-requisite visual aids, a stereopticon with views of Hawaii. Weedon had broken ground; a Joint Tourism Committee was founded with authorization by the Chamber of Commerce and got under way with $1,500 in 1903. Oddly enough, the $1,500 came from a "public health tax" of 10 cents per ton on incoming freight. This tax had been instituted by shippers in the wake of the bubonic plague of 1899 and 1900 and was kept alive as a kind of public emergency health fund to be used in cleaning up the wharves and maintaining supervision on the waterfront. It could also be used to promote industry and business, and the Joint Tourism Committee happily took the $1,500 check "for the benefit of the community," and began promoting the islands as a tourist destination area worth visiting.

And the visitors kept coming.

In 1910, Matson's S.S. *Wilhelmina* entered service and offered fine accommodations, and other cruise vessels brought the Beautiful People to Hawaii's shores. In Hawaii the beat went on *con brio* as the Honolulu Symphony Orchestra was organized and

↑ If old Don Francisco de Paula y Marin could return to see the growth in the hotel business which he probably started, even that entrepreneurial soul would be startled to find 53,000 hotel rooms and close to 20,000 condominium units catering to Hawaii's visitors. Another 3,000 to 5,000 hotel rooms are on the drawing boards, as the visitor count continues to remain impressive.

gave its first public performance in 1902. The Honolulu Community Theatre was established (as the Footlights) in 1915. The College of Hawaii (to become the University of Hawaii) students gave their first performance in 1912. The Waikiki Aquarium was built in 1904 by the Honolulu Rapid Transit and Land Company, and the Honolulu Zoo opened in 1914 in Kapiolani Park. In 1927 the Honolulu Academy of Arts opened and would expand exponentially in prestige. The promotional entity was now called the Hawaii Tourist Bureau and grew along with the times.

In 1921 the Bureau began collecting data on visitor arrivals and laid the foundation for a systematic reporting system that, eventually, also impacted the type and amount of promotion the Bureau undertook. There is one significant gap in the compilation of the statistics: for the years 1942 through 1945, tabulators have entered a single sentence — "the visitor industry was suspended during World War II."

The return was glorious. The Matson flagship *Lurline*, wearing the biggest *lei* ever made, approached Diamond Head on April 21, 1948, while Army and Navy aircraft roared overhead, and more than 80 surface craft sailed out to greet her, blowing whistles and flying flags in full dress-ship. Thirteen outrigger canoes raced out to accompany the other craft, and girls in the canoes scattered flowers in the cruise ship's path. At Pier 11 a *kahuna*, a Hawaiian priest, invoked the old gods of Hawaii while Governor Ingram M. Stainback and Mayor John H. Wilson waited to greet the ship and her captain, Frank E. Johnson. There were 777 passengers aboard and at least 100,000 Hawaii residents crowding the shoreline to see the *Lurline* on her first passenger voyage since reconversion from wartime service.

The great ship's trans-Pacific crossing was symbolic of an industry that was recovering from the war years, but few, if any, could predict the incredible changes that were in the offing. By 1950 air travel accounted for about 70 percent of the total visitors to Hawaii, and in 1959 — the year of statehood — jet aircraft began bringing visitors at an ever-increasing rate. From less than 300,000 in 1959 the visitor count leaped to 1,527,012 in 1969, and the construction industry exploded with hotel and resort development.

The Hawaii Visitors Bureau, evolved from its hard-working predecessors, expanded its efforts (but

↑ Hawaii's charms aren't confined to geography.

in 1959 stopped giving a *lei* to each arriving visitor). In 1972 the visitor total was more than 2 million for the first time, and only four years later was 3,220,151. In 1990 the visitor count was a record 6,971,180, and the visitors spent more than $9 billion in Hawaii.

As the visitor industry strode like a colossus, some in Hawaii feared that some things of value would be smashed in its footsteps. Projections indicate the visitor count could well rise to more than 11 million a year by the year 2010, and that hotel and condominiums might increase from a little more than 53,000 to more than 100,000. Environmentalists worried about the effect on Hawaii's tender environment, and businessmen and civic leaders — perhaps a little belatedly — also began to realize that the most important attraction to visitors was a pristine environment, an unspoiled, non-commercial and

↑ Some children of Hawaii take to the water more easily than others.

↑ **One resident makes his loyalties clear.**

natural ambiance accompanied by quality hotels and plenty of activities. A tall order, but the state of Hawaii acknowledged this necessity in a state Functional Plan for Tourism:

The major theme for these physical Functional Plans focuses on the promotion of a balanced growth approach in the use of our limited resources. This recognizes the need for economic development while preserving our fragile environment and multicultural lifestyles throughout our island state. It also means enhancing our natural environment and cultural resources through actions aimed at protecting, preserving and promoting their significance.

Meanwhile, the factors that lure visitors remain constant — the genuine friendliness of Hawaii's people and the perpetuation of that old *"aloha* spirit" that speaks of warmth and affection; Hawaii's affordability compared with many European, Asian, and Latin American destinations; and what is arguably the world's best climate.

Hawaii is a place that still allows dreams, and dreamers. It is equally a place that gives birth to pragmatic souls who stretch their minds in a world growing increasingly complex. The song of Hawaii is a polyrhythmic presentation that includes the languorous offerings of the old South Seas, but also the quick beat of the future.

That future is in the hands of *na po'e,* who are entrusted to keep in balance the islands' robust economy and fragile environment. It is a challenge accepted by those who love the islands, and they are a legion. They are not only born here but come from elsewhere, practical souls and romantics, beachcombers and scientists, artists and engineers — all pulled by the magnetism of the undefined that lies at the core of the islands and on the edge of every man's consciousness. The islands are the realization of the dream, and all who know them understand the words of Coleridge...

Weave a circle round him thrice
And close your eyes with holy dread,
For he on honey-dew hath fed
And drunk the milk of Paradise.

5
Holo I Mua

To Go Forward

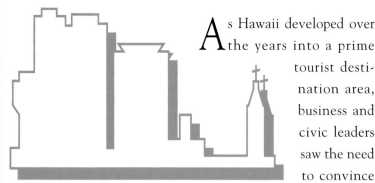

As Hawaii developed over the years into a prime tourist desti- nation area, business and civic leaders saw the need to convince others that the islands were also a place where serious work could be done and was, in fact, being accomplished.

Toward the end of the 1980s a public relations/ marketing firm produced a paper detailing some of the reasons Hawaii was a good place to do business. Hawaii was described as a booming commercial center for the Pacific Basin. The paper highlighted some industries and noted that over two decades, Hawaii has become a major center of international commerce, attracting more foreign investment per capita than any other state, investments that ran the gamut of an expanding economy.

The paper focused on government's role in attracting investments, and listed these actions: a streamlining of the State Department of Business and Economic Development (now with Tourism added); a tax revision that reduced corporate income tax rates and exempted business from the General Excise Tax on exports; a reduction of the tax rate for unemployment insurance financing; expansion of funds available for new business start-ups and expansion; a new loan fund to finance small business innovations; a new training program to tailor the work force and specific needs of new incoming companies, especially high-tech companies; and the establishment of high-tech parks.

Other factors were presented in a positive light: Hawaii is distant, but this becomes irrelevant in an age of expanding communications techniques, and, in fact, the geographic location of the islands is a plus. Secondly, Hawaii's location away from major markets is not the detriment it may appear because the islands do not produce heavy machinery, and do not need to obtain raw materials or ship finished goods. Instead, Hawaii relies on business transactions by telecommunications and by personal contact, both in Asia and on the U.S. mainland, to conduct business that does not involve heavy manufacturing.

The paper discussed the cost of living and the cost of doing business in Hawaii. Such costs are relative. While Hawaii's prices may run higher than most mainland cities, they are lower than many other cities of the Pacific Rim, where business is done. As examples, Tokyo, Hong Kong, and Singapore all are more expensive to do business in than Hawaii. And the cost of maintaining an office in Honolulu is still cheaper than San Francisco or Los Angeles.

Maintaining a staff is cheaper too, according to the Economic Development Corporation of Hawaii (EDCH), which compares the cost of keeping a staff of 12 in 1,800 square feet of space in Tokyo ($1.1 million) and Honolulu ($400,000). Vacancies in downtown Honolulu traditionally are rare, but by 1995 another 1 million to 2 million square feet of space will be available.

Business pays its share of taxes. Hawaii has had an average annual budget surplus of more than $375 million since 1989 because of a strong economy; this showed signs of dropping in early 1992, but traditionally the state has maintained a strong surplus. The largest source of revenue for the state coffers is the 4 percent General Excise Tax on sales and services, but the EDCH notes that a third of the dollars collected through this tax comes from the visitor industry, lessening the burden on local taxpayers. The corporate tax rate is 4.4 percent on net income to $25,000, 5.4 percent to $100,000, and 6.4 percent on income exceeding $100,000. The capital gains rate is 4 percent for corporations. The state has a maximum personal income tax of 10 percent (for taxable incomes of more than $40,000 per year), and a maximum capital gains tax for individuals of 7.25 percent.

In supporting business, the islands provide an interesting and helpful network, in both private and government sectors. Always effective is the Chamber of Commerce of Hawaii, founded in 1850 and today the largest association of business and professional men and women in the state, with a membership of 4,500 individuals representing 2,500 firms (and at least 70 percent of them are small businesses). The Chamber is the parent board to affiliate organizations — the Retail Merchants of Hawaii and the Manufacturers Association of Hawaii — and also maintains 20 program committees and councils; these programs are the Chamber's primary thrust, and the Chamber has proven effective in addressing any issue affecting the economic and social life of the community. The Chamber is funded privately via a dues structure, and over the years has merited the loyalty of local businesses.

↑ **The H-1 Freeway at sunset.**

The Economic Development Corporation of Honolulu is a private, not-for-profit organization working to attract new business to Hawaii. Its mission also is to promote Honolulu as a location for international business activities, thereby expanding and diversifying the economic base. Similarly, the Pacific Basin Economic Council exists to promote the expansion of trade and investment in the area by open markets, and is composed of more than 800 corporations from 14 countries. The Council creates forums for business leaders to develop better networking and communications.

Headquartered in Washington but with offices in Hawaii is the Pacific Forum/Center for Strategic and International Studies; this organization is a joint venture partner with the Pacific Basin Economic Council, and its purpose is to provide research and analysis of political, economic, and security trends in the Asia-Pacific region. Another private, non-profit organization, the Pacific International Center for High Technology Research, has primary capabilities

↑ Behind the palm trees, hula dancers, and sunshine, Hawaii has a thriving business and research and development community.

in alternate energy, information technology, and education/training. It assists Hawaii companies in applying new technology to business, in addition to its broad purpose of applied research.

The Hawaii Business Roundtable, also non-profit, is a group of top business leaders who provide a high-level resource of information and ideas; its most recent focus has been on improving Hawaii's public education, and it is notable for establishing in 1984 the Economic Development Corporation of Honolulu, the EDCH. Another group proving its worth is the non-profit Bilingual Access Line, offering translation and interpretation services. It claims more than 150 translators operating in a dozen or more different languages.

Support for business also comes from the state government, in a manner more quietly efficient than eye-catching. The state does not trumpet massive tax breaks for business firms, but year by year it has managed to improve the business climate with a series

of laws that offer incentives for companies to relocate to Hawaii, or for existing Hawaii companies to expand. As an example, all exported computer software is exempted from the General Excise Tax, as is revenue from securities trading. There also is a revolving fund to help companies set up new operations on the islands.

The state agency that all new or expanding businesses become familiar with is the State Department of Business, Economic Development and Tourism (DBED). This department can provide capital loans up to $1 million or loans of up to $100,000 for "innovative development." It does so via the Hawaii Capital Loan Program within the Financial Assistance Branch of the department. The interest rate is pegged at 7.5 percent per year or 1 percent below the prime rate, whichever is lower. In DBED's Government Marketing Assistance Program, businesses learn which federal, state or county organizations buy goods and services from the private sector. The assistance program then helps the business firm establish a relationship.

For firms that look beyond the U.S., the International Business Center of DBED has been set up to help expand those international opportunities. The center introduces overseas businesses to the resources and expertise available on the islands, works to generate new business, and, in essence, becomes the single starting point for information, assistance, coordination and/or referrals for businesses interested in being active in international trade. (The governments of Australia, Canada, Japan, Korea, Taiwan, and the Philippines have major trade/diplomatic enterprises in Hawaii, and at least 30 other nations of Asia, Europe, Latin America, and the Pacific maintain representatives here. All are geared to provide business information on the countries they represent.) Through a Trade Finance Program, the International Business Center can help firms prepare and submit applications for federal trade finance and insurance guarantees.

Other assistance to business comes from academia, as the University of Hawaii at Manoa offers management and technical assistance to companies, entrepreneurs, government agencies, and community development organizations. The Pacific Business Center is supported by diverse professional faculty of the university and is equipped to develop business plans and feasibility studies, identify suppliers and sources of equipment for market research, provide marketing strategies, engage in strategic planning, and provide other services. Fees are reasonable.

The Pacific Business Center also is internationally-minded, and offers its expertise beyond Hawaii to American Samoa, Guam, the Federated States of Micronesia, the Commonwealth of the Northern Mariana Islands, the Republic of the Marshall Islands, and the Republic of Palau. One of the center's notable success stories was, in fact, assistance to the state of Yap. Invited to conduct feasibility studies on nine separate projects, the center organized teams of professors and students who went to Yap and made in-depth assessments which the government used to develop the various projects, including a tourism plan.

Two other programs help employers recruit and train workers according to the specific requirements of the job. They are the Aloha State Specialized Employment and Training, a state-level program, and Work Hawaii, a county-level operation. Both programs are federally funded.

An enterprising businessman quickly notes that some programs are designed to help him through the licensing and permit process and to put his firm in operation as quickly as possible. A "one-stop" license and permit center is the Business Action Center

↓ Keeping the best of both worlds, business leaders in Hawaii bring the *aloha* spirit to work with them.

SEA CHANGES IN THE PACIFIC ECONOMY

By Dr. David L. Ramsour
Senior Vice President and Chief Economist
Bank of Hawaii

For a number of years observers have referred to a coming Age of the Pacific or a Pacific Century — an era lying ahead in which the shifting weight of world trade and finance from the Atlantic hemisphere to the Pacific Rim communities produces dynamite growth in the region.

Much of the prediction has seemed to exceed reasonable possibility, even to be self-serving when coming from spokesmen with Pacific interests. But now events are transpiring that make this scenario appear far more likely than it could have before.

The critical events essentially involve a massive geopolitical restructuring of the Pacific region that could not have taken place until well after the unique results of the revolutions in Eastern Europe and within the Soviet Union began to be felt. Some of the new perceptions of a more independent Pacific could not have been developed even until the summer of 1991, following the confirmation of perestroika's survival. And now that the new realities of waning Soviet military and political power in the Pacific are more fully grasped, not only do military arrangements change meaning but

entire commercial and financial patterns within this region of the world begin to take new shapes.

The abrupt end of the Cold War of the past 45 years suddenly made certain U.S. defense arrangements less essential than they appeared to be only months before. This not only produced the disintegration of Philippine base talks but significantly altered assumptions about Southeast Asia defense requirements and their associated commercial parameters. It accelerated the weakening sense of defense interdependence in the rest of the Pacific and particularly that of the already softening U.S.-Japanese mutual defense understandings. The direct impact on economic arrangements related to existing as well as potential bases and repair facilities throughout the Pacific and Asia will be substantial.

More dramatic, however, is the effect that the sense of a new world order is having on purely civilian commercial and financial arrangements in the Pacific. Commercial networks ranging from Japan to Vietnam are being rethought and developed in ways that until recently might have been considered unattractive to the participants. Notions of new regional trading agreements have strengthened beyond what would have been thought

politically or diplomatically reasonable only months ago. Within these concepts lies the hotly debated call by many in the region for a clearly defined trading bloc of Asian countries. The development of such a trading bloc implies breaks in traditional trading arrangements with the United States and Europe that had survived a great deal of friction within the more tolerant alliances of super-power struggle.

Without the sense of urgency of defense strategies in a bipolar-polar world, and with the even more uncertain meanings that Europe '92 holds in the wake of Eastern Europe's recent revolutions, countries in Asia have begun to pursue aggressively new market niches and more reliable trading alliances. The formation of the North American Trade Agreement by the United States, Canada, and Mexico has intensified those efforts. There is ongoing debate over the extent to which Asian nations should attempt to penetrate these alliances or, instead, form a powerful bloc of their own in defense against feared exclusionary practices by Europe and North America.

Divided Asian opinion and market realities should keep the debate unsettled indefinitely, especially if an Asian trading bloc appears likely to take on the disliked trappings of a resurrected Japanese co-prosperity sphere. Nevertheless, the dynamics for a more powerful Asian market have been cast, and the Pacific communities including Hawaii will feel this force intensely for many years. To the extent that these nations, and Japan in particular, continue to run surpluses with the rest of the world, some of the impact will come in the form of continued capital investment in Hawaii. But current commercial patterns already indicate that broader product and service exports from Hawaii will come with these developments, and with them, a broader and more robust economic structure for the state.

operated by DBED, which provides help to all with no fees involved.

An excellent resource is the Small Business Center, operated by the Chamber of Commerce of Hawaii in conjunction with DBED. This center exists to advise businesses through consultation and seminars. Similar expertise is available through an all-island Small Business Development Center Network, a support service geared toward new and small businesses. The federal government's Small Business Administration is represented on the islands, with the mission of stimulating business via loan guarantees, training, and counseling.

Again through the University of Hawaii, the no-fees Office of Technology Transfer and Economic Development offers business and marketing planning. The Honolulu Minority Business Development Center provides similar assistance to ethnic minorities, and native Hawaiians receive training and technical assistance through the *Alu Like* program, where the ideal is *E alu like mai kakou, e na 'oiwi o Hawai'i,* "let us work together, natives of Hawaii."

Not the least of programs here has been SCORE, the Service Corps of Retired Executives, sponsored by the Small Business Administration. Its corps of highly-trained and respected retirees provide their skills and long experience to businesses in Hawaii and the South Pacific. In a state where people are relatively long-lived, SCORE has an impressive list of retired but still active businessmen who have valuable knowledge and insights, and are willing and eager to share them.

Starting in the 1970s some islanders began to think in high-tech terms and to develop industries that employed or contributed to a new era of technology. New products in computer software, electronic circuit boards, new tools for aquaculture and other, similar products began to come on the market. Hawaii's Legislature took the long view: a state that probably would never get into heavy manufacturing could, instead, carve a niche with high-tech products and programs. This also would mesh well with environmental concerns, for the high-tech industries tend to be non-polluters.

In 1983 the Legislature created the High Technology Development Corporation (HTDC) to support such high-tech industries, and entrepreneurs were encouraged to think in global terms. A year later the Hawaii Institute of Electronics Research surveyed local companies and found 67 commercial firms with 1,800 employees and annual revenues of $90 million. Four years later another survey showed 191 high-tech firms and support companies employing 9,485 people and producing $908 million in revenues.

↑ The Hawaii Legislature has kept an eye on Hawaii's long-term future by encouraging high-tech projects.

Between 1988 and 1991 Hawaii's high-tech industries blossomed — a 33 percent increase in employment, a 10 percent increase in annual revenues, and 50 new companies starting up or relocating. Late in 1991 there were 300 companies involved in high-tech production, services and support, employing 12,204 workers and contributing more than $988 million to the local economy.

Significantly, through the end of 1991, the Legislature had appropriated more than $40 million in Capital Improvement Program funds to create or expand Hawaii's infrastructure to support high-tech development. More than $2 million went to complete the Manoa Innovation Center on Oahu, with its 46,000 square feet of space for up to 50 firms. One of the anchor tenants there is another HTDC creation, the Hawaii Software Service Center, set up to link Hawaii's software development companies and their clients. A recent count showed some 130 companies in Hawaii involved with software development. On the island of Maui, the 330-acre Maui Research & Technology Center opened in Kihei as a multipurpose facility that can do business worldwide with state-of-the-art telecommunications and computing capabilities.

Two older high-tech parks are the Hawaii Ocean Science and Technology Park, developed by HTDC on 322 acres of the Big Island of Hawaii, and the Mililani Technology Park on Oahu, a 346-acre site that is a project of Castle & Cooke Properties, Inc. That firm along with HTDC has entered into a joint venture with the Chamber of Commerce of Hawaii to market and promote Hawaii as a site for commercial high-tech development. Mililani has been a resounding success, the location of some of Hawaii's most successful high-tech companies. Yet another high-tech center is the Kaimuki Technology Enterprise Center in Honolulu, (KAITEC) a 7,500-square-foot site developed by HTDC to help establish new companies in software development, electronics, telecommunications and other high-tech enterprises. In 1992, there were 19 companies in KAITEC.

In 1991, through Act 288 of the State Legislature and strong public support from Hawaii's governor, the strategic plan drafted by the HTDC for 1990–1995 became the official direction for high-tech development on the islands. The goals are at once sweeping but succinct — to create an environment that will support high-tech development in Hawaii; to determine which companies to support with programs

← Not unlike their predecessors, modern residents of Hawaii look to the stars to gain knowledge and tangible data. With man-made satellites orbiting the earth, today's voyagers aspire to similar feats as the Polynesians who mastered the unimaginable by navigating the Pacific Ocean in double-hulled canoes.

← ↓ There is no lack of solid achievement in this tropical paradise. Professors at the University of Hawaii have gained national attention in a wide range of fields; ocean scientists and volcanologists are breaking new ground in research; companies in the high-tech parks are on the cutting edge of their specialties; political scientists have established Hawaii as a splendid site for East-West relations to flourish; and the Hawaii State Legislature has passed landmark bills in health care and land use that are now being adopted by other states. Left: the University of Hawaii at Manoa's Electronics Laboratory. Below: Caltech's Submillimeter Observatory at Mauna Kea on the Big Island.

and services; to develop support for start-ups as well as existing companies; to develop the ability to evaluate high-tech companies interested in relocating to Hawaii; and to take the lead (without duplicating other efforts), in stimulating the development of high-tech industries in Hawaii.

At a point in its recent history, a point perhaps too swift or too subtle to receive much focused attention at the time, Hawaii underwent a transformation. It stopped being *only* a playground and became a place where serious business got serious attention from other places in the world. Part of the reason for this transition was the overlapping time zones that allow businessmen to connect with East and West. The working day in Hawaii overlaps the working day in major cities from New York to Hong Kong. In the three to four hours between the closing of the New York Stock Exchange and the opening of the Tokyo Stock Exchange, it is the middle of the day in Hawaii, and 24-hour securities trading is possible.

Contributing to the transformation is the frequency of contacts with other Pacific Rim places: 75 flights a week to Tokyo, 41 to Sydney, 14 to Hong Kong, 143 to Los Angeles, 83 to San Francisco. Flights to New York total some 40 a week, 21 others

reach Atlanta, and there are more.

In orbit over the Pacific are three satellites accessed by Hawaii; three others orbit over the Indian Ocean, and seven others over the Atlantic. Hawaii is served by 10 of the 13. Columbia Communications, a Hawaii-based company, has inaugurated satellite service over both Atlantic and Pacific Oceans, and has applied for authority to provide "domestic" telecommunications services via its Pacific Ocean area satellite in joint venture with TRW. International connectivity is provided by AT&T and GTE Hawaiian Tel, and domestic satellite service is provided by US Sprint, GTE Spacenet and AT&T earth stations.

GTE Hawaiian Tel is the only telephone operating company in Hawaii and has undergone a five-year modernization that included digital switch conversion and other upgrading. In 1992, the company began another five-year program at a

THE EAST-WEST LINKAGE

By Michel Oksenberg
President, The East-West Center

The East-West Center is an international research and educational institution that focuses on Asia and the Pacific and on the growing interdependence of those regions with each other, the United States, and the rest of the world. The U.S. Congress created the Honolulu-based Center in 1960 to serve as a bridge between the United States and the vast region from Afghanistan to Japan, including Australia, New Zealand, and the Pacific Island states.

Today, largely funded by the U.S. government, the Center sponsors research, international meetings, and training about problems of contemporary significance in the region. Our purpose is to contribute to the long-term stability, responsible development, and human dignity of all peoples in the region. Each year, through conferences and research projects, the Center brings together intellectuals, business executives, educators, journalists, legislators, and government officials to explore problems of mutual and regional concern, often in partnership with other Hawaii institutions. More than 27,000 men and women have participated in Center programs as graduate students, fellows, and research colleagues. Our alumni, many of whom now hold influential positions in business, government, and education, are part of a growing network of expertise that extends to all corners of the globe.

Leading specialists from both sides of the Pacific join with our staff in examining major economic, demographic, environmental, and cultural concerns. Over 60 Center researchers publish books and articles on critical issues, providing analysis and policy alternatives to business and government leaders. Over 250 students from throughout the region pursue advanced degrees in a multicultural environment. The Center also conducts training for American teachers from kindergarten through the undergraduate level, helping them infuse information about Asia and the Pacific in their classwork.

In addition, the Center has designed seminars on the region specifically for the needs of business executives, diplomats, journalists, and senior government officials from Asia, the Pacific, and the United States. In the near future, the Center will also offer half-day and full-day briefings on the region as part of the many business and professional conventions that take place in Hawaii.

All of these activities are driven by the need for that elusive understanding that Congress recognized when it established the Center more than three decades ago. Now, because of the region's phenomenal growth and change, we must intensify this process of learning. Consider the dramatic transformations that have taken place in the past three decades:

• None of the four great powers in the region — Russia, China, Japan, and the United States — is militarily expansionist. For the first time in this century, all have basically constructive relations with one another.

• The economic potential of the region, already evident in the late 1950s and early 1960s, has been realized. As a result, while still important to the region, the United States has lost its economic dominance.

• Trade and cultural exchanges among Taiwan, Hong Kong, and the Chinese mainland are expanding rapidly. A "Greater China" is emerging.

• The percentage of gross national product that is in the foreign trade sector has risen significantly for all countries, and intra-regional trade and investment flows are increasing rapidly.

• Regional economic and political organizations are being formed, and many disputes are resolved through regional consultation and action.

• Telecommunications and transportation revolutions are affecting the entire region, creating similar patterns of cultural change and generating shared aspirations.

• Social and demographic changes are forcing new issues onto national agendas everywhere, such as women's rights, care for the aged, and provision of public services in urban areas.

• The importance of the region in world affairs has increased. Today, events in this region are decisively affecting world affairs and the fate of other regions.

• Common challenges confront our entire region: dangers posed by dissemination of weapons of mass destruction; environmental degradation; global climactic change; the need for increased efficiency in consumption of energy; the persistent danger of narcotics; the spread of AIDS; urban and rural poverty; and migration within and beyond national borders.

• In increasing numbers, influential sectors of the populace seek to participate in the governance of their countries and in the selection of their rulers. Many people yearn for increased freedom, although in each country liberty assumes a somewhat different guise, reflecting distinctive indigenous intellectual and cultural traditions.

In short, partnerships are replacing the former patron-client relations that pervaded the region. No nation in our region can develop in isolation from others. Instability in one area creates difficulties elsewhere. None can enjoy long-term stability if any are mired in hopeless poverty.

Unfortunately, in many respects, the awareness of interdependence is lagging. A major challenge of the East-West Center is to encourage Americans to learn from the Asian experience as well as to convey the American experience to Asians.

The multicultural setting of Hawaii is the ideal venue for the Center's mission. It provides a convenient and disinterested meeting ground far removed from the emotions that pervade national capitals. In addition, Hawaii offers an extraordinary concentration of regional experience and expertise through the East-West Center, the University of Hawaii, and other public and private institutions with a tradition of working in the region.

The central message guiding all these endeavors must be that the futures of the people in this region are now tightly intertwined. At the East-West Center, we will continue to participate in the formation of a community of Pacific nations and help to cultivate a consciousness among governments, nations and people of our interdependence. We also will work to develop a shared analytical framework for understanding our earth and to foster networks of human relations that will transcend cultural differences and bind the region in peace.

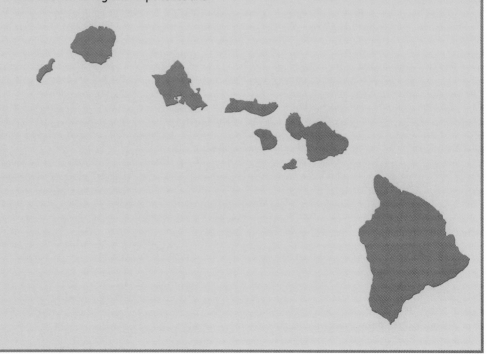

projected cost of $707 million; the expansion and upgrade program will include installation of fiber-optic cables linking Oahu and the other major islands.

Proponents of fiber optics call it the technology of the '90s, as compared with the satellite technology of the past, and contend it performs better than any other medium available. Voice transmission is high in quality, digitized over fiber, and data transmission is better than satellite, they claim. There is no interference by sun spots, or weather problems, and a fiber-optic cable requires maintenance that may prove far less costly in the long run than any other system.

The first fiber-optic cable in the Pacific went through Hawaii in 1989 and branched out to Japan and Guam. It consisted of 40,000 voice-trade circuits and linked San Francisco, Hawaii, and Asia. The next generation is scheduled to come in 1993, linking Los Angeles to Hawaii and on to New Zealand. It will have a capacity for 70,000 circuits. In 1995 the third generation will come from the mainland — actually two fiber systems laid concurrently — and will further link the U.S. mainland, Hawaii, and Asia with another 130,000 circuits.

AT&T made Hawaii the hub of its operations in 1989, and other companies are choosing Hawaii because of its cost-effectiveness. Adding to the international flavor of the operation, the cables are not owned by AT&T alone but by a consortium that consists of AT&T, some other carriers, and foreign telecommunications companies (including European companies who use the system to reach customers in Asia). The cables connect through two stations on Oahu, at Makaha and Keawaula (near Kaena Point), providing one back-up system if something goes awry with the first. The inter-island fiber-optic system will connect with the international circuits.

Currently, the cables link the mainland and Hawaii to Japan, Guam, the Philippines, Korea, Taiwan, Hong Kong, Singapore, and Brunei. Malaysia, Thailand, and Indonesia are expected to be serviced

↗ **Researchers in the islands are actively exploring alternative energy sources through wind farms, solar heating, and ocean water conversion experiments. Right: wind farm on the Big Island.**

in 1993, and 1994 will see the addition of China, India, and Sri Lanka. Vietnam is scheduled to join the network in 1995.

Cost of the first network, the link from San Francisco to Hawaii to Asia, was $700 million, but costs on the second and third networks are likely to

↑ Gauging from the enthusiasm of the fans and quality of world-class athletes participating in such events as the annual IronMan Triathlon, above, Hawaii is often noted as the sports center of the Pacific.

drop dramatically due to the greater capacity and better technology. AT&T stands ready for maintenance by keeping a cable ship at Sand Island on Oahu, but the company expects few maintenance problems, citing the relatively "benign" ocean floor. The glass cables are lighter to carry on a ship than copper cables, and the cost of transport aboard ship is lower. Proponents of the system cite all these reasons for anticipating a long-lived, relatively maintenance-free and reliable system, one built to last at least a quarter-century.

As the gateway between East and West, Hawaii already fulfills an important role, so much so that one Japanese investor in Hawaii once told the much-

respected local journalist, A.A. (Bud) Smyser, that "I consider Hawaii a part of the world, not a part of the U.S." The investor's remarks came during preparation by Smyser of a definitive work a few years ago, *Hawaii as an East-West Bridge*.

Smyser's booklet delved into communications and transportation advantages, and enumerates other possibilities including: Hawaii as a meeting place, a site for international conferences because of better-than-adequate support facilities; Hawaii as an education, training, and information center (a pursuit that Smyser estimated could provide 3,200 jobs and $93.5 million in income); the islands as a center for food research and production for export (an example cited was the Oceanic Center at Waimanalo, on Oahu, a private non-profit center for applied aquaculture whose 300 employees are involved in worldwide projects); Hawaii as a Pacific center for diplomatic and government activities which could be expanded because of a strong international base, both civilian and military; and Hawaii as a center for business, administrative, marketing, and consulting services.

Other potential industries were noted — the islands are in a position to become a sports center of the Pacific, a health and fitness center, a culture and arts center.

The thrust of both government and private sector is to find non-tourism industries, while encouraging and protecting the visitor industry. The buzz word in the past few years and probably into the next few: diversification.

With an ambitious future, Hawaii has begun taking sometimes difficult and often costly steps. One of the first was initiated in the late 1980s with a new airport systems development program that will not be completed until 1996 or later. Statewide, the development plan is estimated to cost some $2.5 billion, with almost $2 billion of that earmarked for Honolulu International Airport, which is to get a 1.6-million-square-foot terminal building and an automated "people mover" to connect all the current terminals. Some airports on other major islands are to be updated, with runways lengthened to accommodate large jets and allow them to return to the U.S. mainland without a Honolulu refueling stop.

The state government contends the costly airports program is not simply to enhance tourism but is necessary for the state's future economic health, to provide transportation services for expansion of local products. They also point to 23 million passengers flowing through Honolulu International in 1990 and an estimated 30 million in the year 2000.

At sea, Matson Navigation Company is investing heavily in the future, with $21 million in new gantry cranes at its Sand Island docks, a $129 million new container ship and an increase in its inter-island barge services. Sea-Land Service, which hauls cargo between Hawaii and the West Coast, also is increasing its service.

On land, the H–3 Freeway project, linking Windward and Leeward Oahu, is well under way and likely to continue despite some community opposition.

There were also some voices in opposition to one part of the state's efforts to find alternative sources of energy, but no argument to the fact of Hawaii's need

↑ Quick transitions from carrying freight to passengers keeps local airlines on schedule with their ever-increasing traffic.

↑ Hawaii is set to be a business and communications hub for the Pacific Rim within the next decade.

to secure a substitute for oil. In the Puna rain forest on the Big Island of Hawaii, wells were drilled to find and exploit geothermal energy, and environmentalists charged it would result in destruction of the rain forest. While the battle raged, Hawaii was consuming the energy equivalent of 49 million 42-gallon barrels of oil each year, and while this was 25 percent less than the national average, it was worrisome. More than 90 percent of the state's energy comes from oil,

contrasted with a national average of 43 percent. Almost all of Hawaii's electricity is generated by oil, but only 4.6 percent nationally. The great oil dependency leaves the islands vulnerable to high oil prices and oil shortages. With no local oil, ocean-going tankers are necessary to supply oil to the two Hawaii refineries, and such tankers may not always be available.

There is no question that the coming years will see the rise of the oft-talked-about Pacific Century; some say it has arrived, others that it may be slower than expected in making its impact on the world, but impact it will.

The statistics identify growth: the Pacific Basin already accounts for almost half of the world's Gross National Product, and contains 2.1 billion people, or some 42 percent of the world's population. The NICS — the Newly-Industrialized Countries — may well lead the GNP growth rates in the coming years, as Singapore and Thailand, Malaysia and Indonesia and others continue to develop their resources. Japan is likely to grow at a rate surpassing that of the United States, even though the U.S., by the year 2000, is expected to have a GNP total that is twice Japan's.

And Hawaii rapidly is gaining experience in international activities. At the beginning of this decade, 29 of the largest 250 businesses on the islands were owned by foreign companies, a situation that gives local banks and business firms strong experience and extensive contacts in Asia. A part of the United States, Hawaii is developing a well-deserved aura of internationalism, a cosmopolitan air, that is one of its most charismatic characteristics. This internationalism will be supported into the future by strong economic growth; the U.S. Department of Commerce has forecast that Hawaii will be ranked sixth nationwide in economic growth through the end of this century.

As Hawaii continues its growth, and as it takes its place in that vast and exciting Pacific Century, these islands will become more and more familiar to an international community as the regional center it deserves to become, and will become. And as it joins that fast-paced and far-flung worldwide business network, it will be equally important to recall the voices of the past, to remind all islanders of what must remain the most vital facet of island lives. The late Edward Joesting, one of Hawaii's finest writers, spelled it out in his *Hawaii, An Uncommon History*, saying:

Most important is the preservation of that particular quality which is Hawaii's first right to fame. That quality is summed up in a sense of tolerance, a willingness to accept others who do not hold a particular tradition and who look different physically. It is the quality of being willing to listen when instinct says to lash out. These are the qualities which make Hawaii unique.

Those who make the islands their home, wherever they come from originally, are indebted to maintain this quality. It is the heritage willed to all of us by the native Hawaiians.

↑ The transformation that has seen Hawaii move easily into a world of high technology has opened people's minds to other possibilities. Many are wondering, "If Hawaii is more than merely a playground, what else can it be? How far can it go in other directions?" The early responses to these questions have prompted Reuters, the oldest and largest financial information service in the world, to open an office in Honolulu so its staff can explore Hawaii's potential as a financial center of the Pacific.

6

Reprise

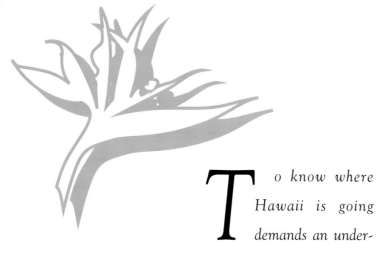

To know where Hawaii is going demands an understanding of where it has been and where it is now.

In 1928, Hawaii author Andrew Farrell transcribed John Cameron's Odyssey *for the Macmillan Company, which then published the sea captain's memoirs. In the book, Cameron muses:*

> Life in Honolulu in those days was one long holiday. The climate could not be surpassed; the people, both native and foreign, were pleasant; customs were free and easy. Doors of residences were seldom or never locked; money or valuables could be left lying about a house in perfect security. In this paradise the one diversion was the arrival or departure of a steamer. Hawaiian girls were there with wreaths of flowers for sale; the band played under the direction of Henri Berger....When a vessel had sailed a depression settled upon the city, isolated from the sinful, remote, yet still interesting world.

That was Hawaii, once upon a time.

More than 60 years later, in a message to the Chamber of Commerce of Hawaii, Governor John Waihee wrote:

> It is a rapidly changing world. There are exciting opportunities. The walls of totalitarianism are collapsing. Telecommunications link people as never before. The potential for new business and trade is enormous. At the same time we are living in a society facing enormous federal deficits and issues ranging from global warming to revitalization of public education. Today's world calls for new private and public sector partnerships and the willingness to constantly challenge 'the old formulas.'... Together we have improved the State's business climate.... Together we will turn the corner of the 21st Century, ready for the world around us and leading it.

Hawaii is no longer isolated from the "sinful, remote, yet still interesting world." And it was no hyperbole for the governor to speak of leadership in the century to come, for Hawaii arguably is in a position to take a quantum leap forward, to seize a leadership position in the Pacific.

And yet...

To read Cameron's adventures in Hawaii is to yearn for a slower pace and a rather more gracious era. The realist must then put such yearnings in perspective: there is no going back. The indicated course of action becomes clear — Hawaii must move into that high-tech, interdependent, swift-moving world and carve out its proper niche. At the same time Hawaii must preserve for future generations the old, wild, romantic, turbulent, and colorful past that gives these islands a flavor found nowhere else on earth.

It is possible to do both. Hawaii has undergone a transformation, but it has not discarded its memories. With the passage of years, the accomplishments and relationships of the past grow more worthy of preservation, more valuable, and more resonant. In the genes of Hawaii's people are preserved not only the history but the legends, not merely the chronicles but also the folklore. As the islands move confidently toward that glittering future, they take along the irreplaceable memories. This is because libraries are as important as data banks, songs as valuable as spreadsheets, art and music and other cultural manifestations on a par with securities trading.

The people of Hawaii have made it so, and will make it continue.

As Hawaii stands on the threshold of the third millennium, and concurrently at the flowering of the Pacific Century, it is perhaps in the most advantageous position of its history. It is vital to look back; it is mandatory to look forward. The coming years will demand men and women of vision and understanding, of intellectual scope and dedication to Hawaii Nei, to the beloved islands. And Hawaii will provide such people.

Early in this book it was noted that "lyrics tell of an incandescent future, a song of Hawaii that will be heard across the seas and down the years." It is a song ever the same but ever changing, confident and clear, echoing from islands that are no long hidden, islands that continue to beckon from a shining sea.

PART II

Partners in Hawaii

By Merlyn Holmes,
Lee Cline, and Roger Coryell

7
Networks, Professions & Services

Hawaii's transportation and communication firms, as well as its business networks, keep people, information, and power circulating throughout the islands. And professionals from all fields provide essential services.

CHAMBER OF COMMERCE OF HAWAII

As part of the celebration of its centennial in 1950, the Chamber of Commerce of Honolulu (now the Chamber of Commerce of Hawaii) published *Building Honolulu*, a history of its first hundred years as the premier advocate for Hawaii's businesses.

The book is a nostalgic chronicle of an organization and a community growing up together through war and peace, six forms of government, economic booms and depressions, natural disasters, and social upheavals.

The Chamber is more than ever an integral part of the fabric of the islands. Its 4,100 members represent all kinds of businesses and organizations from Bishop Street corporations and the military, tiny neighborhood stores to trendy shops and generations-old family businesses, airlines and auto dealers, hotels and manufacturers.

Since its inception, the Chamber has been an organization with an agenda that touches all the people of Hawaii – sometimes in unexpected ways. It rescued a circus stranded here by the 1937 dock strike and launched an insect-pest control project in 1949. It fought tirelessly for statehood. It raised funds at the turn of the century to combat bubonic plague and help victims of a fire that left 4,000 homeless. It rallied support for a modern sewer system in 1920 and organized a food committee to plan production, distribution, and conservation of supplies during World War I.

Over the years, the Chamber has been instrumental in the development of many institutions dedicated to the community. These include the Hawaii Visitors Bureau, Better Business Bureau, Aloha United Way, the Blood Bank, the Tax Foundation of Hawaii, Crime Stoppers Of Hawaii, and the Mental Health Association.

The Chamber of the '90s is positioned for the social, economic, political, and technological challenges of a new century, using up-to-the-minute research and communication equipment and techniques. Its

↑ Honolulu and Waikiki are the heart of Oahu — "the gathering place."

Mission: Provide leadership to create an environment in which businesses will prosper in Hawaii's unique community.

committee structure changes with the needs of the times – bubonic plague is no longer an issue of concern, but a Health Care Reform Task Force is grappling with the contemporary healthcare cost crisis. Instead of wartime food distribution, the Military Affairs Council and Armed Services Committee today work to keep our vital military industry viable. The Pacific Region Institute for Service Excellence is providing resources to help organizations achieve continuous quality improvement. Over the years the Chamber has led myriad "Keep Hawaii Beautiful" campaigns, and now a committee has been formed to address the complexities of environmental protection and enhancement.

The state Chamber counts 16 ethnic, neighbor island, and local community chambers as family, coordinating efforts to achieve common goals and solve shared problems. Their collective strength gives business the credibility and influence necessary to help shape public policy on commercial and community issues. 🌺

GRANT THORNTON

Grant Thornton is one of the largest accounting and management firms in the United States, providing a comprehensive range of professional services to growing companies of all sizes. Concern for clients and a commitment to the highest professional standards have earned the firm a reputation for distinctive service and dedicated work.

Founded in 1924 as Alexander Grant & Company, Grant Thornton currently maintains 50 offices throughout the United States and serves clients in 70 countries through Grant Thornton International — more than 17,000 professionals in 500 offices around the world. This extensive network offers clients access to resources that are both global in scope and local in flavor.

The Honolulu office of Grant Thornton has been serving Hawaii individuals, businesses, and government entities for over 35 years. Established in 1956 through a merger with a local CPA firm, the Honolulu office currently has nearly 60 professional and administrative personnel. It is one of the largest public accounting firms in Hawaii, serving local companies as well as mainland and foreign companies doing business in the state.

Grant Thornton's Honolulu office provides a full range of services — audit, tax, management consulting, accounting — to meet the needs of a wide range of industries, from construction and real estate to education, financial services, and health care. The firm specializes in servicing small businesses and middle-market companies, offering international expertise with a personal touch.

In today's competitive environment, the small- to middle-scale markets face some of the greatest challenges in terms of keeping up with increasingly complex accounting and tax requirements, and in dealing with issues such as quality improvement, international trade, and market expansion. Grant Thornton's reputation for distinctive, high quality work in helping clients face these challenges sets them apart from the others.

Much of Grant Thornton's success in these two growth-oriented markets can be attributed to the firm's commitment to a high degree of partner/manager involvement in client matters. Recognizing the power of the entrepreneurial spirit, Grant Thornton remains committed to servicing clients in these markets.

Grant Thornton also encourages personal involvement in community activities and has seen a growing number of partners and employees at the Honolulu office reach out to community organizations as diverse as Hawaii Foodbank, Junior Achievement, Honolulu Japanese Chamber of Commerce, Japanese Cultural Center of Hawaii, American Cancer Society, American Red Cross, African American Chamber of Commerce, Building Industry Association of Hawaii, Hawaii Tax Institute, Retail Merchants of Hawaii, Better Business Bureau, Honolulu Youth Symphony, Office of Hawaiian Affairs, Task Force to Re-Organize the Department of Education, and Hawaii Society of Certified Public Accountants.

By consistently building upon its already vast resources, Grant Thornton is able to help clients stay ahead of the complex business challenges of the future while staying in touch with the needs of the community today. ✿

↑ The partners of Grant Thornton. From left to right: Patrick Tanigawa, Roy Morihara, Norman Chong, Garrett Serikawa, Managing Partner, and Howard Hanada.

PACIFIC RIM PRODUCTIONS, LTD.

First conceived in 1969 in a small loft on 6th Avenue in New York City, Pacific Rim Productions, Limited is now a highly esteemed Honolulu-based visual communications firm.

Preceded by Abraham and Dunn, Ltd., the premier presentation and audio/ visual company in Hawaii in the 1970s and '80s, Pacific Rim Productions was formed in 1988 in answer to the demands for more extensive photography, filming, and production services across the Pacific Rim.

↑ Aerial photography assignments have taken Pacific Rim's photographers over Hawaii and across the Pacific Ocean.

Pacific Rim's growing reputation for excellent travel, aerial, and underwater photography has led the creative team to various parts of the Pacific. Aerial photography has taken them over Rarotonga in the Cook Islands. Underwater assignments have taken them to another of the Cook Islands, Aitutaki. The staff photographed the encircling islets, or "motus," off the island of Moorea in the Society Islands... a shark-feed in Bora Bora... the rowdy charm of Papeete on Tahiti... and the open markets of Nukualofa, capital of the Kingdom of Tonga.... All these assignments helped promote Pacific Rim's reputation as a producer of travel and adventure multi-media shows.

Retaining the focus on creative uses of words and images, principal Bob Abraham has surrounded himself with an exceptionally talented staff, which is capable of handling all aspects of photography, production, sound, and presentation needs of corporations, advertising agencies, and civic institutions.

Soon after being formed, the staff of Pacific Rim Productions dove into producing a wide variety of projects for numerous Pacific countries. Their first work reflected the diversity of assignments they have enjoyed producing since: a 45-minute documentary on the South Pacific Commission, on the island of Saipan in the Northern Marianas, followed by a 15-minute multi-image show for American Samoa to promote tourism and tell the story of Samoan culture.

While keeping its sight on the Pacific nations, Pacific Rim Productions also has accepted special assignments to produce images of London, Rome, and Zurich as well as Des Moines, Cincinnati, and Dallas.

Despite the thrill and excitement of working on overseas projects, Pacific Rim's heart remains in Hawaii. The principals have been residents of Hawaii for

↖ ↑ ↗

Multi-projector slide shows, video production, still photography... Pacific Rim Productions can produce whatever visuals clients may need. Above are a series of images of *Keiki Hula* (children's hula) at Iolani Palace.

almost two decades and were creators of the long-popular "Waikiki Calls," a fully automated multi-media show that ran every day of the week for more than six years. Thus, it comes as no surprise that Pacific Rim

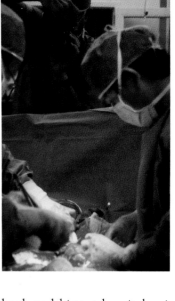

← From laser eye surgery to organ transplants, Pacific Rim Productions' photographers aren't afraid to get close.

Photos by Bob Abraham and Mary Van de Ven.

The beauty and poetry of the images, words, and music in Pacific Rim Productions' traveling multi-media shows of Hawaii are applauded by travel agents as the best they have ever seen.

Productions has an expansive photo library of images of Hawaii, and the staff continues to build the multi-faceted collection — out of a desire to capture on film Hawaii's many fascinations.

Pacific Rim's Hawaii-based work includes presentations on health care for almost every medical organization in Hawaii and five shows telling the story of the 100th anniversary of Hawaii's first Japanese immigrants. Add to these: sales presentations for airlines and hotels... orientation programs for Hawaii's biggest

bank and biggest hospital... information shows for the phone company, the Board of Water Supply, the blood bank, the lung association, the organ donor program, and children's special education.

The staff expresses a clear fascination with Hawaiian culture and Hawaii's special ethnic mix, so when Pacific Rim was asked by the Hawaii Visitors' Bureau to produce a series of traveling multi-media shows, the staff jumped at the opportunity. These highly popular shows toured North America several times and were expanded for showcase events and travel agent events on the Mainland United States and Europe. The beauty and poetry of the images, words, and music were applauded by the travel agents as the best they had ever seen.

Pacific Rim Productions, Ltd. is determined to continue to do extraordinary projects in Hawaii and among the Pacific Island nations.

To add to its scope, Pacific Rim works with the Tai-Pan Group, an elite international communications firm which adds its special talents, knowledge and insights of the Asian world. 🐾

↑ From the top of the world to the depths of the ocean, Pacific Rim has the equipment and the talent.

TROPICAL USA RENT-A-CAR

The Aloha spirit through and through — that's what gives Tropical USA Rent-A-Car a history of loyal customers returning time and time again despite the more aggressive campaigning of larger, national car rental companies. And in an inventive move which reveals a deep strain of resourcefulness, this Hawaiian-born company is headed for the national market — and it's taking its Aloha spirit with it.

After purchasing the assets of Florida's USA Rent A Car in 1992, Tropical began its venture to the mainland. With 530 full- and part-time employees, a fleet of over 6,000 cars, and 23 locations throughout the Hawaiian Islands as well as agencies in Florida, California, Nevada, and Colorado, Tropical is undoubtedly the most successful independent Hawaiian car rental company. And in a uniquely personable fashion, Tropical has made a habit of retaining its previous owners as top managers — a business touch straight from the *aloha* spirit the company encapsulates so well.

It all began in a 6' x 8' booth with the reservation department in a 3" x 5" recipe box. Founders Don and Virginia Hillis had moved to Oahu with two kids under age three and 14 boxes after having fallen in love with Hawaii and seeing a real need for rental car companies.

The first of a $10,000 start-up investment went towards the purchase of four new Toyotas in 1969 which they began renting from their booth on the Nimitz Highway for $7 per day with a $1 damage waiver.

'Tropical became a family, and if it is anything today, it is because of the people, the family of employees behind it.'

— Virginia Hillis Kawauchi
Vice President and Founder

In the second week of business, they bought four used Toyotas, then soon thereafter spent the remainder of their start-up money on a prestigious-looking vehicle for pick-ups and drop-offs — a Ford Station Wagon with wood panel sides.

"It was an informal, tiny operation," Virginia Hillis Kawauchi, former partner and now Vice President, says. "The only money we drew out of the business was for groceries and rent. I'd take the kids and the contracts home at 3 p.m. to do the bookkeeping, and we all started

↑ Tropical began as a family-run operation and has continued to maintain that special personable quality through the years. This Christmas greeting card, like many of Tropical's older photos, came from the founder's family photo album.

taking Hawaiian language classes at night.

"We kept adding a few cars, then a few employees to wash cars, and they soon became family. All of the old

↑ **Fun and Sun: the Tropical way of doing business. Tropical USA Rent-A-Car is known throughout the islands for its quality cars and inventive sense of fun. Not only can Tropical take the credit for having started the convertible market in Hawaii — now practically a state icon — but it was also probably the first to promote mini-vans, an increasingly popular mode of transport for small groups and families.**

Specialty cars such as the Firebird convertible and Geo Tracker, pictured above, as well as 7- and 15-person vans and 4-wheel drives are a hallmark of Tropical's fleet. Special programs such as the free use of video camera with a rental and "Island Hopper" and "Trip Saver" packages reveal the company's family-style flexibility.

company photos are mixed in our family album. Tropical became a family, and if it is anything today, it is because of the people, the family of employees behind it."

William Ong, current chairman and former president of Tropical, was attracted to the company for the same reason. "I was most impressed by the people involved in Tropical," he said of his introduction to them in 1985. "They made me feel confident enough in the company to recommend investment in it to my family."

With survival becoming increasingly difficult for small businesses through the 1980s and fierce competition rising from national car companies in Hawaii, Tropical has been under constant pressure to adapt in inventive ways.

"We've witnessed the demise of small car companies," Ong says. "In Hawaii, there are maybe 10 left when six years ago there used to be dozens; they're just not on a level playing field with the big boys who can offer cut-rate, even below-cost prices here while making their profit elsewhere. Many of them have, in fact, been taken over by auto manufacturers, whose agenda is moving cars."

In a moment of restrained gaiety Ong simply adds, "So we started planning our expansion to the mainland market."

With a *holo holo* mascot, a company *moo moo* and a Hawaiian-born *aloha* spirit, the Tropical USA Rent-A-Car family has something special to offer.

As Kawauchi says, "From one rental company to another, the car can be exactly the same, but the person handling the rental makes a difference. Our people in the field are a vital link — the big edge that we have. Our family and *aloha* spirit are two things that money can't buy. We've earned incredible loyalty from our customers, and that makes me proud."

OCEANIC CABLE

Oceanic Cable was founded in 1969 in response to a real estate developer's concern about unsightly TV antennas. At that time, the Oceanic Properties division of Castle and Cooke was in the process of developing its "planned community" of Mililani Town in central Oahu, and believed that a cable television system would improve the marketability of its project.

In the mid '70s, Oceanic Cable was sold to a group of local private investors. In 1981, ownership passed to American Television and Communications Corporation (ATC).

Although ownership has changed over the years, leadership has been a constant at Oceanic, as well one of the company's greatest strengths. Don Carroll, first assigned fiscal management of the fledgling firm under Castle and Cooke, has led the business through all of its years of development, and now serves as its president.

Jim Chiddix, currently Senior Vice President of Engineering at Oceanic's parent company, ATC, was another key figure instrumental in developing and implementing advanced technologies at Oceanic. Under his leadership as Vice President of Engineering, Oceanic

↑ **Don Carroll, President of Oceanic Cable**

became one of the nation's leaders in computer controlled signal processing and distribution.

Although a latecomer to the cable industry, rapid population growth on the island of Oahu combined with well-timed acquisitions and effective marketing has enabled Oceanic to become the eleventh largest cable operator in the U.S.,

↑ **Oceanic's recently dedicated new administrative office building in Mililani, Hawaii.**

serving nearly a quarter million households, which represents three out of every four homes in Honolulu.

The introduction of satellite delivery systems and the installation of fiber optic trunk lines were significant events in Oceanic's development. The company has adapted rapidly to improvements in technology, steadily enhancing the system's signal quality and reliability, which are now at their highest levels ever. The company was recently awarded the prestigious Seal of Quality Customer Service from the National Cable Television Association.

By aggressively marketing its premium channel services, such as Home Box Office (HBO), Showtime, the Disney Channel, etc., Oceanic has been able to keep its basic service rate as low as possible. Its standard rates are the lowest in the state of Hawaii, and the lowest of the nation's twenty largest cable systems.

Oceanic handles every aspect of its operations in-house, including construction, maintenance, billing and marketing. The company even maintains its own staff of computer programmers to meet the needs of its extensive operations. It was a pioneer in the area of computer controlled cable converter boxes in the home and one of the first cable companies to offer pay-per-view services.

Recognizing a unique distribution opportunity offered by Waikiki and its numerous hotels, Oceanic has also constructed a separate Hotel Trunk system, which delivers a unique multi-channel service to forty hotels, and over 17,000 rooms.

Believing that its success derives from the respect of the people it serves, Oceanic Cable also invests a substantial share of its material and human resources to support community programs and institutions. In addition, the company continues to expand its technological reach by exploring new applications in communications, such as the prospect of linking individuals to international data banks via cable. ❧

HONOLULU CELLULAR TELEPHONE COMPANY

Cellular communication is one of the fastest growing and most rapidly changing industries in the world today. In Hawaii, Honolulu Cellular Telephone Company is setting the pace for the industry.

Honolulu Cellular began operations in 1986 when it was awarded a license by the F.C.C. Since then, it has constructed a cellular network on Oahu covering the entire island and costing millions of dollars. Because of Oahu's unique terrain, more cell sites are necessary to provide quality service compared to most areas on the U.S. mainland. As a result, Honolulu Cellular's system is one of the clearest and most efficient in the country.

Oahu is also one of the most unique cellular markets in that portable phones make up about 90 percent of the cellular phones in use, while mobile phones, or car phones, account for only about 10 percent of cellular phones in service. This mix is completely the opposite of the mainland U.S., where car phones are ideal for long commutes. One reason people in Hawaii opt for portables is there are more cell sites and cell enhancers here, making the small battery found on portables powerful enough to sustain clear conversations.

As the technology matures, the affordability of owning a cellular phone continues to increase. No longer the status symbols they were in the '80s, cellular phones have been enhancing the lives of students, parents, sales people, and professionals alike. In a recent Gallop Poll, 86 percent of cellular users said cellular

↑ People are now able to set up office nearly anywhere, thanks to data transmission through Honolulu Cellular's network.

phones have increased their personal flexibility; 74 percent reported their personal lives have been less stressful with a cellular phone; and 79 percent said they believe cellular phones have enhanced their business relationships with customers.

New applications for cellular technology are also being sought by Honolulu Cellular. Some new uses include portable facsimile machines, laptop computers, even complete cellular work stations.

Honolulu Cellular is also a leader among corporate citizens. Says company president Randy Ogata, "Our commitment to the community goes far beyond providing it with the best cellular service possible." The company participates in a variety of local charity events by providing promotional support, manpower, even cellular communications equipment. Favorite causes include education and drug abuse prevention.

Honolulu Cellular employs more than 100 people. In addition to its corporate offices at Waterfront Plaza, Honolulu Cellular has three retail locations to serve Oahu: Kapiolani, Downtown, and Pearl City. ♥

↑ Honolulu Cellular has built a cellular network on the island of Oahu that is one of the clearest and most efficient in the country.

Sause Brothers, Inc.

↑ This tugboat is one of 10 tugs and three barges in Sause Brothers' Hawaii fleet. The tugs range from 2,000 to 4,000 horsepower with lengths from 75 to 136 feet and a draft of 24 feet. The barges range from 3,600 to 6,000 tons, are 210 to 300 feet long, and have a 20-foot draft. Photo by Bob Abraham.

In the early 1930s, Henry, Curt, and Paul Sause, in the town of Garibaldi on Tillamook Bay, Oregon, put together a company to tow log rafts a distance of 75 miles down the Columbia River. They started with a single tugboat. In the six decades since, the little one-tug company has grown to 64 tugs and barges servicing the American West Coast, Hawaii, and the islands of Micronesia. Today, Paul serves as CEO with his son Dale serving as President and Curt as Vice President/ Treasurer.

In 1947, the brothers incorporated as Sause Brothers Ocean Towing Company (SBOTCO). In 1951, the company began servicing the ports of Southern California, and in 1966 it extended its routes to Hawaii. In 1984, a wholly-owned subsidiary, Sause Brothers, Inc. (SBI), was incorporated in Hawaii to service the neighbor islands out of the Port of Honolulu. The company also runs a shipyard, Southern Oregon Marine (SOMAR), in Coos Bay, Oregon; and a stevedoring company, Crescent City Marine Way (CCMW), in San Pedro, California.

Sause Brothers' service from the West Coast to Hawaii is comprised of lumber and related products such as poles, plywood, and paper products, as well as rebar, chemicals, liquid asphalt, and fertilizers. It carries no containerized cargo on its barges from the West Coast. Sause Brothers, Inc. carries cargoes between points in Hawaii and the South Pacific. SBI tows Matson's barges *Mauna Loa, Haleakala,* and *Waialeale* to the smaller, less accessible outer island ports. Sause also tows Matson's barge *Islander* to Johnston, Majuro, Kwajalein, and Ebeye Islands.

Pepeekeo, Sause Brothers' 50,000 barrel capacity oil barge, carries 200 million gallons a year of "clean" petroleum products for Chevron — aviation fuel, jet fuel, and #2 automobile diesel — to the neighbor

↑ **A Sause Bros. barge transported the gargantuan Spruce Goose from Long Beach Harbor in 1992.**

islands. This barge carries no "black oil" or heavy crude.

For the Military Sealift Command, SBI makes 30 to 40 round trips a year between Honolulu and Kawaihae on the Big Island, transporting heavy equipment for military training maneuvers.

Sause also employs three harbor tugs for ship assist, harbor work, and miscellaneous opportunities throughout the state. All told, Sause Brothers' Hawaii fleet amounts to 10 tugs and three barges. The tugs range from 2,000 to 4,000 horsepower with lengths from 75 to 136 feet and maximum drafts of 24 feet. The barges range from 3,600 to 6,000 tons, are 210 to 300 feet long, and have a 20-foot draft.

Sause Brothers, Inc. takes pride in the fact that it is a *kamaaina* company, employing local people, buying local goods and services, and contributing to the community. The company employs 78 people and has a reputation for being an outstanding corporate and civic neighbor.

The company has been a member of the Chamber of Commerce of Hawaii for 25 years. Its employees participate in the activities of the Maritime Committee of the Chamber, monitoring the state Legislature's activities in the maritime field, as well as testifying at legislative committee meetings and public hearings. Sause Bros. also works cooperatively with the city and county of Honolulu, and with state and federal agencies such as the Harbors Division of the United States Department of Transportation, the Coast Guard, the Army Corps of Engineers, the Navy, and the Army.

Over the past decade and a half, employees of the company have become increasingly involved in various Hawaii Department of Transportation ad hoc committees in their examination and planning of improvements and maintenance of Hawaii's deep draft harbors. The company also participates in the Maritime Advisory Group to the state of Hawaii. In addition, it is an active member of the Propeller Club of Honolulu and a supporter of the Hawaii Maritime Center at Pier 7, where the *Cory Sause*, a large playboat for children, is located on the dock adjacent to *The Falls of Clyde*.

Perhaps the most remarkable thing about this company is that, even through the most frenetic age of bidding competitions, Sause Brothers has remained a privately-owned company...and more than that, a family-owned company.

Sause Brothers is at the heart of Hawaii, supplying the building materials, machinery, and fuel that are the lifeblood of the islands. 🐟

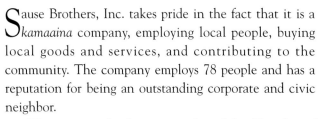

← Henry, Curt, and Paul Sause's original one-tug company has grown to 64 tugs and barges servicing the West Coast, Hawaii, and the islands of Micronesia. Here, the *Mikihana* leads a barge across the waters off the island of Oahu. Photo by Bob Abraham.

HAWAII STEVEDORES, INC.

Hawaii Stevedores, Inc. is one of the oldest companies of its kind in Hawaii. Under different owners and different names it has been in business for 70 years. It was founded in 1922 as Matson Terminals. Then in 1936, the assets were acquired by Castle and Cooke, Ltd. who changed the name to Honolulu Stevedores and some years later to Castle and Cooke Terminals, Ltd.

For 48 years this veteran stevedoring company was part of Castle and Cooke. Many of these were turbulent years of sometimes acrimonious adjustment between all the stevedoring companies in Hawaii and maturing labor unions along the waterfront.

In 1984, at the beginning of a new era for management and labor, a group of Castle and Cooke Terminals management employees bought the company from the parent corporation and renamed it Hawaii Stevedores, Inc., the name it still uses.

Today, Hawaii Stevedores is the only independent stevedoring company in Hawaii.

At present, Hawaii Stevedores serves all the major ports on Oahu. At Honolulu, Barber's Point, and Pearl Harbor (where Hawaii Stevedores currently holds the contract for handling military cargo) the company provides qualified personnel and modern equipment for serving a variety of carriers.

Over the years these stevedoring specialists have served major customers like Sea-Land, NYK Line, Hawaiian Marine Lines, American Hawaii Cruises, Blue Star Line, Nissan, P.M.&O. Lines, Columbus Line, Hawaii Pacific Industries and Hawaiian Cement Co.

For these customers Hawaii Stevedores loads and off-loads container cargo, breakbulk cargo, vehicles, lumber, and a variety of heavy lifts. With specialized equipment the dock workers are able to put conveyors deep into the holds of ships and handle bulk cargoes like silica sand and gypsum, needed by cement plants, or coal, needed to supply Hawaii's energy needs.

The days are long gone when sling-loads of mixed cargo were lifted out of ships' holds by the ships' cranes and deposited dockside to be moved away by mostly unskilled labor. Over the 70 years of its existence, Hawaii Stevedores has offered more sophisticated services and now uses only its own dock workers employed by the company.

Modern stevedoring has become a complex business. Some of the services offered by the company include the receiving, delivering and auditing of cargo. Mechanics, carpenters, riggers, welders and maintenance personnel are needed for fabrication, transfer and care of equipment. Skilled specialists must draw up cargo plans and coordinate container and general cargo loading.

In the office, other trained personnel process all sorts of employee and industrial relations matters. Others handle financial accounting, budgeting, forecasting, tariff development, time-keeping and billing.

To deal with all these complexities, the company conducts appropriate training programs for its personnel, a staff with an average age of only 39 years.

Looking into the future, the company foresees both physical and operational changes. The maintenance operation on Sand Island is being moved adjacent to the office site at Pier 35, off Nimitz Highway. Meanwhile, operations are being increasingly computerized, a change which management believes will provide more efficient service for its customers, while at the same time increasing the profitability of the company.

The management of Hawaii Stevedores looks to the future with optimism. They are constantly planning for the inevitable changes in cargo handling that have been evidenced by the previous 70 years of experience. ♥

↑ Today, Hawaii Stevedores offers a full range of professional services to assist in the receiving, delivering and auditing of cargo.

GBC BOXES & PACKAGING

The story of GBC Boxes & Packaging is typical of many small businesses in the state of Hawaii. It's the story of a single man's desire to be the owner of a successful business, and to control his own destiny. It's also about the desire to develop something of value for his family.

In 1972, George Chu was at the peak of his career as General Manager of Boise Cascade's HOPACO when he decided it was time to move on and be his own boss. Using personal savings and a loan from a friend, he purchased a Hawaiian souvenirs distribution business. This small business with five employees and annual sales of $200,000 was the beginning of a life-long dream.

The souvenir business did reasonably well, but George began looking for other opportunities to complement the operations. He used his past experience and contacts to stock a complete packaging line to fill his customers' needs for such items as paper and plastic bags, gift boxes, wrapping paper, tags, labels, tapes, and

↓ The Malaai Street retail store occupies 6,500 square feet of space and offers a complete packaging products line, packing materials and party goods.

specialty designed packaging. The packaging operations outgrew the souvenir business very quickly, and in 1982, the souvenir portion of GBC was sold.

In 1980, a small 200-square-foot store was opened in a corner of the warehouse facility, which was located in Kalihi. The retail store grew to 1,000 square feet within a year and three years later it was expanded to 2,500 square feet. Presently, the store occupies 6,500 square

feet of space in the main facility at Malaai Street. To complement the packaging products line, the company added packing materials and party goods.

GBC has three retail outlets operating outside its main facility. The Royal Hawaiian Center store offers gift wrapping and packing for shipping and mailing services. It also has a post office substation and mail box rentals. The two other outlets are located at Sears Roebuck's Ala Moana and Pearlridge Center stores. Future plans call for development of additional retail

↑ The GBC Board of Directors: Lester, Georgiana, Bertha, George, Nannette, Walton, and Sanford.

outlets. In June 1990, GBC moved into its present 32,000-square-foot Malaai Street facility. This will allow the company to grow and expand in the years to come.

In addition to the distribution operations, GBC is committed to offering more services to its customers. It invested in foam packing equipment which encases any item in a foam mold for ultimate safety and protection from breakage. In addition, GBC recently installed hot stamping equipment to do custom printing of bags, boxes, and other items for its customers.

In October 1973, the company's name was changed from Baray & Co. to GBC (George and Bertha Chu) Inc. to reflect its family nature. If you ask George and Bertha, the real key to their success is the family atmosphere that they have created. Sons Sanford and Walton both work full-time at the company, as does Walton's wife, Nannette. Their daughter, Georgiana, and son, Lester, provide their input and assistance where they can. All of them are members of GBC's Board of Directors. This feeling of *ohana* extends to the other employees as well, many of whom have been with the company for many years. ❦

CARLSMITH BALL WICHMAN MURRAY CASE MUKAI & ICHIKI

↑ The firm's main office in Honolulu is one of 10 Carlsmith offices in and around the Pacific and Washington, D.C.

The nations of the Pacific Rim, through profound political, economic, and social change, have transformed into the world's most economically dynamic region. These developments strongly suggest that the 21st century may indeed be the "Pacific Century."

Carlsmith Ball Wichman Murray Case Mukai & Ichiki has positioned itself to play a vital role in the future of the Pacific. In a decade of exciting growth and strategic mergers, the 145-year-old firm has become the Pacific region's premier law firm — and Hawaii's largest. It is no coincidence that Carlsmith Ball's evolution into a Pacific legal powerhouse parallels the modern emergence of the Pacific Rim nations. By the mid-1970s, the original Carlsmith firm already had a growing practice in the Pacific, with offices in Guam and Saipan.

In the late 1970s, a long-range planning committee led by current chairman of the firm Tom Van Winkle foresaw the potential rewards for an international firm that is fundamentally committed to the Pacific Basin. Carlsmith moved decisively to strengthen its position, entering into a series of mergers with firms whose attorneys shared the vision of building a strong practice in the Pacific.

In 1984, Honolulu attorneys Stan Mukai, Andy Ichiki, Frank Mukai, and other attorneys from their former firm joined Carlsmith, significantly augmenting its Australian, Hong Kong, and Japanese client base. The following year on Maui, Paul Ueoka and Martin Luna, a past president of the Hawaii State Bar and an active leader in local politics, joined the firm. Their addition expanded the firm's Maui base and brought land use and planning expertise.

A 1988 merger with Los Angeles attorney Duane Zobrist added 11 attorneys to the firm's California office. Zobrist, president of the U.S.–Mexico Chamber of Commerce, works extensively with Mexican, Brazilian, and other South American clients, and provides important access to those markets.

These mergers created the foundation Carlsmith needed to bridge the Pacific-Hawaii-U.S. and South American mainland markets.

The firm was further strengthened in 1990 when it merged with the Los Angeles and Long Beach firm of Ball Hunt Hart Brown & Baerwitz. The merger added a host of legal luminaries to the firm's ranks, including Tony Murray, a former president of the State Bar of California; John McDonough, a former Stanford Law School professor; and Joe Ball, a renowned trial lawyer who was special counsel to the Warren Commission and a former head of both the prestigious American College of Trial Lawyers and the California Bar.

The considerable skills of one of California's leading litigation firms were now combined with the business and commercial law proficiency of Hawaii's oldest law firm.

Carlsmith Ball's origins reach back to 1857 when David Howard Hitchcock, raised on Molokai and a graduate of Williams College in Massachusetts, established a small office in Hilo, Hawaii. He was joined in 1888 by his daughter Almeda, a graduate of Michigan University Law School and the first woman lawyer in Hawaii. Carl S. Smith, one of the first students to attend Stanford University and a graduate of Northwestern University Law School, joined in 1898. Smith continued the practice after Hitchcock's death in 1899 (changing his name to Carlsmith to avoid confusion with other Smiths in Hilo), and was later joined by his sons Wendell and Merrill.

↑ Carlsmith Ball's Honolulu headquarters overlook the Hawaii State Capitol, Iolani Palace, and Honolulu City Hall.

Today Carlsmith Ball is a full-service firm with more than 150 attorneys, nearly 300 support staff members, and 10 offices in Hawaii (including Honolulu, Hilo, Kona, and Wailuku), Guam, Saipan, Washington, D.C., Los Angeles, Long Beach, and Mexico City.

The firm provides its Pacific Basin clients with a wide range of legal and business services. Its Corporate and Business Group offers analysis and advice on structuring business and commercial transactions and in antitrust and intellectual property matters. The Administrative and Government Relations Group counsels clients on regulatory, administrative, and legislative matters.

The Litigation Group provides services in virtually every area of business litigation. The International Group counsels foreign clients on transnational tax, immigration and customs, and other matters — in languages that include Japanese, Mandarin, Cantonese, Taiwanese, Korean, Malay, Portuguese, Spanish, French, and English.

Carlsmith Ball's Real Property and Land Use Group typically represents developers in major real estate projects. The Tax, Trusts, and Estates Group offers advice on federal and local tax matters under the laws of Hawaii, Guam, Saipan, California and Mexico. It also assists in multinational transactions related to foreign investments and operations, trusts, estate planning, and probate.

The Labor and Employment Group provides counsel on complex employment relations issues. The Banking and Finance Group works with financial institutions and commercial lenders and borrowers. The Environmental Group assists clients in environmental legal matters and toxic tort litigation. Finally, the firm offers specialized services in maritime transactions and alternative dispute resolution, including arbitration and mediation.

Carlsmith Ball's clients have played a major role in the development of Hawaii, and the firm has now broadened its vision to encompass those who will shape the destiny of the Pacific Rim. In this spirit, the firm enthusiastically anticipates a dynamic future in this exciting region of the world.

↑ Carlsmith Ball is a full-service firm with more than 150 attorneys and nearly 300 support staff members.

United Airlines

The Friendly Skies of United have never covered so much of the globe. Today, United's wings span five continents, 34 countries, and 169 airports throughout the world.

But a closer look at United's route map reveals the carrier's continued commitment to its "little corner of the world": Hawaii. United ranks as the first domestic air carrier to serve Hawaii from the mainland and offers the most service to the islands today.

United traces its roots to the historic flight of a predecessor company, Varney Airlines, in 1926, which initiated air-mail service from Pasco, Wash., to Elko, Nev. The United name first appeared in 1928 as United Aircraft & Transport Corporation, and United Airlines was organized in 1931.

Just 16 years later, on May 1, 1947, a DC–6 took off for a record 9-hour-19-minute, non-stop flight from San Francisco to Honolulu, marking United's first scheduled service to Hawaii. On board was "Pat" Patterson, United's founder and longtime chairman. He was born

↑ For the last 28 years, United Airlines has underwritten the Hawaiian Open, which raises funds for local charities, while providing challenging golf and spectator fun. Photo by Bruce Chinen.

in Honolulu in 1899 and raised in the plantation town of Waipahu.

Today, United's service within Hawaii extends beyond Oahu's Honolulu International Airport to the Big Island's Keahole Airport in Kailua-Kona, Kauai's

↑ United serves the residents and visitors of the Hawaiian Islands with widebody Boeing 747 and McDonnell Douglas DC–10 aircraft.

Lihue Municipal Airport, and Maui's Kahului Airport. As a major connecting complex for United, Honolulu serves as a pivotal link between North America and the Pacific.

More than 2,600 dedicated United employees work on the islands, serving more than 2 million visitors each year. United's widebody 747 and DC–10 fleet offers comfortable, non-stop service between Hawaii from the mainland gateway cities of Chicago, Los Angeles, San Francisco, and Seattle, and beyond to Auckland, Osaka, and Tokyo.

In addition to passengers, more than 5,000 tons of cargo pass through the islands each month in the form of meat products, dairy goods, and electronics equipment, and United is proud to deliver the Aloha state's pineapples, flowers, and sugar to destinations around the world.

United's commitment to Hawaii has been strong over the last 46 years. That same dedication exists today, and United continues to explore ways of deepening and broadening its involvement in Hawaii. United actively supports and promotes the state's community projects.

For example, over the last 28 years, United has underwritten the United Airlines Hawaiian Open, which raises funds for local charities. United employees also contribute thousands of dollars each year to social agencies through donations to the Aloha United Way.

And in the fall of 1992, United brought hundreds of Honolulu's Farrington High School students under its wing through the Adopt-A-School program. Adopt-A-School brings the corporation to the classroom through presentations by employees such as flight attendants, mechanics, and pilots, as well as through field trips to United facilities, including airports, flight kitchens, and reservations offices.

In recognition of Hawaii's importance to the Friendly Skies, last year United named a senior vice president who resides in Hawaii to oversee United's operations to, from, and within the state.

From Bangkok to Buenos Aires to Brussels, United will continue to sing Hawaii's praises and urge travelers to experience this Pacific paradise in its "little corner of the world." Among the world's airlines, Hawaii has no stronger booster than United. 🌺

↓ More than 2,600 Hawaii-based United employees share the Aloha spirit with customers flying to, from, and between the islands of Hawaii, Kauai, Maui and Oahu.

8
Business & Finance

Banking institutions, insurance, securities, and diversified holding companies provide the foundation for a host of enterprises in Hawaii.

Bancorp Hawaii, Incorporated

Bancorp Hawaii, Inc., the largest Hawaii-based financial organization, was established on December 17, 1897, as the Bank of Hawaii, Limited. It all started with Peter Cushman Jones who, in mid-1893 with his son Edwin, organized the Hawaiian Safe Deposit & Investment Company in Honolulu.

The Bank of Hawaii grew out of Cushman's vision of the great future that lay ahead for Hawaii. In 1897, Cushman, along with friends Joseph Ballard and Charles Montague, founded the Bank of Hawaii, the first bank chartered and incorporated to do business in the republic of Hawaii. The bank opened for business in downtown Honolulu with an initial capitalization of $400,000, and a stock par value of $100 per share.

With a staff of four, including Cushman as president, Bank of Hawaii grew and prospered. By 1899, the bank had established a savings department and Hawaii's first safe deposit boxes. In December 1903, Bank of Hawaii opened its first branch office in Lihue, on the island of Kauai.

↓ In 1897, Bank of Hawaii opened for business in downtown Honolulu. Its first home was this building which cost $12,000.

↑ From statehood and through deregulation, Bancorp Hawaii, Inc. Chairman and CEO H. Howard Stephenson (left) and President Lawrence M. Johnson have seen the bank grow over the years.

By 1930, Bank of Hawaii had opened branches on most of the neighboring islands. When statehood arrived in 1959, the bank had more than 30 offices and was beginning to expand into the Pacific Basin with branches on Kwajalein and Midway Island. In 1961, Bank of Hawaii was one of two banks serving the people of Guam. During the 1960s and 1970s, it further expanded into Asia as well as the Southern and Western Pacific. Bancorp Hawaii, Inc., was established in 1971 as the state's first bank holding company with Bank of Hawaii as its principal subsidiary.

Today, Bancorp Hawaii has more than 100 offices located throughout Hawaii, the Pacific, and Asia. Bank of Hawaii remains the principal subsidiary with more than 60 branches in Hawaii, 11 throughout the Pacific Basin, and 10 international locations, primarily in Asia.

Other subsidiaries include:

• FirstFed America, Inc. — A savings and loan holding company acquired in 1990. FirstFed has 27 full-service offices throughout Hawaii, Guam and Saipan.

• First National Bank of Arizona — This Arizona bank was acquired in 1987. First National Bank of Arizona provides commercial banking services and has four branch offices.

• Bancorp Investment Group, Limited — Formed in 1991, this subsidiary provides full-service brokerage and investment services.

• Bancorp Leasing of Hawaii, Inc. — This subsidiary provides leasing services, primarily to Hawaii's commercial sector.

• Hawaiian Trust Company, Ltd. — the state's oldest and largest trust and investment company has offices throughout the state and in Guam.

From the initial staff of four in 1897, Bancorp Hawaii has expanded its staff to approximately 4,000. The company, with more than $11 billion in assets, ranks among the 50 largest banks in the nation.

↑ Hawaii's first and only mobile ATM, introduced in 1991, is popular at fairs, sports activities and other community events.

SERVICES

The banking industry has changed dramatically during the bank's near 100-year history. Today's financial services environment is highly competitive and requires skills and knowledge in a number of disciplines, from finance and accounting to marketing and information and computer services. Over the years, Bancorp has developed expertise and leadership positions in a number of areas.

Bancorp Hawaii was one of the first banks to use automated teller machines (ATMs) back in 1970. Today, Bancorp has more than 150 ATMs, known as Bankoh BankMachines, located at branches, shopping malls, most major supermarket chains and other convenient locations. ATMs offer Bancorp customers convenience and are popular among Hawaii residents — so much so that monthly ATM transactions total more than one million dollars. Bancorp leads the state's financial institutions in number of ATMs. In addition, Bancorp was among the first financial institutions to introduce ATM instructions in Japanese and Korea.

In 1991, Bancorp introduced Hawaii's first mobile ATM, known as the Bankoh BankMobile. Because Bancorp's ATMs accept so many cards, their mobile ATM has been extremely popular at fairs, sports activities, and other community events.

Bancorp's leadership role in electronic financial services extends to other products, including its debit card. The debit card, known as Bankoh Access Card, is gaining popularity among bank customers who find it convenient to carry a bank card that is connected to their checking account.

The bank has a 24-hour Customer Service Center to assist customers with questions about their accounts, plus a service called Bankoh BankPhone, which allows customers to get account information via a touch-tone telephone.

COMMUNITY SUPPORT

Bancorp Hawaii is recognized statewide for its community involvement and support. The company's commitment to the people of Hawaii extends to the thousands of staff members who are active in the community and who regularly volunteer at bank-sponsored events.

Each year, the company sponsors the premier outrigger canoe racing competitions for men and women. These international races highlight Hawaii's skilled paddlers and attract some of the best crews in the world. Bancorp Hawaii also sponsors music festivals that feature the state's best performing artists in the unique Hawaiian style of guitar playing known as slack key.

Bancorp Hawaii's mission is to be the premier, high performance financial services organization in the state of Hawaii and the Pacific markets the company serves. The bank's basic business strategy is to identify, understand and then satisfy the financial needs and wants of consumers, businesses and governments. Its emphasis on quality has helped earn Bancorp its reputation for safety, security and convenience. ❧

↓ Every fall, canoe clubs from around the world gather in Hawaii to compete in the premier outrigger canoe paddling race — over a 41-mile stretch between the islands of Molokai and Oahu.

BISHOP INSURANCE OF HAWAII, INC.

When Bishop Insurance was founded, the Hawaiian Islands were best known as a place where whaling ships stopped for provisions and where sailors were given shore leave after months at sea. The year was 1859, and the company was then a department of Bishop & Co. (now First Hawaiian Bank). As the economy of the islands grew, so did the pioneer insurance department.

Charles Bishop was co-founder and the leading partner in the bank which bore his name. Bishop married the beautiful Princess Bernice Pauahi, a descendant of King Kamehameha I who had united the Hawaiian Islands. Widely respected, Bishop provided financial help and protection from the earliest days of commercial activity. These services grew as the islands expanded economically.

In 1886 a disastrous fire swept through a large part of Honolulu. Soon after, a board of underwriters was established; among the founding members was the insurance department of Bishop & Co.

Legislation was passed in the early 1900s which restricted banks to banking business only. As a result, Bishop Insurance was incorporated in 1907 as a separate company.

From its earliest years, Bishop Insurance safeguarded the shipment of sugar cargoes to the United States and foreign countries. Sugar was Hawaii's major source of income for over 100 years. Wool has been a lesser export of the islands, yet a consistent source of income since the mid-1800s when sailing ships carried it to Boston and Bremen, Germany. The company still insures these cargoes.

Arthur Berg, manager of Bishop Insurance since 1896 when it was a department of the bank, became president and manager when the agency became a separate company. During his years of leadership Bishop Insurance took important steps forward in modernization and growth. Berg retired in 1928.

In 1925 Bishop Insurance moved into the mezzanine offices of the new Bishop Bank headquarters in Honolulu. At that time the staff consisted of 22 people, and the agency represented 13 different insurance companies.

Founded in the days of the monarchy, Bishop Insurance has continued to grow through the years as Hawaii progressed from a republic to a territory — and now to the 50th state of the Union. Through this long history the people who make up the agency have given time to many different community activities — a tradition which goes back to Bishop Insurance's founding days.

In 1926 the Bishop Insurance Co., Ltd. became a wholly-owned subsidiary of Bishop Trust Co., Ltd. and operated as such until 1965 when it was sold to Employees Liability Insurance Co. This company was later acquired by the Commercial Union Assurance Co. of London, with U.S. headquarters in Boston. In 1979 Bishop Insurance formed a domestic insurance company under the name of Bishop Insurance of Hawaii, Inc.

Hawaii's growth since the achievement of statehood in 1959 has been phenomenal. To keep its place of historic leadership, Bishop Insurance has offices on the neighbor islands of Maui and Kauai and two offices on Hawaii in Hilo and Kona.

In mid-1984, a group of prominent Hawaii business leaders, headed by Clarence G. Philpotts, purchased the Bishop Agency from London-based Commercial Union, thus returning it to Hawaii ownership.

Clarence G. Philpotts, born and raised in Hawaii, has been president since 1965. ❦

↑ **Present-day lobby of Bishop Insurance, founded in Honolulu in 1859. Photo by David Franzen.**

HAWAII NATIONAL BANK

It's a classic rendition of the "Hawaiian dream" — a distinctive, ethnically harmonious adaptation of the American dream. Beginning in the mind and heart of a barefoot Chinese boy from a Kohala plantation in the 1920s, Hawaii National Bank has come to represent the best of American business and Hawaiian temperament graced with a strong but subtle Chinese heritage.

Hawaii National Bank is the largest federally chartered bank in Hawaii. Run by a father and son team, Kan Jung and Warren K. K. Luke, the business retains a personal touch while building on its reputation as a solid, reliable bank with nine offices on Oahu and one on the Big Island.

Known as the "Home of the Warm-Hearted Bankers," Hawaii National Bank was founded on the corner of King and Smith streets in historic Chinatown in 1960 by Kan Jung Luke, the boy from the plantation who by then had received an MBA from Harvard and had, in fact, been lecturing for the previous 21 years on finance, investments and banking at the University of Hawaii Business School — in his free time.

The bank subsequently moved but returned its headquarters and main branch to a new building on King Street in 1989 during the bicentennial year of the Chinese arrival in Hawaii. During the bicentennial celebration, Hawaii National hosted and co-sponsored a number of events, including the exhibit "Masterworks of Ming and Qing Paintings from the Forbidden City" at the Honolulu Academy of Arts, the most heralded exhibition of paintings ever to leave China. More than 100,000 people visited the exhibit during its showing in Honolulu. Today, the Bank's lobbies and offices display traditional Chinese art, screens, and a Chinese robe.

In true Hawaiian fashion, Hawaii National Bank's management, employees, and customers have reflected Hawaii's diverse ethnic groups since its opening in 1960, and the Bank has served its customers and community professionally and sincerely.

↑ Although Kan Jung Luke (sitting) remains Chairman of the Board of the Hawaii National Bank, many of the daily operations are now managed by his son Warren K. K. Luke, Vice Chairman of the Board and President and Chief Executive Officer.

Hawaii National Bank has a fine collection of firsts in service in Hawaii; it was the first bank to offer educational loans — within one month of opening its doors in September 1960. It was the first to offer daily interest on savings, the first to give free personal checking accounts, the first to reproduce on its checks Hawaiian money from King Kamehameha III's reign, and the first to sponsor All-American Auto Loans. It has also been the first to give seniors a discount on checking fees, to provide instant ATM-card encoding and one-hour consumer loan services.

Hawaii National Bank, through its officers, has also been active on a national level. Kan Jung Luke has served as a member of the Comptroller of the Currency's National Advisory Committee on Banking Policies and Practices. Recently, Kan Jung was also honored with Harvard Business School's Alumni Achievement Award, the highest honor conferred by the school.

Warren Luke has the distinction of being the first representative from Hawaii to be elected to serve as a director of the Twelfth Federal Reserve District. Warren also served as president of the Western Independent Bankers and as a member of the National Board of Governors of the American Red Cross. ✤

↑ Hawaii National Bank returned its fully modernized headquarters and main branch to historic Chinatown in 1989.

FINANCE FACTORS FAMILY

In 1952, seeing the need for home financing, a small group of local Hawaii businessmen pooled their capital and founded Finance Factors, Ltd. Business development has continued to be the natural result of identification of customer need. This commitment to meeting needs resulted in the creation of company after company. With the increase in activity, it found an internal need for a holding company to provide financial leadership to the Family of Companies. Thus, Finance Enterprises, Ltd. was created in 1976.

Today, the most prominent members of the Family are Finance Factors, Finance Insurance, Finance Realty, Grand Pacific Life Insurance, Finance Home Builders, Mahalo Nui Management, and Finance Investment. The Family of Companies' growth has been significant. Highlights in the development of these companies are provided below.

Finance Factors, Ltd. opened its doors for business in Downtown Honolulu at King and Smith Streets in July 1952. From its small beginnings, it has weathered the volatile economic and industrial changes of four decades to become one of Hawaii's largest finance companies.

Today Finance Factors, Ltd. has 20 branch offices on Oahu, Maui, Kauai, and the Big Island of Hawaii. The company's financial products include mortgage loans on residential and investment properties, home equity credit lines, and personal loans. Its savings accounts and investment time certificates offer the security of insurance by the Federal Deposit Insurance Corporation (FDIC). Finance Factors is also a member/stock-

holder of the Federal Home Loan Bank of Seattle (FHLB of Seattle) which provides expanded opportunities to serve their customers. Earlier this year, it began an extensive renovation project to upgrade branches and operating systems. Finance Factors is committed to continuing improvements in service capability.

When Finance Factors entered the automobile loan business, customers wanted to obtain car insurance quickly, easily, and economically. In the early years, the company provided insurance from a division within Finance Factors. In 1984, Finance Insurance, Ltd. joined the Family of Companies as a full-service insurance agency providing property and casualty insurance to a variety of business and individual customers.

To remain a strong contender in a competitive market, Finance Insurance strives to give the community and its policyholders personalized service, technical expertise, and a high degree of professionalism. In 1992, Finance Insurance introduced another in a series of insurance packages created specifically to meet the insurance needs of Hawaii's professionals. It continues to stand behind the community by providing a full range of cost efficient products.

Post-war development resulted in a housing shortage. Finance Realty Company, Ltd. was formed in 1953 to help meet this need. Its first project was a 12-acre Manoa subdivision, followed by 435 homes in Waipio Acres near Wahiawa.

As the building programs of Finance Realty grew, so did the need for construction support

↓ The Family of Companies' founders (left to right) — Fong Choy, Daniel B.T. Lau, Clifford H.N. Yee, Hiram L. Fong, Mun On Chun and Lup Quon Pang — as photographed at an annual Christmas party in the '60s. Although Fong Choy and Lup Quon Pang passed away in recent years, each of the remaining founders continues to be actively involved. The next generation of these six founding families are also represented in Finance Factors' current operations.

services. In 1957, Finance Home Builders, Ltd. became the general contractor for Finance Realty with the Waipio Acres project. In addition to the residential units built for Finance Realty, the company developed extensive experience in commercial and renovation projects for clients outside the Family of Companies.

By 1962, Finance Realty had enough project experience to take on the development of Hawaii's first planned residential community — Makakilo. Growth was steady, and by 1973, it saw the need for a company to assist homeowner associations and other community development projects in Makakilo. Mahalo Nui Management was formed to provide these services in addition to property management and grounds maintenance for residents.

In August, the company celebrated Makakilo's 30th anniversary. In those years, it developed more than 3,600 homes and home sites and is still growing. Views from Makakilo are some of the best on Oahu — ocean views and vistas across the Ewa Plain to Pearl Harbor, Downtown Honolulu, and Diamond Head. In February, the first gated, luxury project in Makakilo opened. The completion of Makakilo will bring the total number of residences in this community to more than 6,000.

By 1957, families were growing and needed insurance to provide for future financial security. In that year, Grand Pacific Life Insurance Company was established, offering a variety of life insurance products. Today, it is one of the few locally-owned, locally-operated life insurance companies in Hawaii. As part of its dedication to the community, GPLI invests in local residential mortgages to assist in filling the need for home financing. In this way, the company furthers the first goal of the founders — meeting the home loan needs of Hawaii.

GPLI's focus has always been on facilitating service and providing products to meet the changing needs of its customers. It recently embarked on a program to streamline home office operations and improve service to policyholders and agents. With 35 years of operations this year, it continues to explore opportunities for growth.

In 1958, the year before statehood became a reality, Finance Investment, Ltd. was founded to participate in any sound investment opportunity. Finance Investment has specialized in the purchase, development, and management of real estate. The majority of its current holdings are in office buildings, with substantial investments in industrial, commercial, and residential rental property. The company's most recent investment was the 1164 Bishop Street Building in Downtown Honolulu. The purchase of this building brings the company's total inventory of prime office and commercial space in the central business district to approximately 300,000 square feet.

↗ The Family of Companies would not have grown and developed these four decades without very special, dedicated employees. What started as a small group of nine has turned into a diverse force of 355 with an average of 8.49 years of service to the company. Over 13% of the employees have given more than 25 years of service.

Through the Finance Factors Family of Companies Foundation and the charitable contributions of individual companies and employees, the Family has maintained its committment to Hawaii's community. The company also encourages active participation in events such as the Food Bank Drive, Walk America, and the Bobby Benson Relays, activities that not only benefit the community, but promote employee camaraderie as well.

What began as a small lending business in 1952 has now become a Family of Companies. Business activities have expanded from lending into savings, insurance, real estate development, investments, property management, and account servicing.

During its 40 years of growth, the Finance Factors Family has seen its many companies' headquarters located in six different buildings in downtown Honolulu. They look forward to their future in a reconsolidated Family of Companies home address — 1164 Bishop Street. From this new home, they will continue to grow with Hawaii. ✿

PACIFIC INSURANCE COMPANY, LIMITED

A Standard of Excellence — Second To None. It is a standard by which Pacific Insurance Company, Ltd. delivers quality insurance products and services to meet the risk management needs in Hawaii. This standard today observes the principles set forth by its founders over 64 years ago.

Founded by a select group of Honolulu businessmen on October 25, 1928, this *kama'aina* company was dedicated to provide sickness and accident insurance for Hawaii's plantation employees. At the time, mainland insurers were discontinuing that type of coverage, leaving Hawaii's workers financially vulnerable. The founders recognized the issues and formed Pacific Insurance Company, Ltd. with the intention of providing the much needed protection. The company was devoted to servicing this special need and continued to specialize in this type of insurance for many years. Success was marked at the end of the first decade with reported assets of over $85,000.

In the next decade, spurred by an ever-tightening mainland market for workers' compensation insurance, services were expanded to offer "all lines" casualty and fire insurance. Pacific Insurance met these challenges philosophically and maintained its service base, though slightly handicapped by regulatory restrictions on the amount of general agents a company could have.

In the following years profits were kept in surplus to ensure stability, and nearly half a million dollars in new capital was invested in the company. In addition, a 1944 U.S. Supreme Court decision allowed Pacific Insurance, among other companies, to increase the number of general agents beyond the previous limit of two. All these factors brought substantial growth to Pacific Insurance. By the close of 1947, Pacific Insurance was a fully licensed, well-staffed and mature company with assets of over $1.08 million. Today, Pacific Insurance Company boasts assets of more than $252 million, making it one of the top carriers in the state.

With noteworthy assets and strong competitive leadership at the helm, Pacific Insurance Company thrived and in 1963 joined the Hartford Insurance Group to further broaden its scope of insurance products and services.

Today, as in the past, Pacific Insurance Company stresses service excellence and customer satisfaction with a focus on teamwork and professionalism. As a wholly owned subsidiary of ITT Hartford, Pacific Insurance combines personal, localized service with an impressive record of dependability and financial security. The company has shaped its current business philosophy on Hawaii's diverse cultural base. Pacific Insurance knows that Hawaii is a unique state with unique insurance needs and that special attention must be given in order to cultivate the consumers' trust. In everything it offers, innovation is tantamount. In everything it does, the standard of excellence prevails.

Little could the founders have imagined that the seed they planted back in 1928 was to survive through the Depression of the '30s, the milieu of wars, the advent of statehood and the next 40 years of economic explosion and technological advancement. Since its modest beginnings over 64 years ago, the spirit for excellence and the commitment to serve the people of Hawaii has guided Pacific Insurance Company to become Hawaii's standard for stabile and dependable insurance services. 🌿

↑ The people of Pacific Insurance embody the standard of excellence set forth in the company's corporate philosophy.

ISLAND INSURANCE COMPANIES AND NATIONAL MORTGAGE LTD.

Masayuki Tokioka

Island Insurance and National Mortgage have elected to dedicate this page to chairman and founder Masayuki Tokioka.

"When you go back home to work, don't work for a big company — pick a small one. In a big company, sometimes you are placed in a corner and it is difficult to show

↑ **Masayuki Tokioka and his wife when he was awarded an Honorary Doctor of Laws.**

them what you can do." Such was the advice given to Masayuki Tokioka as he left Harvard, armed with an MBA in International Commerce in 1929.

One of the first Asians to graduate from the prestigious Business School, Tokioka heeded the word of his advisor and looked for a small company. "My friend told me that International Trust Company was looking for an operations man. I was around 25 or 27 years old… so I went for an interview. As I had been told by my advisor, I said 'Yes, Sir!' And I listened to him. Then the time came when I was asked what I thought about the company's operation. I told him what I thought… and they were good enough to give me a chance to do whatever I wanted to do. My report was accepted favorably. They had an internal reorganization right after that."

So began the business career of a local legend — a man who still goes to work every day at the age of 95. Masayuki Tokioka took the chance given him by a small company, and built his experience — his ability to listen and take action — into a family of not-so-small companies that serve the financial and business needs of Hawaii's local people today.

Born in 1897 in Okayama-ken, Japan, the young Tokioka and his mother returned to Hawaii, where his father operated a nursery, in 1909. Even while dutifully helping his father in the nursery, Tokioka displayed a robust love of life and adventure. One of only two Japanese surfers seen on the beach at

Waikiki, he also played football at McKinley High School. Unbeknownst to his parents — who could not afford the insurance to pay for potential injuries — their 112-pound son was McKinley's fullback — playing under the name of Baron Kato.

As a young family man, Tokioka turned his energy to business and community work. He was instrumental in the founding and rapid growth of numerous local companies, including the New Fair Dairy, the Hamakua Coffee Plantation on the Big Island, International Trust, International Savings and Loan, National Mortgage and Finance, and Island Insurance. Each of these companies was founded with local people and their needs in mind.

In 1986, Tokioka was given a Humanitarian Award by the University of Hawaii Alumni Association for 50 years of community service. Those who know him remember that he was instrumental in providing artifacts and support for the Bishop Museum exhibit on Japanese immigration to Hawaii, and for building the Makiki Christian Church. Similarly, he was instrumental in building San Francisco's Japan Cultural and Trade Center and its Peace Pagoda.

Masayuki Tokioka is a man of his word who has brought honor and credit to his race and to all the people of Hawaii. Ask him about it, and he will tell you: "I had a little dream, but not exactly as it is now."

Not exactly. ✤

↑ **Masayuki Tokioka and his mother in Japan.**

↑ **Masayuki Tokioka on the occasion of his 37th birthday.**

BANK OF AMERICA HAWAII

On August 1, 1992, residents of Hawaii awakened to find a new addition to the islands' financial landscape: Bank of America, FSB. The previous day, after more than a year of negotiations to acquire Honfed Bank, BankAmerica Corporation had closed the deal. Within days, what were once Honfed Bank signs now read Bank of America.

Honfed Bank, the state's third largest financial institution, had served Hawaii for over 63 years, and had set a strong foundation of trust and quality service throughout the banking community, making the acquisition and transition smooth for BankAmerica Corporation.

Much of Honfed's growth had been due to Gerald M. Czarnecki, the chairman and CEO of the bank in the years leading up to the acquisition. Hired by Honfed Bank owners to rebuild the institution, Czarnecki, with his "can do" reputation, set to work refining the bank's systems of operations and management, establishing quality service as its highest priority. The dedication and support of the bank's associates, fueled by a booming real

←
**Gerald M. Czarnecki,
Chairman and CEO,
Bank of America Hawaii.**

estate environment that enabled the bank to sell off assets at a handsome profit, allowed Honfed Bank to rebuild the strength of its net worth and substantially improve profitability.

This major accomplishment drew the attention of the financial community around the country, and it wasn't long before BankAmerica Corporation expressed interest in acquiring Honfed Bank.

Today, Bank of America customers can take advantage of the expansion of services, not just in Hawaii, but everywhere in the United States where they see a Bank of America Versateller sign. Indeed, its customers enjoy the benefits of a local touch with a global reach.

BankAmerica Corp., today's second largest financial services company in the nation — and one of the largest in the world — had its beginnings as a small neighborhood bank. Thirty-four-year-old Amadeo Peter Giannini founded "The Little Fellow's Bank" in San Francisco, California on October 17, 1904, and his family continued to run it for the next 50 years.

By 1913, the bank had expanded to southern California, and by the end of the '20s, the bank had 292 branches throughout California. In the mid-'30s, Lawrence Mario Giannini, the founder's son, became the president of the bank; under his leadership, the bank expanded to 487 branches.

After World War II, branches were set up in Manila, Tokyo, Yokohama, Kobe, Bangkok, and Guam. In

↑ From left, Gerald Czarnecki, Chairman and CEO, and Mendel Borthwick, Vice Chairman, outside the Kahala branch on its first day of operation as Bank of America Hawaii.

↑ Kahala branch associates watch the Bank of America Hawaii blessing.

addition, Bank of America New York, a wholly-owned subsidiary for international banking under the provisions of the Edge Act, was organized.

By 1954, the bank had 548 branches in California and overseas. Throughout the next 30 years the bank continued to grow. The acquisition of Nevada First Development Corporation in 1989 positioned BankAmerica as the West Coast's largest bank holding company.

By the end of 1991, branch offices were operating in nine western states, and a merger with Security Pacific Corporation — the largest bank merger in U.S. history — was under way. The merger was completed in the first half of 1992.

With the acquisition of Honfed Bank in August 1992, BankAmerica, through its network of banking subsidiaries, provides consumer banking services in 11 western states, fiduciary and consumer financial services nationwide, and expanded commercial and corporate banking operations throughout the United States. Its reported assets were $188.6 billion and total deposits were $139.2 billion.

BankAmerica Corporation's principal banking subsidiaries operate branches in California, Washington, Arizona, Oregon, Nevada, New Mexico, Texas, Idaho, Utah, Alaska, and Hawaii, with corporate offices and representatives in 37 countries. With its recent unprecedented expansion, the company is well-equipped to meet the future challenges from a position of strength and stability.

Bank of America continues to be a leader in innovative products, services, techniques, and practices. Today, Bank of America Hawaii is better positioned to deliver outstanding customer service, offer new products, and contribute to the growth of the state of Hawaii.

Bank of America Hawaii has 30 branches statewide. To make banking more convenient, 14 branches are open on Saturday; customers can talk to a "real person" 24 hours a day via the customer satisfaction center; and Versateller ATMs will be installed at 48 convenience store locations in the state.

Concludes Czarnecki, "We will continually evaluate and add services for our customers in our ongoing effort to meet the bank's philosophy of 'We're not satisfied until you are.'" ☙

9
Building Hawaii

Real estate and construction industries shape tomorrow's skyline, providing working and living space for Hawaii's people and attracting new business and residents to the islands.

CASTLE & COOKE PROPERTIES

Both Samuel Northrup Castle and Amos Starr Cooke were attached to the eighth company of American missionaries who arrived in Honolulu in 1837. Castle was a manager of secular affairs for the mission. Cooke started out as a teacher and subsequently joined Castle in the business management of the mission. In 1851 both were released from their responsibilities to the mission and formed the partnership of Castle & Cooke, which became one of the giants of business in Hawaii in the areas of agriculture, shipping, real estate, and other aspects of Hawaii's business community.

James Drummond Dole, a relative of Sanford Ballard Dole, Hawaii's first governor, arrived in Hawaii in 1899

↑ Castle & Cooke Residential, Inc. is the developer of Mililani Town, a master-planned community in the plains of central Oahu. In 1986, Mililani won the prestigious All-America City Award. It is the only city in Hawaii to win this award.

and joined a group of California homesteaders in Wahiawa to pioneer the pineapple industry. In 1901 he established the Hawaiian Pineapple Company, Ltd. and packed his first crop in 1903. In 1906 he established what would become one of the largest canning operations in the world in the Iwilei section of Honolulu.

By World War II, Castle & Cooke, Inc. acquired controlling interest in the Hawaiian Pineapple

Company, and in time, taking advantage of the worldwide recognition of the "Dole" name, Castle & Cooke, Inc. changed its name to Dole Food Company, Inc., thereby becoming the parent company of Castle & Cooke Properties, Inc.

Today, Dole Food Company, Inc., more than 141 years old, is a major food and real estate development company. Dole is one of the world's largest producers and marketers of high quality fresh fruit and vegetables, juices, packaged fruits, and nuts. Through its subsidiaries, Dole is also engaged in the development of residential, commercial, and industrial real estate in Hawaii, California, and Arizona, and in the development and operation of resorts on Lanai.

Based in Honolulu, Castle & Cooke Properties and its Hawaii affiliates have operations on the islands of Oahu and Lanai where they are actively building homes, shopping centers, industrial parks, a high technology park, tourist centers, and hotels. The company has assets in excess of $350 million and a total work force of more than 300.

The major affiliates of Castle & Cooke Properties are Castle & Cooke Residential, Inc., Castle & Cooke Retail, Inc., Oceanic Construction, Inc., and Lanai Company, Inc.

With all of its activities, Castle & Cooke Properties continues a tradition of being a Hawaii company. Witness the fact that they are the largest home-builder in the state, and the first to build master-planned communities of homes for thousands of families.

For example, Castle & Cooke Residential, Inc. is the developer of Mililani Town, a fee-simple, master-planned community in the plains of central Oahu. In 1986, Mililani became the first community in Hawaii to win the prestigious All-America City Award. Construction of homes and sites for business and community services have continued to expand at Mililani.

Castle & Cooke Properties was selected by the state

↑ Lanai Company, Inc. an affiliate of Castle & Cooke Properties, has developed the Manele Bay Hotel, a spectacularly beautiful resort at Hulopoe Bay on the island of Lanai.

of Hawaii as the developer of the first increment of the state's affordable housing project at the Villages of Kapolei. Current projects for Castle & Cooke Residential include developments at Waikele and Royal Kunia in Leeward Oahu and Waikoloa on the island of Hawaii.

Castle & Cooke Retail, Inc. was formed in 1987 with interests in tourism, retail, and packaged goods industries. It provides visitors with an opportunity to see some of Hawaii's fastest growing visitor attractions, the Dole Cannery Square and Dole Plantation.

Oceanic Construction, Inc. was the general contractor for the first two buildings at the Mililani Technology Park and for Dole Cannery Square. In 1991, Oceanic Construction completed the Ellison S. Onizuka Space Center Memorial at Keahole Airport in Kona, Hawaii, to commemorate the life of Ellison Onizuka, a Kona resident who lost his life in the Challenger disaster in 1986.

Commercial/Industrial development projects currently include the 232,000-square-foot Town Center of Mililani, the Mililani Technology Park, and the Iwilei commercial/retail center. Plans are underway to enlarge the Town Center of Mililani to become one of the largest shopping complexes in the state. Mililani Technology Park has been developed as part of the master-planned community to be a major employment center for central Oahu. It is expected that about 6,000 to 9,000 people will work at the park eventually. Development of the Iwilei Dole Cannery Square includes retail shops, food courts, and commercial office spaces.

Dole has owned a major part of the island of Lanai for many years, growing pineapples for its cannery in Honolulu. However, the difficult economics of the

pineapple industry in recent years have dictated that a different use should be found for the island. As a result, Lanai Company has developed two spectacularly beautiful resort hotels on the island of Lanai.

At Hulopoe Bay is the 250-room Manele Bay Hotel, named for the adjacent cliff-ringed harbor at Manele Bay. In the center of the Lanai highlands, surrounded by Norfolk Island pines, grassy slopes and forested mountain sides is the 102-room Lodge at Koele. Koele boasts an 18-hole championship golf course while at Hulopoe Bay, a second golf course designed by Jack Nicklaus is under construction.

The difficult task of converting from agricultural to resort use has been skillfully handled by Lanai Company, resulting in at least 70 percent of the plantation workers being retrained and employed in many areas, including resorts, retail, construction, diversified agriculture, medicine, and education.

Castle & Cooke Properties is determined to be a good corporate citizen of the islands in which it has roots going back 141 years. On Lanai this commitment can be seen in the preservation of Hawaiian archeological sites and the granting of a conservation easement to the Nature Conservancy of Hawaii.

State-wide, the company has been a leader, offering support for community organizations like the Aloha United Way, the Bishop Museum, the Honolulu Symphony, Special Olympics, and many others. Castle & Cooke also helped establish the first village for the homeless of Oahu, built in Haleiwa. It donated land, cash, and construction management services.

Over many years, the company has been a major contributor to countless other charities.

Such is Castle & Cooke Properties, a Hawaii company, originating almost a century and a half ago to serve Hawaii through all these years of shifting economic, environmental, and cultural change. 🖋

↑ The impressive Lodge at Koele in the Lanai highlands.

Fletcher Pacific Construction Co., Ltd.

↑ **Grand Hyatt Wailea Hotel**

In January of 1939, with $100,000 and a handful of contracts totaling $276,000, George E. Freitas incorporated Pacific Construction Co, Ltd., in the offices of the Hawaii territorial treasurer. Thus, what would later become Fletcher Pacific Construction, one of the leading construction companies in the Pacific Basin, was launched.

Pacific Construction grew from strength to strength and within a few years it had established itself among the top contractors in the state. After a series of ownership changes, Pacific merged with DMA Hawaii, a Honolulu contracting firm, in 1978.

In the fall of 1986, Pacific Construction was acquired by Fletcher Construction Company, Ltd. and its distinguished *kamaaina* heritage became linked to the equally distinguished heritage of the Fletcher Challenge Group, New Zealand's largest company. On July 1, 1990, Pacific Construction was renamed Fletcher Pacific Construction Co., Ltd.

With the resources of a major construction firm behind it, the company flourished. In 1991, in the wake of a booming construction market, Fletcher Pacific posted record revenues of $530 million and was ranked by *Hawaii Business* magazine as Hawaii's largest general contractor and 12th largest business overall.

Fletcher Pacific re-established itself as a force in Hawaii's civil engineering market and enlarged its markets geographically. An ambitious expansion program led to the opening of an office in Guam and the completion of many substantial projects in the region. In 1990, Fletcher Pacific was named Contractor of the Year by the government of Guam.

The legacy of Fletcher Pacific's work is evident throughout Hawaii. The company has built much of modern downtown Honolulu's skyline, including the Grosvenor Center complex, Pauahi Tower, Pacific Trade

Nauru Tower →

Center, and 1100 Alakea. Condominiums such as Nauru Tower and One Waterfront, the state's tallest buildings, were also constructed by Fletcher.

The company has also been active in Hawaii's visitor industry. Among its projects are the Hilton Hawaiian Village Tapa Tower, Kapalua Bay Hotel, Sheraton Kauai, Embassy Suites Maui, Kea Lani Hotel, and the 787-room Grand Hyatt Wailea, the most expensive private sector construction project in Hawaii's history.

Fletcher Pacific has built housing projects as well, including the 1300-home Village Park community on Oahu and exclusive homes such as the luxurious Toyota corporate retreat on the Big Island. The company also built Pearlridge Shopping Center and medical facilities that include Wilcox memorial on Kauai and Moanalua Medical Center and St. Francis Medical Center on Oahu.

While Fletcher Pacific has access to valuable financial, human, and technological support from the Fletcher Construction Co., its corporate culture remains rooted in Hawaii. Drawing on the superb quality of its local work force, the company expects to continue its tradition of pride, excellence and achievement well into the future. 🐾

ASSOCIATED STEEL WORKERS, LTD.

Associated Steel Workers, Ltd. is beginning its 45th year of providing reinforcing bars, usually called "rebar," for the construction industry of the state of Hawaii.

The firm traces its humble beginnings to 1941 when Takao Togami, the company's founder, and five of his future partners were employed on the Tripler Hospital project. Installing all the rebar, they completed the Tripler project shortly after the war ended. They formed Associated Steel Workers, Ltd. in 1948. With surplus U.S. government equipment, the founding partners fabricated rebar, loaded it up, delivered it, then unloaded it and installed it at the job site from their base in Kalihi.

↑ Takao Togami, founder and former president and CEO of Associated Steel Workers, Ltd.

In the early years, their salaries, if any, barely put food on their tables. However, the booming years of postwar construction in Hawaii were good years of steady growth for Associated Steel. Profits were reinvested back into the company, and a crane rental department was established. The mobile cranes were used on their construction projects, as well as being rented to general contractors, and were used unloading cargo at the piers in Honolulu harbor. This aspect of the business has grown until Associated Steel has 20 rough terrain and boom trucks.

In 1961, Associated Steel Workers, Ltd. moved to Waimalu close to the shores of Pearl Harbor. On the new two-acre site, the staff set up a modern fabrication shop and office facility, where major hotel and condominium projects during the 1980s kept the shop busy with two shifts fabricating rebar.

In 1971, Associated Steel Workers, Ltd. anticipated the construction boom on the island of Maui, and it set up operations in Kahului. The timing for this move was a good one. Through the '70s and '80s there was rapid resort growth in Kaanapali and Kihei as the visitor industry grew.

In 1990, Associated Steel Workers, Ltd. set up a new shop and office facility at the Campbell Industrial Park. With the future growth of Honolulu heading towards the leeward plains beyond Ewa, this new shop location could expect to be in the center of growth for the next 15 or 20 years. The H-3 highway projects kept both Waimalu and the Campbell shops operating full time.

Takao Togami, the founder of the company, officially retired in 1988, although he remained active in the company until his death in 1992.

When the world-wide economic slowdown reached the construction industry in Hawaii, Associated Steel took steps to adjust it. The Waimalu shop and office facility was closed in 1992 and consolidated at the Campbell site.

Some of the major projects in which Associated Steel has had a part include the H-3 freeway; Hospital Rock Tunnel; Windward Viaduct; the Haiku tunnels and approaches; the H-1 airport viaduct; Waikiki landmark; the Ilikai; Hyatt Regency Waikiki; and the Ala Moana Hotels; One Waterfront Plaza and Towers; Honolulu Towers; and Honolulu Park Place.

Now, the company has some 200 employees on Oahu, Maui, and Hawaii with Ronald Fujikawa as President and CEO. Many of these are the sons and daughters of the founding partners as well as many veterans of 15 or more years with the company.

While supplying a current yearly total of about 30,000 tons of rebar to Hawaii's construction industry and enjoying about $35 million in gross sales, Associated Steel Workers looks forward to many years serving the growing community of Hawaii.

← Windward Oahu Twin Viaducts, about 1.25 miles each, a part of a $1 billion H-3 Highway being built by SCI/E.E. Black.

MidPac Lumber Company, Ltd.

↑ **Wallace Jun Duck Lai.**

What would Honolulu be without the many services of its favorite lumber company? Less than paradise, customers and friends agree. In this land where people all over the world come to pursue their most extravagant visions, MidPac Lumber Company has provided an invaluable service to residents building their dreams.

MidPac brings to Oahu the highest-quality glass products, wood and vinyl windows and doors, and accessories for every residence. The company's household fixtures display room is a wonderland of modern designs. The floor bustles with builders and homeowners wandering from display to display, mixing and matching items to complement a new or rebuilt Honolulu home.

MidPac not only offers products that can endure the islands' particularly demanding conditions; it offers them at an affordable price.

High-end traditional and contemporary cabinetry, top-of-the-line hardwood flooring, decorative doors, and plumbing fixtures are displayed in naturalistic home surroundings so that customers — architects, designers, contractors, and homeowners alike — can make accurate and informed decisions.

Over the years MidPac has added a glass department, a roof truss plant, a wood-treating plant, and a pre-hung door plant.

And, of course, there is the lumber. MidPac maintains several million board-feet of lumber in inventory in various species; Douglas fir is the most popular, but the company also carries ample quantities of redwood (notably its famous 1 x 8" clear redwood tongue and groove), cedar, hem/fir, and pine. MidPac imports

the lumber "green" and treats it in its own, state-of-the-art OSMOSE wood treatment plant.

As Oahu's essential homebuilding materials supplier, MidPac works closely with the architectural, engineering, and designer communities to explore solutions to the ever-increasing costs of wood products. Steel framing systems might well be an alternative to the costs involved in wood products today. Exterior finish systems offer solutions to the shrinking siding market as the "stucco" look continues to be a favorite with home buyers. MidPac provides an array of alternatives.

The company is also sensitive to the unique stresses that the islands place on home building materials. Hawaii's demanding weather and termite conditions require particularly high grade materials, and MidPac has made it their number one priority to research and offer durable yet inexpensive products for island homes that will last.

MidPac is presently nurturing a new branch operation on the island of Kauai. With this second convenient location, Hawaii residents today are finding it even easier to see their dream homes become a reality.

MidPac's founding father, Wallace Jun Duck Lai, rose from simple roots to a community and industry leader in a rags-to-riches tale that would have made Horatio Alger envious. He spent his childhood years among the small frame homes and narrow streets typical of Hawaii at that time. During his college years, he worked part time in a pineapple cannery and in a

↑ **High-end traditional and contemporary cabinetry, top-of-the-line hardwood flooring, decorative doors, and plumbing fixtures are displayed in naturalistic home surroundings so that customers — architects, designers, contractors, and homeowners alike — can make accurate and informed decisions.**

Chinatown vegetable stall owned by his uncle. He walked away from the University of Hawaii in 1939 with a bachelor's degree in business and economic accounting.

Like so many young Hawaii men in that period, Lai was swept up in the whirlwind of World War II. He served two years with a Navy Construction Battalion, the Seabees, on Guam. Returning to civilian life after the war, he began raising a family even as he was preparing to nurture MidPac into a blossoming business.

By the late 1940s, Lai had become the successful General Manager of Pacific Lumber Company, when he learned that the company planned to close its Hawaii store. His distress at the loss of his job was short-lived: soon, he recognized it as a glistening opportunity.

Lai immediately began working to purchase the assets of Pacific Lumber. And when he realized he didn't have the funds to meet the owners' demands, he turned to some friends, family, fellow employees, and business associates to invest in a new company to take the place of Pacific Lumber Company. With their support, MidPac Lumber Company, Ltd. was incorporated in 1956.

Those who trusted Lai's judgment have known the rewards of faith in this unusual man. Against entrenched competition from other building suppliers, MidPac has become a watchword in the industry.

MidPac was saddened at Mr. Lai's passing on January 28, 1991. Yet the company Mr. Lai created continues to flourish and remains a leader in Hawaii's building materials distribution business. 🦜

↓ Douglas fir is MidPac's most popular wood, but the company also carries ample quantities of redwood (notably its famous 1 x 8" clear redwood tongue and groove), cedar, hem/fir, and pine. MidPac imports the lumber "green" and treats it in its own, state-of-the-art OSMOSE wood treatment plant.

PAN-PACIFIC CONSTRUCTION, INC.

It is difficult to go anywhere in Hawaii and not be in sight of one of the projects created by Pan-Pacific Construction, Inc. There are few, if any, construction challenges that Pan-Pacific hasn't accepted, and it is unlikely that one will find a more impressive marriage of engineering technology and artistic taste anywhere in Hawaii, or indeed across the Pacific Basin.

The story of Pan-Pacific starts in Hawaii in 1948. In that year, the former entity of Pan-Pacific Construction was founded on the island of Oahu. These were the post-war years when Hawaii was turning to the pressing needs of a civilian population. The company was one of the pioneers in the construction of much-needed modestly priced private homes.

As this first need was met, it quickly became evident that Hawaii was going into a period of booming economy. The central "hub" of the Pacific community was becoming an international business center, a tourist center, a center for research and education and indeed a community requiring all the complex construction of a sophisticated metropolis. The original body of Pan-Pacific Construction, by the year 1964, had widely increased its capabilities to meet the needs of this era of growth with a spectrum of building services to individuals, corporations and agencies of the city, the state, and the federal government.

As its capabilities broadened and its reputation for versatility became more widely known, the company

↑ Hotel Ihilani Resort and Spa

caught the attention of giant Tokyu Construction, a member of the powerful Tokyu Group of Japan. Looking to the future, a merger was completed in 1979 that gave the new company, now called Pan-Pacific Construction, Inc., huge resources of capital, technology, and equipment with which to serve its clients' needs from the ground up.

When this merger was completed, the new company assured the public that the addition of the impressive influence of the Tokyu Group was not going to be used to bring about a disruptive upheaval in the construction industry. On the contrary, the new company made it clear that it planned to blend in with the Hawaii community, contributing to the economic balance of the islands as they moved into the 21st century.

↓ Mauna Lani Bay Hotel and Bungalow

↓ Sheraton Moana Surfrider Hotel

In keeping with that determination, Pan-Pacific continues to employ about 500 men and women in Hawaii. Only nine of that total are Japanese nationals.

A brief overview of the staggering number of activities of the Tokyu Group includes the following:

- The Transportation Group builds and repairs railway carriages and specialized vehicles. It also operates two airlines.
- The Development Group, of which Pan-Pacific is a part, develops land for housing and recreation. It also builds, maintains, and leases office and commercial facilities.
- The Retailing and Distribution Group operates a wide variety of department and general merchandise stores, as well as offering information and physical distribution services.
- The Recreation and Leisure Group develops and operates a variety of hotels, inns, movie theatres and a planetarium. It also operates golf courses, tennis courts, and ski grounds.
- The Educational Group operates a number of foundations including schools, a university, a library, an environmental foundation, and others.

Finally, Tokyu is involved in general research, a cable television service, and other activities around the world, aimed to create a well balanced life for the 21st century.

During the decade or so since Pan-Pacific Construction was founded, Pan-Pacific has completed or is nearing completion of nearly 200 major projects of every possible description. A few of the more prominent examples include: the towering Pearl Ridge Square, the Kapiolani Community College at Diamond Head, the Liberty House at the Windward Mall, the Mauna Lani Racquet Club on the Big Island, the Mauna Lani

↓ Waianae Sewage Treatment Plant

↑ Pan Pacific Plaza

Terrace, the Waianae Sewage Treatment Plant, the renovation of the Sheraton Moana Hotel, the Mauna Lani Bay Hotel and Beach Club, the renovation of the Ala Moana Hotel and the Kamaoa Windfarm on the island of Hawaii, Pan Pacific Plaza in the heart of Downtown Honolulu, and the Hotel Ihilani Resort and Spa in Ko'Olina Resort, west beach.

Pan-Pacific, backed by the Tokyu Group, looks to the future with some mindboggling concepts. The staff are designing buildings that will be far more resistant to earthquakes. They are using their research into the acoustical sciences to design better auditoriums. On their drawing board is a dome-covered athletic facility that is more than 600 feet in diameter and which can be opened to the sunlight or totally closed against the weather.

Underground cities are being studied and designed. Fast, modern transportation between population centers is under research. And of special interest to Hawaii is the development of waterfronts and the utilization of the sea for recreation, science, and food production.

What started as a modest construction business in Hawaii less than three decades ago has become a benevolent giant with limitless capabilities, and with vision that sees beyond the horizons of space and time. ❦

HAWAIIAN DREDGING & CONSTRUCTION COMPANY

With over 90 years of high quality construction achievements in Hawaiian Dredging & Construction Company's cap — or famous blue hard hat to be more precise — all President James R. Perry has the modest ambition for is: "To do the same for the next 90 years. We simply want to continue to serve our children and future generations, to serve the needs of a growing Hawaii.

"As we enter our tenth decade with a service-minded team in place," he says, "we have the expertise, the manpower, and the vision to build Hawaii's future for the next century."

After the Wall Street troubles of the '80s with a leveraged buy-out and sell-off of the parent company Dillingham Corp., the management, employees, and a Japanese 45 percent partner, Shimizu Construction, bought the construction side of the company to return it to the community.

The Hawaii-Pacific arm of Dillingham Construction Corp., Hawaiian Dredging & Construction Company (HD&C) has a tradition of fathers and sons working for the business. Many of the employees have been with the company for 25 or 30 years, as has President James Perry, a 25-year veteran. Every working day sees the company contribute to the community as it constructs the buildings and infrastructure necessary for residents and visitors.

Beginning with reclaiming thousands of acres of land from swamp and dredging the Pearl Harbor channel in 1902, HD&C has been entrusted with most of the major construction projects in Hawaii, including the Honolulu Airport Reef Runway, the Ala Moana

James R. Perry, President

Shopping Center, and the Aloha Stadium.

Since the spin-off from Dillingham Corp. in 1987, the new owners (the management) have set HD&C firmly back on its feet. Projects completed in 1992 include construction of the luxury resort hotel Ritz-Carlton Kapalua (at a cost of $112 million); the AES 180-megawatt coal-fired energy plant at Barbers Point ($84 million); the Imperial Plaza, a 35-story condominium ($74 million); the widening of Kalanianaole Highway ($37 million); and many other smaller projects. Still under construction is the Halawa Valley approach and tunnels on H-3 Highway ($89 million) with plans for completion by February 1994. HD&C has also recently completed 2,000 affordable housing units throughout the islands.

When people jokingly refer to the construction crane as the state bird, they could more properly identify it as the Hawaiian Dredging & Construction Company species of crane — as recognizable an inhabitant of the islands as many of the now-naturalized species of birds and animals. 🐾

→ Hyatt Regency Waikoloa

← Hyatt Regency Kauai

The Hawaiian Dredging & Construction Company, now in its 10th decade of building Hawaii, takes the credit for building about 60 percent of Hawaii's most beautiful hotels and resorts as well as much of the infrastructure for the state, including highways, homes, the City Financial Tower, the new state office building, and the AES coal-fired power plant at Barbers Point.

10
The
Marketplace

Hawaii's retail establishments, service industry, and leisure/convention facilities offer an impressive variety of choices for Hawaii's residents and visitors alike.

COFFEES OF HAWAII

Early in the morning of September 25th, 1992, a small crowd gathered in a field of young plants near the Kualapuu Reservoir, on the island of Molokai, for an intimate ceremony: the first harvest of beans from the new Coffees of Hawaii plantation. Farmers, community leaders, friends, and neighbors came to try their hand at picking and, of course, for the complimentary cup of fresh Molokai gourmet coffee.

The seedlings, a progeny of Coffee Arabica cultivar developed with the Kualapuu fields in mind, were planted in the fields only a year and a half before. The plants thrived in the favorable climate and soil, and with Vice President and Manager Dan Kuhn's extensive agricultural skill, the beans were ready to harvest 18 months earlier than predicted.

Kuhn and Jack Magoon, President and CEO of Coffees of Hawaii, Inc., welcomed the visitors and read letters of congratulation from Senator Dan Inouye and Governor Waihee. Councilman Patrick Kawano emphasized the importance of the plantation to the people and the economy of Molokai. Afterwards, each participant was briefed on the basics of coffee harvesting, given a baggie and turned loose on the fields. As the guests returned the red, ripe beans, they were poured into a gunny sack and blessed by Auntie Lehua Mokuilima.

The reason for the celebration: Coffees of Hawaii is unusually poised to propel Hawaiian coffee into the forefront of the international gourmet coffee market. The company is determined to introduce the exceptional coffee that Molokai alone can produce, and the rest of the island is behind it all the way.

Superior quality beans is only part of the story. By emphasizing purity, simplicity, and attention to detail, the staff has rediscovered the traditional art of coffee cultivation, and it shows in their product. Coffees of

Coffees of Hawaii is presently the only plantation in the state — and the country — that grows, processes, and roasts its own coffee. It also offers 100 percent Hawaii beans, rather than the usual blends.

Hawaii is presently the only plantation in the state — and the country — that grows, processes, and roasts its own coffee. It also offers 100 percent Hawaii beans, rather than the usual blends.

↑ Several varieties of coffee have been selected to grow in the fields of Kualapuu, including seedlings of Coffee Arabica cultivars, which took only a year and a half to produce harvestable beans. The plants will grow to a height of 10 to 12 feet.

Coffees of Hawaii currently employs approximately 30 people, including a management staff, full-time and part-time field workers, and seasonal workers who perform special planting and harvesting tasks. With nearly 400 acres planted and another 400 in the planning stages, Coffees of Hawaii looks forward to a flourishing and fruitful future of coffee farming on Molokai. ♥

WYLAND GALLERIES HAWAII

The collaboration of family talent which has created the success of Wyland Galleries began in the rustic town of Haleiwa. Bill Wyland, brother of America's leading environmental marine life artist — known simply as Wyland — decided that his brother's art had a market in Hawaii. Wyland's environmental art debuted in Hawaii on August 1, 1988. Bill and his wife, Kelley, devoted an immeasurable amount of time and energy in the early days of the gallery. Bill attributes much of the galleries' success with pride to Kelley, who has been his greatest supporter for the past ten years.

Wyland Galleries Hawaii has come a long way since then, and has earned Bill quite a reputation as an astute businessman in the state of Hawaii. Moreover, his marketing savvy is surpassed by few in the art business in Hawaii. Gross earnings for 1992 were approximately $13 million with 12 galleries on Oahu, Maui, Kauai, and the Big Island. "I have a brother who is an incredible environmental artist, and I also have the best array of internationally acclaimed talent ever housed in one gallery in the history of Hawaii," says Bill.

Known as Bill to most, William A. Wyland was born in 1958 in Dearborn, Michigan. He has three brothers, Wyland, Steve, and Tom, and has given the family name new perspective in the world of art without even lifting a brush. By starting a new chain of art galleries in

↑ **William A. Wyland**

Hawaii for older brother Wyland, he's brought years of marketing experience to a crescendo of success for America's leading environmental marine life artist, and made quite a mark of success of his own in the process. William A. Wyland now operates and owns the largest gallery chain in the history of the Hawaiian Islands. Wyland Galleries Hawaii is the only fine art gallery in Hawaii to have galleries on all four of the major islands.

Wyland Galleries Hawaii is a major sponsor and contributor to many different events in the community. In just one year, sponsorship included the World's Fair in Seville, the Wahiawa General Hospital Summer fund raiser, The Dolphin Research Center, the Surfrider Foundation, the Triple Crown of Surfing competition on the North Shore of Oahu, and an array of additional programs for the environment including "Adopt-A-Highway" and "Recycle Hawaii," to name a few. Bill Wyland is constantly giving back to the community the benefits he has reaped from success; he values the importance of "environment," making the public continually aware of the "art of environment."

In less than four years, Wyland Galleries has fueled the Hawaiian economy with 12 locations, three of which are on Oahu, in Haleiwa and Waikiki. The others are Kauai Village I and II, Kapaa, and Anchor Cove on Kauai; 697 & 711 Front Street, 136 Dickenson Street, and Whalers Village on Maui; and Waikoloa and Waterfront Row Kona on the Big Island. In addition to these outlets, Wyland Galleries also has five collection stores located on Kauai, the Big Island, and Oahu that sell retail items ranging from T-shirts to 14 karat gold jewelry. As many as 15 new collec-

↓ **Wyland Galleries Hawaii, Haleiwa**

tion stores are expected to open within the next five years. At present, Wyland Galleries Hawaii has more than 110 full- and part-time employees. In addition to Wyland, other internationally acclaimed artists are featured, such as Roy Tabora, John Pitre, James Coleman, Janet Stewart, Walfrido Garcia, Doug Wylie, Dale Evers, and Peter Ehrlich.

With Bill Wyland's impressive track record, Wyland Galleries Hawaii is expected to see continued growth. Bill hopes to complete the chain with a total of 15 galleries and 18 collection stores. Wyland Galleries Hawaii has had an incredible success rate since the opening of its first gallery on Oahu in 1988. Judging by the slew of that success, Bill Wyland certainly possesses the talent for the "art of success."

WYLAND — AMERICA'S LEADING ENVIRONMENTAL MARINE LIFE ARTIST

Wyland is recognized by millions as America's pioneer in the marine art movement. He has been painting his way into the collective consciousness of people around the world for over 25 years. He has truly mastered the art of painting his favorite subject, the oceans, above and below. His extraordinary paintings, sculptures, and internationally famous "Whaling Wall" murals have exposed millions to the graceful beauty of whales, dolphins, and other marine life, as well as the fragile ecosystems of our precious oceans.

Last year, Wyland completed Whaling Wall XXXIII,

↓ **Wyland with "First Breath" in the Haleiwa Gallery.**

entitled "Planet Ocean," in Long Beach, California. This giant mural, which is ten stories high, covers the entire 116,000 square feet of the Long Beach Convention Center; it is the largest mural in the world, as certified by the Guinness

↑ **Wyland in front of the Haleiwa Gallery on Oahu.**

Book of World Records on May 4, 1992. Wyland was also selected to represent the state of Hawaii at the World's Fair in Seville, Spain in September of 1992.

As a diver and devout environmentalist, Wyland spends much of this time underwater, researching what is reflected in his paintings. His unique perspective, gained by 14 years of diving all over the world, brings to each of his murals, paintings, and sculpture an insightful quality that separates his work from that of other artists in his genre. To date, Wyland has completed approximately 35 life-size Whaling Walls, with a goal of painting 100 of the murals during his lifetime. Each of his works speaks of our beautiful but fragile marine ecosystem and conveys the spirit of its undersea life.

Dedicated to saving our oceans through art and education, Wyland's art is collected by people from various countries, including the United States, Canada, Australia, Europe, and Japan. Wyland and his family have art galleries in numerous locations throughout the United States. Wyland owns galleries in both Laguna Beach and San Diego. Wyland's brother Bill owns and operates galleries on four of the Hawaiian Islands; brother Steve Wyland owns and operates galleries in Portland, Oregon. Wyland attributes much of his success to his mother, Darlene, who runs the California galleries. "My mother has been an inspiration in my life as an artist and a proud son," he says.

There is one message, however, that dominates this fascinating odyssey of a man and his art. And that is Wyland's unshakable vision that in order to save the whales and other creatures of the sea, man must first open his eyes and see that he must save the earth's oceans. "I believe if people see the beauty in nature, they will work to preserve it, before it's too late," Wyland says. 🐳

CHIP & WAFER OFFICE AUTOMATION, INC.

"Service second to none" has been President Linda M. Eto's philosophy since she founded Chip & Wafer Office Automation, Inc. in 1986. With the support of the Minolta Corporation, Ms. Eto and her staff have carved a competitive niche for themselves in Hawaii's office equipment marketplace.

Chip & Wafer is proud to offer fine Minolta copiers at competitive prices. Their most sophisticated equipment provides such cutting-edge technology as color, job recovery, zoom enlargement and reduction, two-sided copies, and collating, all at lightning speed, and all for prices comparable to those of the most rudimentary copiers 10 years ago.

Duty to the customer is far from over when a sale is made. Years after the initial transaction, Chip & Wafer continues to provide its clients with technical assistance and advice.

In order to remain abreast of the rapid changes in office automation technology, Chip & Wafer is dedicated to continuing education in technological developments and maintains a strong bond with the local Minolta representative, so its employees are continually informed and well-equipped to offer practical solutions to their customers' requirements.

President Linda M. Eto has always believed that education and training are the key to individual growth. Chip & Wafer's apprenticeship program and its participation in an annual fundraising drive to fight illiteracy are just two ways Ms. Eto remains true to her word.

Linda Eto is a strong proponent in education and hands-on training, as exemplified by Chip & Wafer's practice of choosing its leaders from among its own personnel, rather than hiring from outside. Eto prefers her managers to be thoroughly familiar with the mechanisms of the company — and likes to watch the company grow with its employees.

The company has also initiated an apprenticeship program for students of Honolulu's Electronics Institute. Students earn academic credit over two years while gaining real-life experience in office equipment repair under the supervision of an experienced technician. The company also donates laser programs, test material, and older copiers for the students' use in their studies.

In other community service, Chip and Wafer works with Minolta in its annual fundraising drive for the National Foundation Fight Against Illiteracy.

The company also supports local business organizations via membership in the Chamber of Commerce, Small Business of Hawaii, the Better Business Bureau, and, on a national level, the National Office Machines Dealers Association (NOMDA).

The employees at Chip & Wafer make it their business to do much more than sell office equipment. The company strives for a high standard of ethics and fairness when dealing with fellow businesses, aiming to cultivate long-term relationships based on trust. 🌺

← Linda Eto takes a hands-on role in providing service to Chip & Wafer's clients. Pictured above with Ms. Eto are George Kawatachi, Senior Vice President of Central Pacific Bank Properties, Inc., and his secretary, Cinda Rickel. Photo by Bob Abraham.

IBM

Mention IBM and what comes to mind? For decades, IBM has been synonymous with computers — mainframe, desktop, laptop, handheld, in voting booths, on the operating table, on flights to the moon — computers any which way you find them.

"But IBM means much more than just computer hardware," says Anton Krucky, General Manager for IBM Hawaii. "In fact, our main focus is providing solutions to some of the most pressing problems facing Hawaii's businesses. We have a tremendous interest in the community here.

"Delivering the hardware is one thing," Krucky says. "Helping individuals and businesses achieve success and realize the full potential of leading edge technologies, well, that's what we are most concerned about — partnering with our customer to meet the challenges of the future as we've done in Hawaii for the past 60 years."

Like when IBM tabulated the election results of the vote for statehood in 1959 — complete with the 97 votes flown in from Niihau by carrier pigeon. And before that with setting up punch card time systems for the Big 5 Plantations in the early '30s.

IBM's involvement goes beyond its formal business ties to the community. The corporation, the management team, and many of the employees volunteer time and resources in a wide variety of worthwhile causes. From Aloha United Way to the Hawaii Special Olympics and

the Great Hawaiian Relay, IBM is present and contributing — as it is in the Chamber of Commerce, Rotary, Friends of the Ballet, Honolulu Symphony, Make-A-Wish Hawaii Foundation, Boy Scouts, Girl Scouts, Junior Achievement, Navy League Sea Cadets. . . the list goes on. Impact '89, chaired by Anton Krucky and Lynn Waihee, Hawaii's First Lady, was a particularly successful program which aimed at forging a stronger community with a focal strategy of strengthening Hawaii's families.

And, of course, IBM is generous with the resource it is best known for — computers and the skill to manage them. Grade schools through universities have received equipment and technical assistance in a number of IBM-sponsored programs. And IBM's joint project with Alu Like, the Hawaii Computer Training Center, has had tremendous success in teaching computer skills as well as providing vocational training and job placement assistance to native Hawaiians. In 1991, this Center was nationally recognized for its excellent community acceptance and job placement rate. 🐬

↑IBM has launched a number of computer training programs in Hawaii such as the Hawaii Computer Training Center pictured above "where tradition and technology meet" on a human level. Photos by Bob Sonoda.

↖ One customer described his working relationship with IBM this way: "When our company merged with three other companies, our data center needed to be expanded to a larger facility. The problem was that no one on my staff had the expertise or time to manage this monstrous project. When IBM offered a total solution, we jumped at it.

"They became our single point of contact for everything. . . the design, construction, site planning, the actual relocation of equipment, the coordination of contractors and architects. . . everything, and we were free to run our business as usual.

"Right now they are helping us align fragmented software platforms to meet the new corporate goals. Through IBM we've gained access to a whole world of resources, which, as you know, it's sometimes difficult in Hawaii to find the right, specialized skills you need."

SCHUMAN CARRIAGE

When Gustave Schuman arrived from Germany more than 100 years ago, he was drawn by the qualities that make America great. Inventiveness. Enthusiasm. The love of excellence. The entrepreneurial spirit. When he put down his roots in Hawaii, he started a love affair with the automobile that has lasted in his family for a full century, and which has swept all of Hawaii along with it.

↑ When customers wanted a surrey, a phaeton, a wagon or, later, a "Tin Lizzy," they knew who to see.

Today, Gustave's grandson "Dutch" Schuman heads up a top quality automotive company that sells Buicks and Cadillacs and is the distributor for Subaru. Because each targets a different audience, Schuman Carriage is able to offer the best car in any price range for any taste.

Cadillac's Seville STS was the 1992 Motor Trend Car of the Year. The Buick Park Avenue Ultra was named "The Best Luxury Car" by *Motorweek*. And Subaru is known for its exceptional value and extraordinary reliability and durability.

Completing the Schuman family of products

is the wholly-owned NAPA distributorship, supplying top quality parts to all 38 NAPA auto parts stores throughout Hawaii. In a move that reflected his ambitious lateral thinking, Dutch Schuman joined the National Automotive Parts Association in 1955, creating a parts distribution center here in Hawaii that has grown to be Hawaii's leading automotive parts supplier.

↑ "Dutch" Schuman

Today, Schuman Carriage Company, Inc. and its subsidiaries, Schuman Carriage Buick-Cadillac-Subaru, Inc.; NAPA Hawaiian Warehouse, Inc.; Schuman Automotive, Inc.; S.C. Ranch Co., Inc.; and S.C. Builders Inc., flourish under the leadership of CEO Dutch Schuman and President Mark S. Oshio.

↑ Buick Park Avenue

↑ 1993 Cadillac STS

Schuman's century-long commitment to quality is reflected in every part of the Schuman product line. From carriages to automobiles and replacement parts, the Schuman name has been synonymous with Hawaii, quality, and American know-how since 1893.

And so the second century begins.... 🐾

↑ 1993 Subaru Legacy Wagon

LIBERTY HOUSE

When Heinrich Hackfeld, an ambitious German merchant, first set up shop in Honolulu, he had a glorious vision of his company's future. But even as Hackfeld placed his first saleable items on the shelves of his new store in 1849 – everything from hardware to parasols, silk waistcoats to bird cages – he could not have imagined how good the Hawaii islands would be to his retail business, now known as Liberty House.

Today, Liberty House is one of Hawaii's premier retailers with nine department stores and 22 resort, Collections and Viewpoint shops throughout the islands. It offers the latest fashions; casual, career and evening wear; accessories from world-renowned designers; and the finest names and labels for men, women, teens, and children.

Liberty House offers a complete collection of cosmetics and fragrances, fine china, gifts, crystal and silver from around the world, plus kitchen, bed, and bath accessories. The gift selection includes works by local island artisans.

At its 310,321-square-foot Ala Moana Center flagship store, Liberty House customers can enjoy a beauty salon and men's hair salon, bridal salon and travel agency, as well as a choice of three restaurants, a bakery and deli.

Along with fashion leadership, Liberty House is committed to first-rate customer service. Personal Shopping Consultants are available as a complimentary service to help customers plan their wardrobes and select clothes for all their needs. The Bridal Registry helps brides with gift preferences and guests with gift selections, and the Baby Registry is a similar service for parents-to-be. Shopping by phone, gift wrapping, package delivery, and a liberal return policy are other services offered to Liberty House customers.

Liberty House has hosted major fairs featuring the fashion, food, and culture of European countries and American cities. Special events such as a bridal fair,

↑ Liberty House, one of Hawaii's premier fashion retailers, features designer clothing and the finest names and labels for men, women, teens, and children. Shoppers are drawn to its fashion shows and special events.

personal appearances by designers, vendor representatives and celebrities, seminars, and product demonstrations are presented regularly. Fashion shows and informal showings of designers' collections take place throughout the year.

The company has diversified into the off-price segment of the retail business through expansion of its Penthouse shops which carry merchandise marked down from Liberty House stores as well as specially purchased items. Its first home furnishings off-price store will open in fall 1993.

Liberty House is active in the community, supporting many statewide cultural and educational programs with monetary and in-kind donations. Past recipients have included the Honolulu Symphony, American Heart Association Hawaii Affiliate, Hawaii Special Olympics, and The Nature Conservancy of Hawaii, among many others.

Committed to being Hawaii's leading fashion retailer with unsurpassed customer service as well as one of the state's corporate leaders, Liberty House continues its 144-year tradition in Hawaii. ❦

↑ Sometimes the best things come in huge packages. At Liberty House, shoppers can find a broad selection of fashions and home furnishings, plus a bridal salon, beauty and men's hair salons, restaurants, a bakery and deli.

DFS HAWAII

Founded in 1961, Hawaii's duty-free concession operator at Honolulu International Airport, DFS Hawaii, has become the number one retailer in the state of Hawaii. Today, Duty Free Shoppers, Limited is the world's largest retailer to the traveling public with retail operations in eight countries and 24 cities, and support operations in three countries and five cities.

The duty-free concept — that magical pastime for foreign travellers — is simple; goods sold in duty-free shops at international airports are free of the country's duty and tax, although they must be exported by the buyer.

After purchases are made, DFS delivers the merchandise to the point of departure at the airport, or at the arrival of the final destination; the merchandise is not available for consumption in the country where the purchase was made.

↑ Stairway from shopping to customer service at DFS Hawaii's Waikiki store.

↑ Delicacies from around the world are available in the gourmet section of DFS Hawaii's Waikiki store. Other departments offer fashion items, jewelry, perfume, alcohol, cigarettes, and much more to international travelers.

From the start, DFS has been committed to making Hawaii a popular destination for international

↓ With retail operations in eight countries and 24 cities and support operations in three countries and five cities, DFS is easily the world's largest retailer for the traveling public. From Hong Kong to Honolulu, San Francisco and Toronto, there's a DFS outlet for visitors.

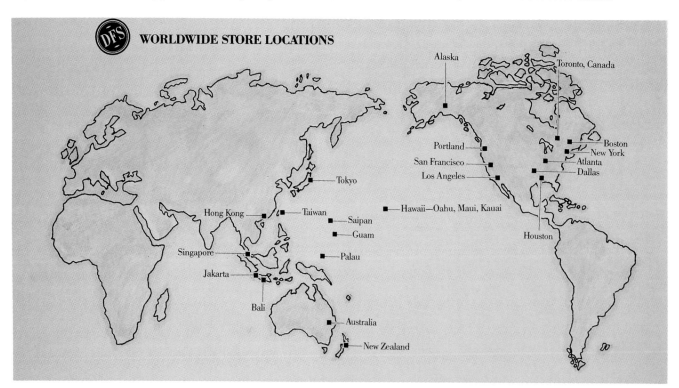

WORLDWIDE STORE LOCATIONS

Alaska
Toronto, Canada
Portland
San Francisco
Los Angeles
Boston
New York
Atlanta
Dallas
Tokyo
Hawaii—Oahu, Maui, Kauai
Hong Kong
Taiwan
Saipan
Guam
Houston
Singapore
Palau
Jakarta
Bali
Australia
New Zealand

DFS' At Your Service Staff is dedicated to attending to all the special needs of their customers. In addition to personal shopping assistance, this multi-lingual staff provides a five-star concierge and information service, complete with advice on recreation and entertainment, currency exchange, international and local telephone services, and travel and tourist information.

travelers. In the three decades that DFS has been Hawaii's official duty-free concessionaire, it has created the world's largest, most successful duty-free store system.

In 1968, DFS opened in the heart of Waikiki the first in-bond, duty-free shop off airport premises in the United States. Sales jumped substantially, increasing revenues and the amount of money DFS remits to the state for financing the airport system.

DFS commits to excellence in everything it does. Foremost, DFS delivers premium and unique products at reasonable prices to its customers with courteous, first-class service. Merchandise includes jewelry and fashion items in addition to the standard duty-free items such as alcohol, cigarettes, and perfume.

The duty-free shopping is for international travelers only, but in every other way, DFS contributes to the communities in which it operates. In Hawaii, DFS gifts help support the arts, education, health care, and civic development, and DFS employees participate wholeheartedly in community activities from team sports to the Aloha United Way.

DFS also strives to be the best employer possible and visibly demonstrates this ambition in the areas of pay, benefits, conditions, and work environment. And, finally, DFS protects and enhances its shareholders' assets to the best of its ability.

↑ The Waikiki store was the first in-bond, duty-free shop off airport premises in the U.S.

JCPenney

Kemmerer, Wyoming and the islands of Hawaii seem like unlikely partners. But both were brought together when JCPenney opened its doors at the Ala Moana Shopping Center in 1966. From humble beginnings in 1902, in a dusty mining town, James Cash Penney's first Golden Rule store pioneered the way for 1300 department stores located in all 50 states and Puerto Rico.

The major portion of the company's business are department stores, which have family apparel, shoes, jewelry, accessories, home furnishings, and catalog departments.

Within the last decade, the company has seen enormous growth and change. JCPenney sharpened its focus on an essential element: fashion. It contracted exclusive lines for its shoppers, and now popular national labels are offered alongside the company's top-quality private ones. Here in Hawaii, unique creations by local designers are in the stores to expand the merchandise mix, as well as support local industry.

Just as JCPenney adjusted to meet its customers' contemporary wants and needs, the local market has become much more than just *muu muus* and *aloha* shirts. Hawaii's stores are helping to promote the quality of the Hawaiian spirit and lifestyle, not only to their mainland

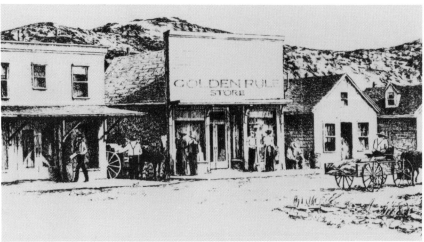

↑ Sales at the end of the first day of the Golden Rule store came to $466.59, an astonishing total considering the store's most expensive item was a $9.95 men's suit. Much more typical prices were 35-cent overalls — 58 cents for a Levi Strauss pair — and 49-cent ladies' shoes.

counterparts, but also to the rest of the world.

While the company continues to evolve, Mr. Penney's original ideals of community service, like our *ohana* spirit, have endured. JCPenney is an active supporter of various non-profit organizations, such as the United Way. In 1991, it was awarded the prestigious "Spirit of America" award, which is given to only one company each year. JCPenney also honors community service volunteers nationwide through its Golden Rule Awards program.

↑ Over the past decade, JCPenney has been presenting exclusive lines by such designers as Allan James, Lee Wright, and Mary McFadden, as well as popular national brands like Haggar, OshKosh B'Gosh, and Vanity Fair.

In its staunch commitment to responsibility and fairness to its communities, JCPenney today reflects the ideals of its founder: "No man or organization can long exist selfishly…the only true community spirit is that which sets up a general improvement plan for the benefit of all. Always remember," James Cash Penney told his associates, "that you are building not just a business, but a community." 🐿

↓ JCPenney Hawaii presents unique creations by local designers to expand the merchandise mix as well as support local industry.

COLONY SURF HOTEL

Every suite at the Colony Surf Hotel views the vast Pacific Ocean, majestic Diamond Head, or Kapiolani Park. At the same time, the delightfully quiet hotel lies just minutes from the urban excitement of Waikiki proper, separated from the action by Hawaii's largest multipurpose park and an avenue of stately ironwood pines.

The hotel's second great claim to fame — after its matchless location on "Life's Greatest Beach" at the foot of Diamond Head — is its world-class restaurant, Michel's, holding such distinctions as the Travel-Holiday Award (given every year since the restaurant opened) and, recently, the title of World's Most Romantic Restaurant from "Lifestyles of the Rich and Famous." Reflected in gilded mirrors and crystal chandeliers, Michel's beachside vista spans the entire Waikiki coastline — blending a mood of formal European opulence with the natural splendor of the islands. Michel's menu spotlights classic French cuisine, but diners may also select such other taste treats as Hawaiian specialties made from fresh local fish of the Pacific.

A few steps inland, the Colony Surf East building holds another of Waikiki's popular dining alternatives, Bobby McGee's Conglomeration, known for its friendly atmosphere and lively disco. Room service presents a

↑ The Colony Surf Hotel is located at the lush green end of Waikiki. Guests enjoy proximity to Honolulu attractions while staying in a quiet elegance a world apart.

third option for meals, available from 7am to 10pm.

The Colony Surf's 50 spacious one-bedroom suites all come with fully equipped kitchen facilities. Living areas surround guests with sophisticated tropical furnishings of white, blue and beige. The color scheme puts the accent outdoors, on the glorious seaside setting that fills one wall with floor-to-ceiling windows.

Air-conditioned studio suites are located in the Colony Surf East and include kitchenettes, color TVs, and balcony-lanais. Colony Surf East also incorporates a beauty salon and penthouse. This deluxe two-bedroom apartment offers 2½ baths, an enormous living room, dining room, and wraparound balcony with 360-degree view of the mountains, sea, and city.

Complimentary services for all suites include twice daily maid service, 24-hour switchboard, daily newspaper, and valet or self-parking. Grocery delivery is but a phone call away. Tennis courts and marked jogging trails with exercise stations wait just across the street, or guests can just relax on the hotel's idyllic white sand beach.

Four Diamonds from the Auto Club underline the Colony Surf's first-class combination of location, cuisine, accommodations and service. Whether for a short vacation or an extended stay, the Colony Surf will always guarantee a peaceful Hawaiian haven combined with sheer luxury. 🐚

↑ Fine French cuisine, classic service and an open-air view of the ocean highlight romantic dining: breakfast, lunch or dinner at the award-winning Michel's.

Outrigger Hotels Hawaii

Outrigger Hotels Hawaii is first and foremost a family business, whose commitment to value has been the principal factor in its growth from a small operation in 1947 to its current position as the largest and most diverse chain in the Hawaiian Islands.

Outrigger is a full-service lodging and hospitality company, operating more than 10,000 rooms and suites in Hawaii and the Mainland United States.

And today, thanks in large part to Outrigger, Hawaii remains one of the world's great travel bargains. No other destination offering so much can be enjoyed as inexpensively as Hawaii. On any given night, some 15,000 people are discovering Hawaii from the vantage point of an Outrigger hotel.

But Outrigger is not a "bargain-basement" operation by any means. Outrigger is a classic example of an operation that keeps its overhead low, passing significant savings on to its customers through the efficiency of its management structure.

That corporate philosophy was born in difficult times for Hawaii and the nation. Roy and Estelle Kelley arrived in Hawaii just before the infamous "Black Friday" stock market crash of October 1929. The Kelleys went into part-time business for themselves in 1932 by constructing a six-room apartment building in Waikiki. Other apartment buildings followed, and then, in 1947, the Kelleys built the 50-room Islander Hotel on Seaside Avenue.

As his hotel empire expanded, Roy Kelley capitalized on his expertise as an architect and contractor to build rooms at a considerable savings over his competition — and to price them accordingly. The Kelleys became famous in Hawaii and on the Mainland for offering "a clean room and a good bed." They concentrated on guest accommodations, allowing outside specialists to provide food

↓ **Roy and Estelle Kelley**

↑ **The Islander Hotel, built in 1947, was the Kelleys' first hotel in Waikiki.**

and beverage services, retail operations, beach services, and other amenities.

The large number of repeat visitors to Outrigger Hotels Hawaii demonstrates the effectiveness of the Outrigger style. From the beginning, Roy and Estelle Kelley were known for their involvement in every phase of the operation. Long after his business successes had made him wealthy, Roy Kelley continued to work at his desk in the Reef Hotel, keeping a vigilant eye on the level of service his hotels were providing.

If someone in need of shelter could not cover the cost of a room, Kelley would charge him what the traffic would bear. One long-time manager remembers, "If guests had six bucks in their pocket and they needed a room, they got a room for six bucks!"

Mrs. Kelley, too, had her own personal style. She handled all the visitor bookings in the early years, writing down reservations on yellow slips of paper. "When the yellow pile reached three finger-widths in height, I knew I had to cut off reservations," she recalls.

These days, one call to Outrigger's STELLEX reservations system (named for Estelle Kelley) provides travel agents, groups, and independent travelers with the ability to reserve rooms at any hotel in the chain.

In the 1990s the Outrigger standard is maintained by Roy and Estelle's son, Dr. Richard Kelley, chairman of Outrigger Hotels Hawaii, and by David Carey, company president.

Like his parents, Dr. Kelley combines a keen business sense with a sensitivity to the *aloha* spirit and its importance to the way business is conducted in Hawaii.

David Carey, who began his career as an Outrigger

↑ **Outrigger Waikiki on the Beach hotel, with Diamond Head in the background.**

program; initiated a scholarship program at Kapiolani community College, to help non-traditional students with everything from tuition to childcare; and donated a computer reservations system to Waipahu High School, to help educate students interested in pursuing a career in the hotel industry.

What about the future? As Dr. Richard Kelley puts it, "The last decade of the 20th century is going to be the beginning of a new era for Outrigger."

The newest areas of expansion are Hawaii's neighbor islands and the U.S. Mainland. On the neighbor islands, Outrigger-managed properties include the oceanfront Outrigger Kauai Beach Hotel, the Plantation Hale, and the Royal Waikoloan, a deluxe beachfront resort on the Big Island's Kohala Coast. An Outrigger affiliate, Outrigger Lodging Services, manages hotels in California, Texas, and New Mexico.

Company President David Carey sums it all up: "We have tremendous organizational strength now, which allows us to capitalize on opportunities that come our way. It's a unique advantage within the hotel industry. So, look for us to grow." ✦

↓ **Lobby of the Outrigger Prince Kuhio hotel.**

desk clerk, holds law and MBA degrees from the University of Santa Clara. His dual expertise has served the company well in a period of reorganization and massive growth. He shares Dr. Kelley's concern for keeping the spirit of *ohana* (family) alive in a rapidly expanding enterprise.

That feeling of *ohana* applies to Outrigger's place in the Hawaii community as well. Roy and Estelle Kelley established the Outrigger policy toward community contributions in the early days of the company. For them, the importance of a gift lay in the good it could do, not in the credit it could reflect back on the giver.

Today the Kelley tradition is expressed through contributions to local, not-for-profit organizations. More than $400,000 was contributed in 1991. Funds were distributed in the areas of education, environmental initiatives, health programs, and community projects. The choices made reflect a concern for the qualities that make Hawaii a place of special beauty.

The programs include Project Delphis, a study of dolphin intelligence; a Waikiki Aquarium-produced videotape about Hawaiian jellyfish species; the Governor's Litter Control Committee; Ronald McDonald House; the American Cancer Society; the Boy Scouts and Girl Scouts of Hawaii; and Kapiolani Medical Center.

Outrigger has provided counsel (and computers) to help Punahou School expand its computer-education

STAR MARKETS

Over 60 years ago, Tsunejiro Fujieki and his wife Mika had a dream of starting a family business. What's come of their efforts has turned out to be bigger than anyone in the family could have imagined.

It began as a simple meat market in 1929, in a modest building on Cooke Street, with Mika doing the butchering and Tsunejiro manning the front. Theirs was a neighborly shop, with friendly service and great deals on quality products. After closing time, the Fujiekis would often stay and work into the night to ensure a pleasant shop for the customers the next day.

Eventually this first Star Market expanded to include groceries, and the Fujieki sons began to help out after school. Soon their little store

↑ Color and variety contribute to the pleasing atmosphere of Star Market stores.

↓ Service and style have long been hallmarks of Star Markets, as evidenced by the bow ties of these clerks in Star's Moiliili store, whose photo was taken in 1954.

↓ Sometimes shopping at Star Markets is a festive occasion… Ice cream, balloons, pastries, and a beautiful Hawaiian day — what more could neighborhood families want?

supermarket. On the corner of Beretania and King Streets, the building offered 13,500 square feet of selling space and remains one of Honolulu's top supermarkets today. The brothers opened a second supermarket at Kamehameha Shopping Center in 1959, the largest supermarket on the islands with 20,000 feet of selling space, air conditioning, a public address system and other modern features. About a year later, they purchased four supermarkets from Western Super, at the Waialae Shopping Center, Kaimuki, Kailua, and Halawa, bringing the total up to six supermarkets.

turned out to be a giant success, and the Fujiekis called a family council to discuss the future of the business.

The Fujiekis retired in 1939, and their sons Richard, John, and George took over. Having had eight years' experience with their parents, the sons knew how the retail grocery business worked. In 1940, they opened a second market on South Beretania Street; five years later, they opened a third, at Liliha and School Streets. Each of the sons managed one store.

In 1948 the brothers began to modernize and enlarge their markets, and by 1949 the chain was four modern markets strong, each offering a complete line of groceries, fresh fruits and vegetables, meats, fish, liquors, frozen foods, and household merchandise. Business had tripled by then, and staff had increased to 25.

Time came again to pull the family together and discuss the future. The brothers realized that the medium-sized markets would quickly become obsolete, and made plans accordingly.

Six years and four hundred thousand dollars later, John and George opened the first Star

The Fujieki family continues to stay at the forefront of technical developments and supermarket trends. In 1980 they computerized their data processing, and in 1982 they added grocery scanners. Star Markets today offers service delis, in-store bakeries, and even reusable canvas grocery bags for the environmentally-concerned.

And yet, with so much growth, George, John, Richard, and Raymond Fujieki still believe in the same values of service and neighborliness that their parents believed in. Now, even as the fourth largest food chain in Hawaii, Star Markets hasn't forgotten its mom-and-pop roots.

↘ The meat market in Kakaako was founded by Tsunejiro and Mika Fujieki in 1929.

11
Quality of Life

Medical, educational, and religious institutions, as well as sports and leisure-oriented companies contribute to the quality of life in Hawaii.

KUAKINI MEDICAL CENTER

Kuakini is a private, non-profit health care organization with a long history of philanthropy and community support in Hawaii. Kuakini's roots date back to charitable activities performed during the last century.

In the late 1800s Honolulu was beset by a series of disasters. First the city was ravaged by an outbreak of bubonic plague, which was followed by a devastating fire that raged through Chinatown, leaving thousands of immigrants homeless. In response to community need, the Japanese Benevolent Society, which was incorporated in 1899, decided to build a charity hospital. With the help of its members, and through generous contributions from the community, The Japanese Charity Hospital was completed. After only two years, it was evident that the 38-bed two-story wooden structure in the Kapalama district of Honolulu could not meet the community need, and a larger hospital was built a few miles away from the original site.

By 1917, a modern facility was constructed at a third location on Kuakini Street — the present site of Kuakini Medical Center. Once again, funding was provided by the Society and public contributions. This new 70-bed facility, simply called The Japanese Hospital, was equipped with the latest medical technology of the time. In 1931, the Japanese Home of Hawaii was developed on

the campus to offer food, shelter and care for elderly immigrants who had no families to provide for them.

During the outbreak of World War II, the hospital was partially occupied by the U.S. Army for military operations. Following the war, the hospital was renamed as Kuakini Hospital and Home.

The 1970s was a period of systematic expansion — new building programs, including remodeling of ancillary facilities, construction of a nine-story parking structure, a physicians office building, which today has over 95 physicians and medical specialists, and a 10-story patient care facility called Hale Pulama Mau ("House of Cherishing Care"). The hospital was renamed in 1975 Kuakini Medical Center, to reflect its expanded services.

KUAKINI TODAY

Today, Kuakini is a major health care institution providing comprehensive acute medical and surgical services, emergency services, outpatient diagnostic and treatment services, rehabilitation programs, and significant educational and research programs. With 1400 employees and a combined medical staff of over 550 physicians, Kuakini is one of the largest medical centers in Hawaii. Kuakini is especially proud of its 300+ volunteers, who donate over 50,000 hours of service each year. Kuakini also has the honor of being the last remaining hospital in the United States established by Japanese immigrants.

Kuakini is also an owner/member of the Premier Hospital Alliance, Inc., an affiliation of 49 private teaching hospitals in the U.S. which have strong tertiary care and clinical research programs. Premier provides a national network for information sharing and for announcing new trends in technology and patient care among non-competing hospitals.

Kuakini is fully accredited by the Joint Commission on Accreditation of Health Care Organizations, a voluntary program which surveys hospitals nationwide.

↓ **Kuakini is a teaching hospital, affiliated with the University of Hawaii School of Medicine.**

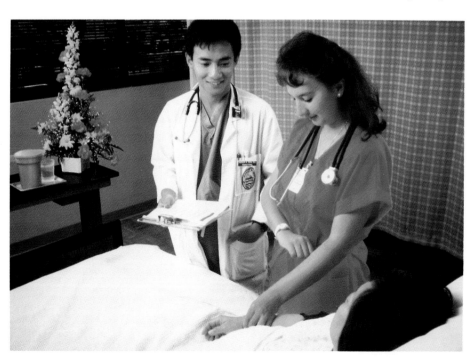

PROGRAMS

In addition to the broad range of traditional medical and surgical care, Kuakini continues to be a major provider of specialized programs that address the three most catastrophic afflictions affecting the population — cancer, heart disease, and respiratory disease.

Cancer Care. Extensive diagnostic, treatment and rehabilitative programs are provided by Kuakini, including Chemotherapy and Radiation Therapy, the latter utilizing the latest linear accelerator for specialized treatments that are available to both hospitalized patients and outpatients.

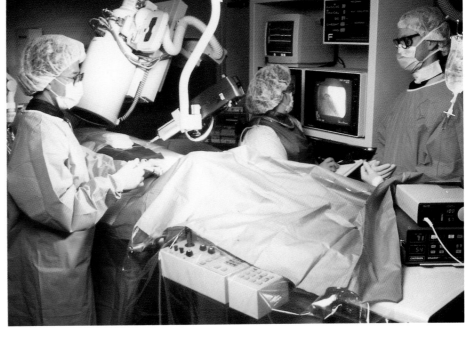

↑ The goal of the Cardiac Catheterization Lab is to provide the most advanced diagnostic and therapeutic capabilities available and to aid in the prevention of disability from cardiac disease.

An Interdisciplinary Oncology Team was established over 20 years ago to deliver an integrated cancer support program for Kuakini patients and their families. Professionals from various fields make up the team and provide a coordinated medical, social, spiritual, and dietary support program for each patient. Oncology Clinical Nurse Specialists provide individualized teaching to patients.

The future holds many promises for new methods of treatment in Chemotherapy and Radiation Therapy. Kuakini's commitment to cancer care also extends to ongoing clinical research and keeping abreast of new medical advances.

Cardiac Care. In July 1992, Kuakini installed a new Cardiac Catheterization Lab to provide state of the art diagnostic and treatment capabilities. This new facility produces high resolution images of the heart and vessels. Kuakini currently performs over a thousand cardiac catheterization procedures annually.

A former general nursing unit was recently remodeled to create a 12-bed Cardiac Care Unit and a 12-bed Progressive Care Unit, which enables specially trained nurses to give personalized attention to their patients, and maximizes patient comfort during recuperation.

Respiratory Care. The Pulmonary Services Program of Kuakini offers the complete spectrum of care for patients with acute respiratory problems or chronic lung deficiencies. It encompasses diagnostic, therapeutic, and rehabilitative services given by a highly trained staff. Services include specialized programs such as the Sleep Disorders Center and the Environmental and Occupational Lung Disease Center.

Since 1988, Kuakini has been a major sponsor of The Smoke-Free Class of 2000. This is a joint project of the American Cancer Society, American Heart Association, and American Lung Association. The Smoke-Free Class of 2000 is an educational project to increase anti-smoking awareness. The 12-year smoke-free campaign is aimed at children who will graduate in the year 2000. Kuakini's funding provides educational material and teaching kits for Hawaii's schools, and health professionals from Kuakini visit local schools to explain the harmful effects of smoking.

Commitment to Research and Education. Kuakini's research staff has received national and international recognition for medical contributions made through the research programs based at Kuakini. The major projects under way are the Honolulu Heart Study, funded by the National Heart, Lung and Blood Institute since 1965, and the Japan-Hawaii Cancer Study, supported by the National Cancer Institute since 1971.

Kuakini is a teaching hospital, affiliated with the University of Hawaii Schools of Medicine, Public Health, and Social Work; the nursing schools of the

University of Hawaii, Kapiolani Community College, and Hawaii Loa College; and the allied health professional schools of Kapiolani Community College.

Commitment to the Community. Kuakini is a sponsor of various health education programs for the community. Through the Kuakini Education and Training Department, community classes for CPR, Diabetes Management, First Aid, and other popular courses are offered throughout the year. Kuakini also sponsors its annual Emergency Medicine Symposium, which provides continuing education for all Emergency Medical Technicians, Paramedics, and Mobile Intensive Care Technicians in the State.

A frequent participant in local health fairs, Kuakini also stresses disease prevention and wellness through screenings, educational material, and various speakers bureau activities.

↑ A patient is monitored at the Pulmonary Sleep Disorders Center. Specially trained staff at the center annually evaluates about 500 patients.

The mission of Kuakini Health System is to: provide comprehensive health care services and programs at reasonable cost to the public; continuously improve the quality of health care services and programs; encourage clinical research; support training and educational programs for health care personnel; and offer health education and community service programs to the community.

From its humble beginnings Kuakini was an institution intricately interwoven into the fabric of the community. Kuakini has always been supported by local residents, and has made great strides to return this community support in the form of superior health care and extended concern for Hawaii's people. This attitude is clearly reflected in the Kuakini mission statement as well as in the services provided to both patients and the community.

To this day Kuakini remains closely linked to Hawaii residents. The Medical Center is not part of a national chain of hospitals, nor is it the beneficiary of any large endowment. This means the acquisition of all new technology and funds for expansion projects at Kuakini have been — and always will be — funded primarily from the contributions of Kuakini's friends — individuals and businesses from the community, many of whom have been faithful, long-time supporters. Being so closely interdependent with the community has enabled Kuakini to retain an approach to patient care-giving that is more personal — similar to the atmosphere established in Kuakini's own beginnings — a greater concern for each individual, as found in the small community hospitals of yesteryear. ▮

REHABILITATION HOSPITAL OF THE PACIFIC

Rehabilitation Hospital of the Pacific, known familiarly as REHAB to the residents of Hawaii, provides comprehensive physical rehabilitation for individuals disabled by illness or injury. Here, patients gain the strength and skills that enable them to return to fulfilling lives.

Established in 1953 by the Kauikeolani Children's Hospital Foundation, REHAB had its humble beginnings in renovated quonset huts on the grounds of Kauikeolani Children's Hospital in Nuuanu. Now, 40 years later, REHAB Hospital has grown into a 100-bed inpatient facility, with seven satellite clinics conveniently located on Oahu (Honolulu, Hawaii Kai, Mililani, and Aiea), on Kauai (Lihue and Kilauea), and on Maui (Kahului). REHAB's modern medical services and state-of-the-art equipment draw patients from around the entire Pacific Basin.

Patients admitted on an inpatient basis enter one of five patient programs: stroke, spinal cord, brain injury,

Rehab's team, comprised of specialists in a wide range of areas from physical medicine to vocational evaluation, strive to help restore each patient's dignity and well-being.

amputee/orthopedic, or general rehabilitation. Patients work with specialized treatment teams consisting of physiatrists, internists, physical and occupational therapists, speech/language pathologists, rehab nurses, recreation therapists, social workers, and psychologists. These specialists are trained not only to provide physical rehabilitation, but to address the emotional trauma and anxiety that can accompany a disabling injury as well. Together, the REHAB team strives to help restore each person's dignity and well-being.

As patients progress in their treatment, REHAB exposes them to real-life physical challenges, both in the hospital and in the home. Staff members assess each patient's ability to handle day-to-day situations and make determinations as to what training each patient will need. After an inpatient stay of approximately three weeks, patients are discharged home, and continue with outpatient therapy as appropriate.

Outpatient services are organized under three different programs: Ambulatory Care, the Comprehensive Outpatient Rehabilitation (COR) Clinic, and the Injured Workers' Center. Via Ambulatory Care, patients are seen in one of REHAB's many specialty clinics, such as the brace, post-polio, and prosthetic clinics. In COR, REHAB provides diagnostic evaluations, driver training, and an aquatics program to supplement their full range of therapeutic services. As part of the Injured Workers' Center, REHAB offers work hardening and simulation, pain management, injury prevention, and loss control programs.

REHAB remains the only rehabilitation hospital in the state, and is accredited by both the Joint Commission on Accreditation of Healthcare Organizations (JCAHO) and the Commission on Accreditation of Rehabilitation Facilities (CARF). ✤

↑ At REHAB, patients gain the strength and skills that enable them to return to fulfilling lives.

Castle Medical Center

↑ Sitting peacefully in the shadow of Mount Olomana, Castle Medical Center meets the physical, emotional, and spiritual needs of Windward Oahu residents.

Though medicine has seen many changes over the years, Castle Medical Center has never lost sight of the human side of health care. Today, Castle's commitment to providing innovative health care is still coupled with concern for each patient's physical, emotional, and spiritual well-being.

Since Castle first opened its doors in 1963, the hospital's primary mission has been meeting the needs of its community. Located in Kailua, Castle Medical Center is a full-service, acute care hospital recognized for both its inpatient care and outpatient programs throughout the state. The 160-bed facility offers a broad spectrum of services, ranging from preventive health programs and maternity care to emergency medicine and critical care. Castle Medical Center is staffed by more than 800 employees, 250 volunteers, and nearly 300 physicians. Each year, Castle cares for approximately 7,000 inpatients, 50,000 outpatients, and 15,000 emergency patients. Castle Medical Center, a non-profit institution, is operated by Adventist Health System-West.

A demonstrated commitment to quality patient care placed Castle Medical Center at the forefront of other U.S. hospitals in the 1992 Commitment to Quality national recognition program, sponsored each year by The Healthcare Forum. A resolution passed by the Honolulu City Council also commended the hospital for its quality initiative.

In 1992, Castle Medical Center became the first hospital in the nation to implement patient-focused care facility-wide. This major strategic effort was launched as a means of both enhancing the value of services provided by Castle as well as positioning the hospital as a leader in the health care arena. PatientsFirst, Castle's patient-focused care program, is designed to achieve these goals by increasing efficiency, reducing costs, and improving patient care and service. Under PatientsFirst, hospital restructuring places patients' needs at the center of the health care delivery system.

Another major accomplishment was Castle Medical Center's completion, in 1991, of a $10 million expansion and renovation program. As a result of the project, Castle opened Hawaii's first single-room maternity care unit, a progressive care unit, and a new, state-of-the-art critical care unit.

Many of Castle's most successful programs are focused on preventive medicine that promotes a healthy lifestyle. The Castle Center for Health Promotion, the employee wellness program, and the vegetarian Pali Gardens restaurant all support this mission.

A wide range of services has been developed to meet the community's health needs, including numerous screening programs, the HEARTBEAT Coronary Risk Evaluation Program, physical fitness testing, stress management training, lifestyle weight management, a smoking cessation program, and aerobics and exercise classes. Castle offers free seminars on health issues as well.

Castle's Alcoholism and Addictions program, which opened in 1985, has successfully treated patients throughout Oahu and the neighbor islands. In 1990, Castle assumed operation of the Bobby Benson Center, Hawaii's first residential treatment center for young people.

The years ahead will, no doubt, bring many changes to health care. But Castle Medical Center's primary mission — to treat the whole person — will remain unchanged. 🐾

ISLAND CARE

← Island Care wants to see its members healthy. The organization focuses on prevention, encouraging healthy lifestyles and regular checkups.

Island Care is committed to keeping Hawaii residents healthy.

As a group model, non-profit Health Maintenance Organization (HMO), Island Care's approach to health care is preventive in nature; it gives medical attention to its members at all times instead of just waiting until something goes wrong then administering treatment after someone has fallen ill or sustained an injury.

Unlike traditional health care insurers, Island Care provides managed health care services rather than merely reimbursing physicians, hospitals, and members for their services. By combining the delivery and the financing of comprehensive health services, Island Care is able to return some control of health care costs to the client employer groups throughout Hawaii.

Thus Island Care, again unlike traditional insurers, is able to provide broad health care services at an affordable price.

As its name implies, Island Care has its roots in Hawaiian soil and ideals. Beginning as a locally-owned and operated HMO on Kauai in 1981, Island Care's founders recognized the need for a quality, service-oriented alternative to traditional health insurance. They developed a system of providing cost-effective, quality-managed health care benefits to Hawaii's work force and families through community hospitals, physicians and health care programs.

Island Care moved its headquarters to Honolulu in 1985 to address the growing demand for an HMO alternative throughout the state. And in 1992, Island Care stepped under the directive of Queen Emma when Queen's Development Corporation, a subsidiary of Queen's Health Systems, became its sole owner. The staff at Island Care has embraced Queen Emma's mission to provide health care services to the people of Hawaii with renewed energy and a spirit of enthusiasm.

Today, Island Care provides 22,000 members from over 700 employer groups with HMO health care services on Oahu, Kauai, Maui, Molokai, and Hawaii.

Members can look forward to enhancements in products and services as well as an expanding network of providers.

Island Care is looking to the future for innovative services it can bring to members while holding onto the local roots and original vision of a managed health care organization dedicated to providing Hawaii's people with

↓ Island Care's expanding network of health care professionals provides convenient and reasonable access to the best health care services available anywhere.

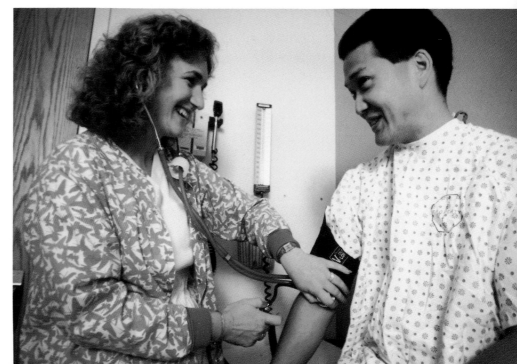

STRAUB CLINIC & HOSPITAL

Straub Clinic & Hospital had its beginnings shortly after the turn of the century when Dr. George F. Straub came to Hawaii from New York to practice general surgery. Dr. Straub's first office was destroyed by fire in 1910, but within two years, he was working out of a two-story residence at 401 South Beretania Street, one block from Iolani Palace. "The Clinic," as the modest structure was later to become known, was the forerunner of today's clinic and hospital.

Dr. Straub, born to one of Europe's most distinguished medical families and a graduate of Wurzburg and Heidelberg Universities, had a gentle and professional manner that soon won him a sizable practice. In fact, his patient load expanded so quickly he feared the quality of his practice would suffer.

"I would sometimes get only four or five hours of sleep per night; oftentimes I had no time to read, no time to educate myself further," Dr. Straub said in a 1952 interview. "With so many new discoveries in all fields of medicine, I felt I simply could not do justice to my patients."

His concern for quality patient care prompted Dr.

← In later years, Dr. George Straub became ever more dedicated to handcrafting violins. Here he displays a part of his collection, circa 1960.

Straub to form a partnership in 1921 with four other prominent physicians whose specialities complemented his own surgical skills. The doctors were obstetrician/

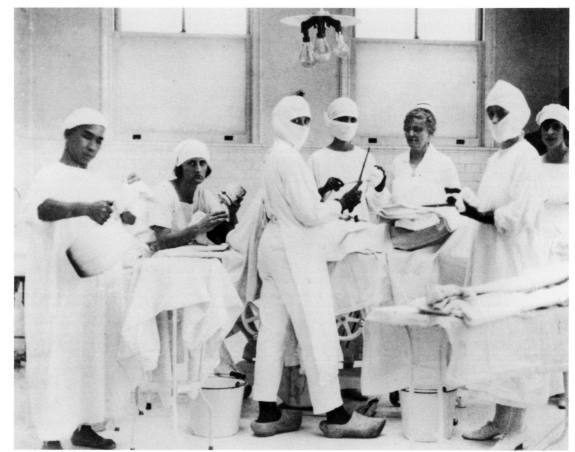

→ Dr. Straub's wooden clogs were de rigueur when he would operate. Unmasked attendants, bare feet and open windows would find no place in today's highly sterile medical environment.

gynecologist Guy Milnor; internist Arthur Jackson; otolaryngologist Howard Clark; and clinical pathologist Eric Fennel.

The Clinic soon became one of Honolulu's premiere group practices, and by the early 1930s, it became evident that the partners would need a larger facility. In 1933, the group moved into a new three-story office building at Ward and Hotel Streets, Straub's current location. That same year, Dr. Straub retired from the practice after having given 25 years of his life in service to the people of Oahu.

Dr. Straub returned to active practice briefly during World War II, but otherwise devoted his retirement years to gardening and to crafting exquisite violins. In 1952, the organization was renamed Straub Clinic in honor of the man with the vision and persistence to turn his dream into a reality.

Meanwhile, business at The Clinic continued to expand. Along with Oahu's increasing population came an increasing demand for services, and so it was in 1950 that a large new wing, called the Milnor Building, was added to the original structure. It was occupied by the departments of pediatrics and obstetrics/gynecology, with the third floor and basement kept vacant to handle expansion over the next decade. Expansion came more

rapidly than expected, and by 1953, there was already a need for more room.

The present registration building and seven story Palma Wing were completed in 1963. In 1970, a new parking garage was completed, and construction was begun on the 159-bed hospital. The hospital was completed in 1973, and the organization became known as Straub Clinic & Hospital, Inc.

Responding to the needs of outlying communities, Straub opened its first satellite clinic in Aiea in 1977. This was later followed by offices in Hawaii Kai, Kailua, Kaneohe, in downtown's financial district, in Kona on the Big Island, and on Lanai.

It was Dr. Straub's ideal that the combined skills of a variety of specialists would provide the finest in quality health care, an ideal that remains to this day the focus of Straub's dedicated physicians and staff, an ideal reflected in Straub's growth and success.

Today, Straub Clinic & Hospital is one of Hawaii's foremost health care providers, with more than 150 physicians representing 33 specialities, carrying on a tradition of medical excellence established in Hawaii so many years ago by Dr. Straub. ✿

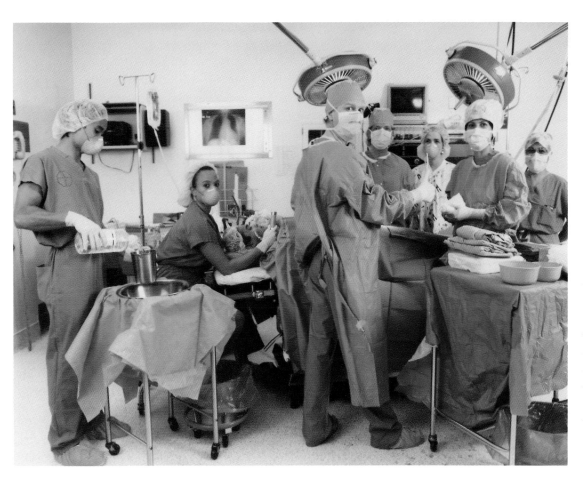

← Cardiologist Roger White, M. D., and team in a modern operating room at Straub. Although health care technology has evolved dramatically since the '20s, the modern world of the healing arts is still one of caring and commitment.

Kaiser Permanente Hawaii Region

When famed industrialist Henry Kaiser retired to the Hawaiian Islands in 1958, he saw a need for affordable, prepaid, quality health care and started the Kaiser Permanente Hawaii Region. Today, 3,500 employees, including physicians, nurses, technicians, and administrators work together as a team to handle the myriad tasks required by over 1 million physician office visits and 12,000 hospital admissions each year.

↑ The centerpiece of the Region's facilities is the 202-bed Moanalua Medical Center, which opened in October 1985. Malama Ohana Skilled Nursing Facility was added in January 1989.

The Hawaii Region owns and operates one hospital, the Moanalua Medical Center, which opened in October 1985, and twelve clinics on the islands of Oahu, Maui, and Hawaii. The Moanalua Medical Center includes a 202-bed acute care hospital, a 55-bed skilled nursing facility, 74 physician's offices, an outpatient clinic, and extensive ancillary support services that include laboratory, pharmacy, and radiology.

The traditional medical community once criticized Kaiser Permanente because members' choices of physicians were limited — the Hawaii group began with only five physicians. Today, members may choose from among 270 physicians from all major medical specialities in the state's largest medical group. When they join the Kaiser Permanente Medical Care Program, members are encouraged to choose a primary care physician to coordinate and oversee every aspect of their care and treatment. Members need never delay seeking medical care because of its cost. Their monthly dues and their broad benefits cover nearly all necessary care.

↑ Magnetic Resonance Imaging (MRI) is a state-of-the-art technology that uses a large magnet, radio waves, and a computer to create a two- or three-dimensional image of what's going on inside a patient's body — without using x-rays.

The Kaiser Permanente Medical Care Program is the largest group practice prepayment plan in the United States and the largest non-governmental health care delivery system in the world. Kaiser offers its more than 6.6 million members in 16 states and the District of Columbia quality, comprehensive medical care at a reasonable, predictable price. Kaiser Permanente members don't have forms to fill out or bills from doctors, hospitals, or laboratories to pay.

Kaiser is a federally qualified non-profit health maintenance organization, or HMO. Its success springs from a joint endeavor between the professions of business and medicine. It is organized into three separate but closely cooperating interdependent organizations: Kaiser Foundation Health Plan, Inc., Kaiser Foundation Hospitals, and the Permanente Medical Groups. It is the Health Plan's responsibility to handle the day-to-day functions of the program, such as enrolling members and organizing, operating, and maintaining a health care delivery system. In turn, Health Plan contracts with Kaiser Foundation Hospitals and the Permanente Medical Groups to provide members with a full range of prepaid health care services.

This arrangement makes Kaiser Permanente attractive to physicians because it allows them to practice together as a group. Within the Hawaii Permanente Medical Group, each physician can focus on his/her speciality and concentrate fully on providing quality medical care and meeting each member's health care needs. Permanente physicians have no incentives to overtreat and no pressures from fellow physicians or any third party to undertreat. Permanente physicians are paid on a capitation basis which means that for a fixed, monthly payment for each enrolled member, the physician group provides for all covered and necessary medical services. This agreement encourages timely, appropriate, and cost-effective care.

As a provider of direct patient care, Kaiser Permanente is continually striving to keep costs down. Some internal cost-containment efforts include the Short-Stay Unit at the Moanalua Medical Center, which allows for the monitoring of patients without hospitalization; the Special Delivery Program, which enables healthy newborns and mothers to be discharged within 36 hours of birth; and other cost-effective programs such as home IV therapy, hospice services for terminally ill patients, and case management for the elderly and the chronically ill.

Even as Kaiser Permanente strives to contain costs, the Program is equally committed to quality of care and quality of service. Kaiser Permanente has made a commitment to devote significant human and financial resources to both quality assessment and quality improvement. By practicing Total Quality Management (TQM), the Hawaii Region is constantly evaluating current methods of providing care and working to gain more knowledge of members' needs. The Hawaii Region's ultimate goal is to be Hawaii's preeminent health care organization in "Caring for Hawaii's People Like Family."

Through its subsidy program, Kaiser Permanente participates in Hawaii's State Health Insurance Program (SHIP) which establishes basic health coverage for part-time workers who do not qualify for either employer-based health plans or Medicaid. Kaiser Permanente provides enrollees with comprehensive health benefits and subsidizes the dues. The Dues Subsidy Program also funds the Aloha Program for uninsured immigrants. As a community service, Kaiser Permanente pays all the dues for medically uninsured immigrants who meet household income guidelines similar to the SHIP program.

The Kaiser Permanente Medical Care Program has made a long-term commitment to actively promote the health of Hawaii members by sponsoring health education and physical fitness programs. It sponsors the Great Aloha Run each year, which is open to the general public, and the Children's Great Aloha Run, a shorter version of the Great Aloha Run open to all children age 12 and under. Waiting areas in some of the pharmacies are equipped with interactive videos which give members information on current health topics such as immunizations and cold and flu season.

As a non-profit HMO, Kaiser Permanente emphasizes prevention and early detection of illness. To encourage members' active participation in their health care, Kaiser Permanente offers the Personal Health Appraisal Program to help members evaluate their lifestyle, health status, and health risks. It offers the Women's Health Clinic which targets women's specific health concerns. The Women's Health Clinic offers family planning services and information on menopause, premenstrual syndrome, and osteoporosis, as well as routine physical examinations, complete with breast exams and pap smears. Nurse Practitioners and Physician

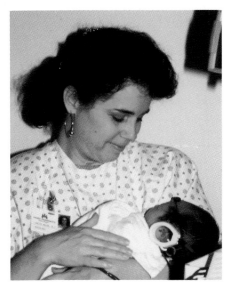

← Judith Mason, coordinator of Audiology Services, uses the sophisticated Algo-1 Plus machine to test newborn Adam Buote's hearing. The machine works by measuring the brain's response to sound.

Assistants in both the Personal Health Appraisal Program and the Women's Health Clinic devote an hour to each member to review their personal health history and address their specific health concerns.

Other prevention and early detection programs include the Heartwise Program and the Flexibility, Fitness and Endurance Testing Program. Kaiser Permanente also offers the Lifestyle Program, which consists of classes in physical fitness, smoking cessation, stress management, CPR training, nutrition, goal achievement, and prenatal and newborn care to members and non-members alike.

Kaiser Permanente also actively promotes good health and fitness through the "Bodywise Star Challenge," an internally produced play aimed at children. The "Bodywise Star Challenge" is a travelling menagerie of characters that perform at elementary schools to educate children about the benefits of living healthy lifestyles and being responsible. It is a program that has been approved by the Hawaii State Department of Education and is an important part of educating and inspiring future members to accept responsibility for their health care. ❧

CHAMINADE UNIVERSITY

Located on a hillside overlooking Diamond Head, Chaminade University of Honolulu is an independent, co-educational, Catholic, Marianist institution serving 800 day session undergraduates, 1,400 evening session undergraduates, and 300 graduate students. The University welcomes people of all faiths. Students come from 35 states and 33 countries. The campus is a vibrant multicultural community.

Chaminade University offers its students an exciting combination of liberal arts, professional arts, and Christian values. The University prides itself on its small classes and the personal, individual attention given to students by professors and staff. The emphasis is on excellent teaching and a strong sense of community among students, faculty, and staff.

Chaminade students choose from 25 undergraduate majors, including biology, business, communications, criminal justice, education, history, international studies, philosophy, and religion. Master's degrees are offered in criminal justice, counseling psychology, Japanese business studies, and business administration. In Hawaii, Chaminade has the only early childhood education program with a Montessori emphasis, the only master's degree in criminal justice, and the only interior design program at an accredited institution. In 1967, Chaminade University became the first university in Hawaii to offer complete degree programs on the military bases on Oahu.

Chaminade University is an NCAA Division II school, sponsoring eight intercollegiate sports. The university gained national renown in 1982 when its men's basketball team beat the University of Virginia,

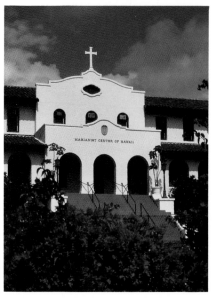

← Freitas Hall, headquarters for the Marianist Center of Hawaii and Chaminade University.

then ranked first in the nation. Subsequent wins against Louisville and Southern Methodist University earned the team the nickname, "The Giant Killers."

Chaminade University is named after Father William Joseph Chaminade, a French Catholic priest who lived through the French Revolution and the wars of Napoleon. In 1817, Father Chaminade founded the Society of Mary, whose members are known as Marianists. Today, there are 111,000 students in 106 Marianist schools and universities in 29 countries.

Chaminade is one of three Marianist universities. The other two are the University of Dayton in Ohio, which was founded in 1850, and St. Mary's University in San Antonio, Texas, which was founded in 1852. Chaminade University was founded in 1955 in Kaimuki, a residential neighborhood situated between downtown Honolulu and Diamond Head. The campus, which is shared with St. Louis School, is known for its Spanish/ Moroccan style buildings with arched windows and colonnades, stucco exteriors, and red tile roofs.

The mission of Chaminade University is to prepare its students for meaningful, productive lives. As part of the Marianist tradition, the university encourages its students to consider careers which help meet the needs of the community. This emphasis on community service has been demonstrated in the lives of Chaminade's graduates. More than half of the students who have graduated from Chaminade with bachelor's degrees have undertaken public service careers in government, teaching, non-profit organizations, medicine, and public health. 🐾

↓ Henry Gomes, Dean of the School of Sciences and Mathematics, with students in the biology laboratory.

SAINT ANDREW'S PRIORY

In 1867, when little was expected from "the fairer sex" beyond sewing and cooking, two uncompromising women saw otherwise. Founded by Queen Emma Kaleleonalani with the help of Mother Priscilla Lydia Sellon, Saint Andrew's Priory was created to provide young women an opportunity to develop their minds and spirits to the fullest.

Today, Saint Andrew's Priory is an independent Episcopal girls school located in the heart of downtown Honolulu. The campus supports 640 girls from kindergarten through 12th grade, and a faculty/staff of 73. This favorable student/faculty ratio, combined with a wide range of courses and extracurricular activities, provides a challenging college prepatory education. Over 96 percent of Priory graduates continue on to four-year colleges, and more than 60 percent of them attend institutions on the mainland. Alumnae consistently report that the study habits and communication skills they learned at the Priory give them an edge in college and later life.

Why an all-girls school? At St. Andrew's Priory, girls are given an opportunity to establish a sense of identity beyond sexual stereotyping. Girls are offered leadership roles and chances to develop an assertive approach toward learning. Studies show that young women attending single-sex institutions have more confidence than their counterparts in coeducational schools; that they complete more homework, watch less television, and are absent less often. Girls from single-sex high schools actually do better in reading, writing, and science than girls in coed schools. According to a national survey, a greater percentage of girls school graduates go on to succeed in their careers. The Priory is committed to providing an educational environment in which girls come first.

In addition to academic development, Priory emphasizes spiritual and emotional growth in each girl. The school's Christian tradition is enriched by the reverence and spirituality inherent in Hawaiian culture. Through classroom discussions, songs and crafts in the early grades, to advanced seminars as the girls mature, students are encouraged to explore the issues of values, ethics, and integrity that are most important to them. These activities are supplemented by weekly chapel services at Saint Andrew's Cathedral, as well as a rigorous program of community service. When students volunteer for Students Helping Out (SHOUT), Ronald McDonald House, and other groups, they learn firsthand the values of loving, caring, and giving of the self.

The school's Camp Timberline, a 10-acre recreational site in the Waianae Mountains, provides an ideal setting for workshops and retreats. Here, students attend values camps which teach problem-solving skills, leadership, and foster a sense of community.

← Through songs and crafts in the early grades to advanced seminars as the girls mature, students are encouraged to explore the issues of values, ethics, and integrity most important to them.

The Priory also administers Queen Emma Preschool, where a faculty of 20 works with 150 young students ages 2–6 years. Achievement is gauged on personal potential rather than peer comparisons, and the curriculum is designed to encourage growth of the whole child.

Though the Priory has seen many changes in its 125 years — from computers to new math, from modern dance to varsity sports to short skirts — the school has maintained a strength of conviction that surely would have made Queen Emma proud. 🌺

HAWAII PACIFIC UNIVERSITY

Hawaii Pacific's unusual blend of varied elements provides for a singularly rewarding learning experience. With one campus on the west coast, in the heart of fast-paced Honolulu, and another on the east shore of Oahu, nestled among the rural hills, the University's settings epitomize its broad approach to student education and experience.

The curriculum provides over 40 liberal arts and pre-professional programs to an undergraduate and graduate student body from all 50 states and over 60 countries. And while its offerings are expansive, the University maintains the intimacy of a small college: a low faculty/student ratio, personal career counseling, and a fierce dedication to the

individual student.

The course of study is designed to give students the skills they need to ask pertinent questions, solve problems, and make decisions. And though liberal arts is the heart of the curriculum, every academic degree awarded is enhanced by hands-on experience. Scholars of international renown are joined by leading business and career professionals to provide a comprehensive balance between theoretical concepts and real-world applications. Students are encouraged early on to explore career options and develop career strategies suited to their individual goals. Career and placement counselors provide guidance to each student throughout his or her University education. The Cooperative Education and Internship Programs offer students the option of paid work experience related to their fields of study.

Student life is lively, internationally-flavored and outdoor-oriented. Students participate in social and

cultural events, intercollegiate athletics, and a number of clubs including honor societies, service clubs, pre-professional organizations and student government. Though a good deal of campus activity is centered around the residence halls — one of a variety of housing options — students also take advantage of the urban and

← ↑ A dynamic downtown campus in the heart of Honolulu's financial district and a rural Hawaii Loa campus eight miles away combine to offer a unique international university, one that emphasizes teaching excellence and individualized attention.

rural environments beyond each of the campuses.

The University admits first-time freshmen, transfer students, and graduate students from around the world each term. The admissions staff considers a combination of factors when making admission decisions: previous academic coursework, grades, test scores, community service, motivation, leadership, and special talents and interests. Certain programs, such as Marine Science and the School of Nursing, have specialized requirements. More information can be obtained by calling (808) 544-0238.

Rated by *Barron's* as one of the "best buys" among American colleges, Hawaii Pacific is affordable, and financial aid counselors are available to assist students applying for the University's extensive aid program, which includes federal, state, and institutional funding.

Hawaii Pacific University is an independent, nonsectarian, coeducational institution accredited by the Accrediting Commission for Senior Colleges and Universities of the Western Association of Schools and Colleges and the National League for Nursing. As a university combining east and west, city and country, theory and practice, Hawaii Pacific's diverse factors comprise one very dynamic whole. 🌺

Photo by Bob Abraham.

A Select Bibliography

Armstrong, R. Warwick. *Atlas of Hawaii.* 2nd ed. Honolulu: Univ. Hawaii Press, 1983.

Bank of Hawaii. *Annual Economic Report, Hawaii 1991.* Honolulu, 1992.

Beckwith, Martha Warren, ed. and trans. *The Kumulipo: A Hawaiian Creation Chant.* 1951; rpt. Honolulu: Univ. Hawaii Press, 1972.

Chamber of Commerce of Hawaii. *Hawaii As a Pacific Regional Center.* Honolulu, 1990.

Coryell, Roger. "The Heritage of the Menehunes." *Hyatt's Hawaii Magazine,* 1st quarter 1986.

Daws, Gavan. *Holy Man: Father Damien of Molokai.* New York: Harper & Row, 1973.

————. *Shoal of Time: A History of the Hawaiian Islands.* Honolulu: Univ. Hawaii Press, 1968.

Day, A. Grove. *History Makers of Hawaii: A Biographical Dictionary.* Honolulu: Mutual Publishing, 1984.

Economic Development Corporation of Honolulu. *Honolulu: International Center of the Pacific.* Honolulu, n.d.

Far Eastern Economic Review. "Hawaii: The Pacific Link." Hong Kong, September 28, 1989. (advertising supplement.)

Farrell, Andrew. *John Cameron's Odyssey.* New York: Macmillan, 1928.

Freuchen, Peter. *Peter Freuchen's Book of the Seven Seas.* New York: Julian Messner, 1957.

Glick, Clarence E. *Sojourners and Settlers.* Honolulu: Hawaii Chinese History Center and Univ. Hawaii Press, 1980.

Hawaii Agriculture Statistics Service. "Statistics of Hawaiian Agriculture." Honolulu, 1990.

Hawaii Ocean and Marine Resources Council. *Hawaii Ocean Resources Management Plan.* Honolulu, 1991.

High Technology Development Corporation. *1991 Annual Report.* Honolulu.

Joesting, Edward. *Hawaii: An Uncommon History.* New York: Norton, 1972.

————. *Kauai: The Separate Kingdom.* Honolulu: Univ. Hawaii Press and Kauai Museum Association, Ltd., 1984.

Kamehameha Schools/Bishop Estate. "Report to the Community." Honolulu, 1989–1990.

Kuykendall, Ralph S., and A. Grove Day. *Hawaii: A History.* New Jersey: Prentice-Hall, 1976.

Lewis, David. *We, The Navigators.* Honolulu: Univ. Hawaii Press, 1972.

Linnekin, Jocelyn. *Children of the Land.* New Jersey: Rutgers Univ. Press, 1985.

M&H Group, Inc. "Strategic Plan for the High Technology Development Corporation, 1990–1995." Honolulu, 1990.

MacDonald, Craig et al. "Ocean R&D Spending Patterns in Hawaii: Analysis and Outlook"; and "Strategic Market Planning for Hawaii Ocean R&D: Comparative Rating and Industry Potential." Honolulu: State of Hawaii, Department of Business, Economic Development & Tourism, Oceans Research Branch, n.d.

Malo, David. *Moolelo Hawaii.* Trans. Dr. Nathaniel B. Emerson. 2nd ed. Honolulu: Bernice P. Bishop Museum, 1971.

McNassor, David, and Randall Hongo. *Strangers In Their Own Land: Self-Disparagement In Ethnic Hawaiian Youth.* Honolulu, 1972. (monograph.)

Murphy, Thomas D. *Ambassadors In Arms: The Story of Hawaii's 100th Battalion.* Honolulu: Univ. Hawaii Press, 1955.

Nordyke, Eleanor C. *The Peopling of Hawaii.* Honolulu: East-West Center, 1977.

Peterson, Barbara Bennett. *Notable Women of Hawaii.* Honolulu: Univ. Hawaii Press, 1984.

Pukui, Mary et al. *Nana I He Kumu, Hui Hanai.* Honolulu, 1972.

Smyser, A.A. *Hawaii As An East-West Bridge.* Honolulu: East-West Center, 1990.

Spectorsky, A.C., ed. *The Book of the Sea.* New York: Grosset & Dunlap, 1954.

State of Hawaii, Department of Business, Economic Development & Tourism. *Annual Report.* Honolulu, 1991.

State of Hawaii, Department of Business, Economic Development & Tourism. "The State of Hawaii Data Book." Honolulu, 1991. (Statistical Abstract.)

State of Hawaii, Department of Business, Economic Development & Tourism. *State Functional Plan: Tourism.* Honolulu, 1991.

State of Hawaii, Department of Education, Superintendent of Education. *1990-1991 Annual Report.* Honolulu, 1991.

State of Hawaii, Department of Labor and Industrial Relations. *Employment Outlook for Industries and Occupations, 1988–1993.* Honolulu, 1988.

State of Hawaii, Department of Transportation. "Port Hawaii Handbook, 1988–1989." Honolulu, 1989.

State of Hawaii. *Hawaii Revised Statutes, 1991 Supplement.* Honolulu, 1991.

Stephan, John J. *Hawaii Under The Rising Sun: Japan's Plans for Conquest After Pearl Harbor.* Honolulu: Univ. Hawaii Press, 1984.

Stone, Scott C.S., *Honolulu: Heart of Hawaii.* Tulsa: Continental Heritage Press, 1983.

Tseng, Wen-Shing et al. *People and Cultures in Hawaii.* Honolulu: Univ. Hawaii School of Medicine, 1974.

Westervelt, W.D. *Myths and Legends of Hawaii.* Foreword by A. Grove Day. Honolulu: Mutual Publishing, 1987.

Worden, William L. *Cargoes: Matson's First Century in the Pacific.* Honolulu: Univ. Hawaii Press, 1981.

Index

Accreditation of Healthcare Organizations, 174, 177
Accreditation of Rehabilitation Facilities, 177
Adams, Alexander, 66
Adopt-A-Highway, 158
Adopt-A-School, 129
Adventist Health System-West, 178
AES, 153
Afghanistan, 98
AFL-CIO, 28
Africa, 38
African American, 67, 71, 75, 115
Agriculture, 18, 20–23, 27–29, 39, 49–52, 54–55, 57, 65, 71, 74, 77, 100, 144–145, 157
AIDS, 85, 99
Aiea, 177, 181
Aitutaki, 116
Ala Moana, 125, 147, 151, 153, 163, 166
Ala Wai, 83
Alakea, 146
Alaska, 54, 141
Alcoholism, 178
Alexander Young Hotel, 83
Alger, Horatio, 148
Algo-1 Plus, 183
All-America City Award, 144
All-American Auto Loans, 135
Allen, Mark, 102
Aloha Festival, 65
Aloha Program, 183
Aloha Stadium, 153
Aloha United Way, 65, 114, 129, 145, 161, 165
American Cancer Society, 115, 169, 175
American College of Trial Lawyers, 126
American Hawaii Cruises, 124
American Heart Association, 163, 175
American Indians, 71
American Lung Association, 175
American Samoa, 29, 71, 93, 116
Anchor Cove, 158
Aquaculture, 20, 27, 29, 39–40, 55, 95, 102
Aramaki, Carol, 11
Arctic, 30
Arizona, 35, 132, 141, 144
Arizona Memorial, 35
Armed Services Committee, 114
Arts, The, 9, 38, 51, 64–65, 79, 81–82, 85, 109, 115, 135, 145, 157–159, 161, 163, 166, 175
Asia, 27–29, 31–32, 38, 50, 64, 68–69, 71, 74, 78, 87, 90–91, 93–94, 98–100, 102, 104, 117, 132, 139
Associated Steel Workers, Ltd., 147
ATC, 120
Atlanta, 97
Atlantic, 66, 94, 97
ATM, 38, 57, 72, 125, 133, 135, 140–141, 167, 170, 176
Auckland, 129
Australia, 32, 65, 93, 98, 126, 159
Auto Club, 167
Ayeshire, 66
Azores, 66
Baldwin, D. D. , 54
Ball, Joe, 126
Ballard, Joseph, 132
Ballet, 161
Bancorp Hawaii, Inc., 132–133
Bangkok, 129, 140
Bank of America Hawaii, 10, 137, 140–141
Bankoh, 133
Barbers Point, 153
Barbour, Gregory, 11
Bass, Bill, 11
Bedford, 30
Belgium, 60

Beretania Street, 171, 180
Berg, Arthur, 134
Berger, Henri, 108
Bethlehem Shipyards, 35
Better Business Bureau, 114–115, 160
Bilingual Access Line, 92
Bird, Isabella, 61
Bird of Paradise, 48
Bishop, Charles, 134
Bishop Estate, 11, 80
Bishop Insurance of Hawaii, Inc., 134
Bishop Museum, 139, 145
Bishop Street, 65, 114, 137
Bishop Trust Co., 134
Black, E. E., 147
Black Friday, 168
Blonde Hotel, 82
Blood Institute, 175
Board of Education, 73
Boat Day, 34–35
Bobby Benson Center, 137, 178
Boeing, 128
Bora Bora, 46, 116
Borthwick, Mendel, 140
Boston, 30, 134
Boy Scouts of America, 161, 169
Brazil, 126
Brewer, C., 11, 49–50
Brigham Young University, 74
Brooke, Rupert, 61
Brown, William, 31
Brunei, 100
Brussels, 129
Buenos Aires, 129
Buick, 162
Building Industry Association of Hawaii, 115
Buote, Adam, 183
Business Action Center, 93
Buyers, J. W. A., 11, 50
Cadillac, 162
California, 16, 51, 53–54, 65, 118, 122, 126–127, 140–141, 144, 159, 169
California Institute of Technology, 97
Cameron, John, 108
Camp Timberline, 185
Campbell, Archibald, 66
Canton, 20, 31, 67, 82
Cape Verde, 66
Carey, David, 168–169
Caribbean, 68
Carlsmith Ball Wichman, et al. 126–127
Carroll, Don, 120
Castle & Cooke Properties, 34, 49, 54, 96, 120, 124, 144–145
Castle Medical Center, 178
Catholicism, 60, 184
Catton, Robert, 66
Caucasian, 66–67
Central America, 27, 53
Central Pacific Bank Properties, 160
Challenger Space Shuttle, 145
Chamber of Commerce of Hawaii, 2, 7, 10, 91, 95–96, 108, 114–115, 123, 160
Chaminade, Father William Joseph, 184
Chaminade University, 74, 184
Chelonia, 40
Chevron, 122
Chicago, 129
Chiddix, Jim , 120
China, 16, 21, 27–28, 30, 51–52, 65, 67, 69–70, 82, 98–99, 102, 135, 163
Chinatown, 135, 149, 174

Chinen, Bruce, 128
Ching, Rocky, 32
Chip & Wafer Office Automation, Inc., 160
Chong, Norman, 115
Choy, Allen, 11
Choy, Fong, 136
Christianity, 139, 184–185
Chu, Bertha, 125
Chu, George, 125
Chun, Mun On, 136
Cincinnati, 116
City Financial Tower, 153
Claudina, Emma, 34
Cobalt, 42
Coffee, 16, 22, 49, 51, 54, 139, 157
Coffees of Hawaii, 157
Cold War, 94
Coleman, James, 159
Coleridge, 87
College of Hawaii, 85, 127
Colony Surf Hotel, 167
Columbia Communications, 97
Columbia River, 122
Columbus Line, 124
Commercial Union Assurance Co. of London, 134
Commissioners of Agriculture, 51
Condominiums, 28, 39, 56, 85–86, 146–147, 153
Congress, 4, 98
Conrad, Joseph, 43
Constitution, 35, 48, 64, 83
Cook, Captain James A., 27–28, 47, 52–53
Cook Islands, 29, 116
Cooke, Amos Starr , 144
Coos Bay, 122
Cory Sause, 123
Craven, Dr. John P., 11, 38
Crown Lands, 48–49
Czarnecki, Gerald M., 10, 140–141
Davies, Theo H., 49
Dawdy, Robert L., 11
de Paula y Marin, Don Francisco, 53, 82, 85
Del Monte Corporation, 54
Demerath, Patrick, 11
Democratic Party, 49
Depression, The Great, 84, 108, 138
Des Moines, 116
DFS Hawaii, 164–165
Diamond Head, 31–32, 39, 56, 84–85, 137, 151, 167, 169, 184
Dickenson Street, 158
Dillingham Corp, 153
DMA Hawaii, 146
Dole, James Drummond, 54, 144
Dole, Sanford Ballard, 144
Dole Cannery Square, 145
Dole Food Company, 11, 54, 144–145
Dues Subsidy Program, The, 183
Eames, Alfred W., 54
East-West Bridge, 102
East-West Center, 11, 75–76, 98–99
Easter Island, 27
Eastern Europe, 94
Ebeye Islands, 122
Echo I, 75
Economic Development Corp. of Honolulu, 11, 90–92
Edge Act, 141
Edinburgh, 66
Education, 11, 21, 40, 49, 56, 64, 66, 73–75, 80–82, 85, 92–93, 95, 97–99, 102, 108, 115, 117, 121, 126–127, 129, 135, 139, 145, 148–151, 159–161, 163, 165, 169–171, 173–176, 180, 183–186
Ehrlich, Peter, 159

Embassy Suites, 146
Emperor Seamount, 46
Erosion, 33, 46–47
Eto, Linda, 160
Europe, 18, 67–69, 77, 87, 93–94, 100, 117, 159, 163,
  167, 180
Evers, Dale, 159
Ewa Plain, 137
Exclusive Economic Zone, 42
Faison, Lois, 10
Falls of Clyde, The, 123
Farrell, Andrew, 108
Farrington High, 129
Fassler, C. Richard, 11
Fennel, Eric, 181
Finance Factors Family, 136–137
First Hawaiian Bank, 134
First National Bank of Arizona, 132
FirstFed America, 132
Fletcher Pacific Construction Co., Ltd., 146
Fong, Hiram L., 136
Food Bank Drive, 137
Forbidden City, 135
Ford Island, 36
Ford Motor Company, 118–119
Foreign Trade Zone, 28, 32
Foreigners, 48–49, 67
Forestry, 55, 77
Fort Street, 20
Four Horsemen, 38
France, 75, 82, 127, 167, 184
Franzen, David, 134
Freitas, George E., 146
Freitas Hall, 184
French Revolution, 184
Front Street, 30, 158
Fuji, 67, 69, 71
Fujieki, Mika, 170–171
Fujieki, Raymond, 170–171
Gallup Poll, 121
Garcia, Walfrido, 159
Garibaldi, 122
GBC Boxes & Packaging, 125
Germany, 66–67, 134, 162–163
Giannini, Lawrence Mario, 140
Giant Killers, The, 184
Girl Scouts of America, 161, 169
Golden Rule, 166
Golf, 28, 38, 55–56, 68, 78–79, 128, 145, 151
Gomes, Henri, 184
Government Marketing Assistance Program, 92
Grand Cayman, 78
Grand Hyatt Wailea, 146
Grand Pacific Life Insurance, 136–137
Grant, Alexander, 115
Grant Thornton, 115
Great Aloha Run, 183
Great Britain, 28, 31, 48, 69
Great Hawaiian Relay, 161
Great Mahele, 48
Gross National Product, 99, 104
Gross State Product, 28, 68, 77
GTE, 11, 97
Guam, 78, 93, 100, 126–127, 132–133, 140, 146, 149
Guangdong, 67
Gulf War, The, 58, 76
H-1 Freeway, 91, 147
H-3 Freeway, 103, 147, 153
Hackfeld, Heinrich, 163
Haiku, 147
Haku Lei, 72
Halawa, 153, 171
Hale Pulama Mau, 174
Haleakala, 47, 59, 122
Haleiwa, 145, 158–159
Halekulani, 83
Hamakua, 66, 139
Hamakua Coffee Plantation, 139
Hanada, Howard, 115
Hanalei, 42, 51
Hang Seng Index, 65

Hartford Insurance, 138
Harvard, 54, 135, 139
Hastings, Barbara A., 11
Haumea, 46
Hawaii, Island of (the Big Island), 28–31, 34, 41, 43,
  46, 51–52, 54–55, 58, 60–61, 66, 96–97, 100, 104,
  123, 128, 135–136, 139, 146, 151, 158, 169, 181
Hawaii Authority, 41
Hawaii Business Roundtable, 92
Hawaii Capital Loan, 92
Hawaii Computer Training, 161
Hawaii Department of Transportation, 123
Hawaii Foodbank, 115
Hawaii Institute of Electronics, 95, 160
Hawaii International Billfish Tournament, 31, 79
Hawaii Kai, 177, 181
Hawaii Legislature, 37, 40, 95, 97
Hawaii Loa, 176, 186
Hawaii Maritime Center, 123
Hawaii National Bank, 135
Hawaii Nei, 109
Hawaii Ocean Science, 96
Hawaii Pacific Industries, 124
Hawaii Pacific University, 26, 32, 74, 91, 94, 100, 102,
  116, 124, 132–133, 138, 151, 186
Hawaii Society of Certified Public Accountants, 115
Hawaii Software Service Center, 96
Hawaii Special Olympics, 161, 163
Hawaii State Bar, 126
Hawaii State Capitol, 127
Hawaii State Dept. of Economic Development, 7, 41
Hawaii State Department of Education, 183
Hawaii State Library System, 74
Hawaii State Student Council, 73
Hawaii Statehood Bill, 55
Hawaii Stevedores, Inc., 124
Hawaii Sugar Planters, 11
Hawaii Tax, 114–115
Hawaii Tourist Bureau, 85
Hawaii Visitors Bureau, 11, 68, 86, 114, 117
Hawaiian Cement Co., 124
Hawaiian Dredging & Construction Company, 153
Hawaiian Green Sea Turtle, 40
Hawaiian Island Packing Company, 54
Hawaiian Marine Lines, 124
Hawaiian Open, 128–129
Hawaiian Pineapple Company, 144
Hawaiian Safe Deposit, 132
Hawaiian Trust Company, 133
Hawaiiana, 71–72
HBO, 120
Health Care Reform Task Force, 114
High Technology, 11, 91, 95, 105, 144
Hilo, 34, 52, 74, 127, 134
Hilton Hawaiian Village Tapa Tower, 146
Hitchcock, David Howard, 126
Hollywood, 84
Holualoa, 54
Honfed Bank, 140–141
Hong, Stanley, 11, 68
Hong Kong, 65, 78, 90, 97, 99–100, 126, 164
Honjo, 10
Honolulu Academy of Arts, 85, 135
Honolulu Cellular Telephone Company, 121
Honolulu City Council, 178
Honolulu City Hall, 127
Honolulu Community Theatre, 85
Honolulu Customs District, 28
Honolulu Harbor, 2, 31, 35–36, 137, 147
Honolulu International Airport, 103, 128–129, 153, 164
Honolulu Iron Works, 66
Honolulu Japanese Chamber of Commerce, 115
Honolulu Minority Business Development Center, 95
Honolulu Park Place, 147
Honolulu Rapid Transit, 85
Honolulu Symphony, 79, 85, 115, 145, 161, 163
Honolulu Towers, 147
Honolulu Zoo, 85
Hotel Ihilani Resort, 150–151
House of Cherishing Care, 174
Hualalai, 60

Hughes, Robert H., 11
Hula, 21, 79, 83, 92, 116
Hula Bowl, 79
Hulme, Kathryn, 61
Hulopoe Bay, 145
Humanitarian Award, 139
Hunnewell, James, 50
Hyatt Regency Kauai, 153
Hyatt Regency Waikoloa, 153
Hyun, Carrie, 11
IBM, 161
Ilikai, 147
Imin, Kanyaku, 69
Imperial Navy, 36
Imperial Plaza, 153
India, 102
Indian Ocean, 97
Indonesia, 32, 71, 100, 104
Inouye, Dan, 157
Inter-Island Steamship Company, 78
International Longshoremen, 28, 49, 78
Iolani Palace, 1, 23, 65, 71, 83, 116, 127, 180
Ironman Triathlon, 79, 102
Island Care, 179
Island Insurance Companies, 139
Islander Hotel, 168
Ivy League, 49
Iwilei, 144–145
Jackson, Arthur, 181
Jamaica, 54
James, Allan, 166
Japan, 21, 28, 30, 32, 35–36, 39, 56, 69–70, 76, 78,
  93–94, 98, 100, 102, 104, 115, 117, 126–127, 133,
  139, 150–151, 153, 159, 174–175, 184
Japan-Hawaii Cancer Study, 175
Japanese Benevolent Society, 174
Japanese Charity Hospital, 174
Japanese Cultural Center, 115
Japanese Home of Hawaii, 174
JCPenney, 166
Joesting, Edward, 105
Johnson, Lawrence M., 132
Johnson, Lyndon Baines, 75
Johnston Island, 42–43
Jones, James, 61
Jones, Peter Cushman, 132
Ka Lae, 26
Ka-iwi-o-Pele, 46
Kaanapali, 147
Kaena Point, 100
Kahala, 140–141
Kahiki, 18
Kahoolawe, 28, 58, 60
Kahului, 129, 147, 177
Kahului Airport, 129
Kai, 177, 181
Kailua, 54, 171, 178, 181
Kailua-Honokahau, 29
Kailua-Kona, 30–31, 40, 86, 128
Kaimuki, 39, 96, 171, 184
Kaimuki Technology Enterprise Center, 96
Kaiser, Henry J., 55, 182
Kaiser Permanente Hawaii Region, 55, 182–183
Kakaako, 171
Kalakaua, 36, 69, 83
Kalanianaole Highway, 153
Kalaupapa, 60–61
Kaleleonalani, 185
Kali, Marilyn E., 11
Kalihi, 125, 147
Kamaoa Windfarm, 151
Kamehameha Day Parade, 84
Kamehameha I, 21, 66, 134
Kamehameha III, 48, 73, 135
Kamehameha IV, 66
Kamehameha V, 66, 82
Kamohoalii, 46
Kamuela, 57
Kanemori, Merle, 11
Kaneohe, 181
Kapaa, 158

Kapalama, 174
Kapalua Bay Hotel, 146
Kapiolani, 85, 121, 151, 167, 169, 176
Kapiolani Community College, 151, 169, 176
Kapiolani Park, 85, 167
Kapolei, 56, 145
Kapuaiwa Grove, 19
Kato, Baron, 139
Kaua, 42
Kauai, Island of, 22, 28, 31, 46, 51–52, 58–59,
    128–129, 132, 134, 136, 146, 148, 153, 158, 169,
    177, 179
Kauai Village, 158
Kaunakakai, 19
Kawaihae, 31, 123
Kawano, Patrick, 157
Kawatachi, George, 160
Kawauchi, Virginia Hillis, 118
Kea Lani Hotel, 146
Keahole Airport, 128, 145
Keahole Point, 41
Keawaula, 100
Keck II, 75
Keiki Hula, 116
Kelley, Dr. Richard, 168–169
Kelley, Estelle, 168–169
Kemmerer, Wyoming, 166
Kewalo Basin, 29
Kidwell, John, 54
Kihei, 96, 147
Kilauea, 46, 177
King Kalakaua, 36, 69, 83
King Kalakaua Jubilee, 83
King Street, 135
Kobe, 140
Koele, 145
Kohala, 52, 135, 169
Kohala Coast, 169
Koloa, 52
Kona, 39, 51, 54, 127, 134, 145, 158, 181
Koolaus, 59
Korea, 28, 70, 93, 100, 127, 133
Krucky, Anton, 161
Kuakini Medical Center
Kualapuu, 157
Kuhn, Daniel, 157
Kumulipo, 43
Kwajalein, 122, 132
Lactawen Laa, 10
Laguna Beach, 159
Lahaina, 30, 52, 58–59, 82
Lai, Wallace Jun Duck, 148
Lanai, Island of, 28, 52–54, 60, 144–145, 181
Land Use, 40, 48, 50, 55, 57, 97, 126–127
Laos, 71
Latin America, 87, 93
Lee, Stephen R., 11
Levi Strauss Company, 166
Lewers, Robert, 83
Liberty House, 151, 163
Lihue, 129, 132, 177
Liliha, 171
London, 116, 134
London, Jack, 61
Long Beach, 123, 126–127, 159
Los Angeles, 90, 97, 100, 126–127, 129
Louis, Robert, 61, 66
Luke, Kan Jung, 135
Luna, Martin, 126
Lup Quon Pang, 136
Lurline, 34, 85–86
Maalaea, 29
MacDonald, Dr. Craig D., 11
Macdonald Hotel, 66
Macintyre, Donald, 66
Macintyre, Janet, 66
Madeira, 66
Magoon, Jack, 157
Mahalo Nui, 10, 136–137
Make-A-Wish Hawaii Foundation, 161
Makiki Christian Church, 139

Malaai Street, 125
Malama Ohana Skilled Nursing Facility, 182
Malay, 127
Malaysia, 27, 100, 104
Mandarin, 127
Manele Bay, 145
Manganese, 42
Manila, 140
Manoa, 51, 54, 74, 93, 96–97, 136
Manoa Innovation Center, 96
Manoa Valley, 54, 74
Marianas, 26, 116
Maritime Committee, 123
Marquesas Islands, 18, 26, 29
Marshall Islands, 93
Martin, William H., 11
Maryknoll High School, 66
Mason, Judith, 183
Master of Ballantrae, 61
Matson, William, 34
Matson Navigation Company, 11, 34, 85, 103, 122, 124
Matsonia, 34
Mau, K. S., 11
Maugham, Somerset, 61
Maui, Island of, 28–29, 46–47, 52, 54, 58–60, 82, 96,
    126, 129, 134, 136, 146–147, 158, 177, 179, 182
Maui Pineapple Company, 54
Mauna Kea, 46, 57, 60, 75, 79, 97
Mauna Lani Bay Hotel, 150–151
Mauna Lani Terrace, 151
Mauna Loa, 46, 60, 122
Mazatlan, 20
McCarran-Walter Act, 49
McCreary, Linda, 11
McDonnell Douglas, 128
McDonough, John, 126
McFadden, Mary, 166
McGee, Bobby, 167
McKinley High School, 139
Medicaid, 183
Meiji, Emperor, 69
Melville, Herman, 61
Mexico, 70, 94, 126–127, 141, 169
Michener, James A., 61
Michigan University Law School, 127
Micronesia, 93, 122–123
MidPac Lumber Company, Ltd., 148–149
Midway Island, 36, 132
Mikihana, 123
Mililani, 96, 120, 144–145, 177
Mililani Technology Park, 96, 145
Milnor, Guy, 181
Milnor Building, 181
Minerals Management, 42
Ming, 135
Mining, 42–43, 166
Minister of Foreign Affairs, 66
Minolta Corporation, 160
Missionaries, 51–52, 66, 144
Mitsui Corporation, 39
Moana Hotel, 34, 83, 150–151
Moanalua Gardens, 66
Moanalua Medical Center, 146, 182–183
Moiliili, 170
Molokai, Island of, 19, 28, 54, 60, 126, 133, 157, 179
Montague, Charles, 132
Montessori, 184
Moorea, 116
Morihara, Roy, 115
Mormon Church, 71
Morocca, 184
Mount Olomana, 178
Mukai, Frank, 126
Mukai, Stan, 126
Murray, Tony, 126
Na Pali Coast, 59
Namakaokahai, 46
Nani Mau Garden, 156
NAPA Hawaiian Warehouse, 162
Napoleon, 184
National Advisory Committee, 135

National Bank, 132, 135
National Cable Television, 120
National Foundation Fight Against Illiteracy, 160
National Mortgage, Ltd., 139
Native Hawaiian Health Act, 81
Natural Energy Laboratory, 41
Natural Resources, 37, 56
Nature Conservancy of Hawaii, 145, 163
Nauru Tower, 146
Navarro, 82
Navatek, 39
Nawiliwili, 31
Neill, John, 66
Nevada, 118, 141
New Fair Dairy, 139
New Mexico, 141, 169
New York, 97, 116, 141, 180
New York Stock Exchange, 97
New Zealand, 27, 29, 98, 100, 146
Nicklaus, Jack, 145
Niihau, 28, 59, 161
Nimitz Highway, 118, 124
Nissan, 124
Norfolk Island, 145
North American Trade Agreement, 94
Northwestern University Law School, 127
Nukualofa, 116
Nuuanu, 177
Oahu, Island of, 20–21, 28–29, 31–32, 36, 51–52, 54,
    56, 58–59, 64, 66, 74, 82–84, 96, 100, 102–103, 114,
    118, 120–121, 123–124, 128–129, 133, 135–137,
    144–148, 150, 158–159, 177–179, 181–182, 184,
    186
Oahu Hotel, 82
Observatories, 75
Ocean Resources Management Act, 37
Oceanic Cable, 120
Office of Hawaiian Affairs, 115
Ogata, Randy, 121
Okayama-ken, 139
Okinawa, 69
Oksenberg, Michel, 11, 98
Olina Resort, 151
Ong, William, 119
Onizuka, Ellison, 145
OPEC, 75
Oregon, 122, 141, 159
Organic Act, 70
Osaka, 129
Oshio, Mark S., 162
Outrigger Hotels Hawaii, 168–169
Pacific Basin Economic Council, 91
Pacific Business Center, 93
Pacific Century, 94, 104, 109, 126
Pacific Concrete, 7
Pacific Construction Company, 146
Pacific Insurance Company, Ltd., 136–138
Pacific International Center, 91
Pacific Islanders, 28, 71
Pacific Lumber Company, 149
Pacific Ocean, 26, 96–97, 116–117, 167
Pacific Region Institute, 114
Pacific Rim Productions, Ltd., 10, 116–117
Pacific Trade Center, 146
Pakistan, 71
Pali Gardens, 178
Pan Pacific Plaza, 151
Pan-Pacific Construction, Inc., 150–151
Panama Canal, 31
Papeete, 116
Pasco, 128
Pau Rider, 84
Pauahi Tower, 146
Peace Pagoda, 139
Pearl City, 121
Pearl Harbor, 35–37, 53–55, 84, 124, 137, 147, 153
Pearl Ridge Square, 151
Pele, 46–47
Pepeekeo, 122
Perry, James R., 153
Philippines, The, 53, 70–71, 93–94, 100

Philpotts, Clarence G., 134
Piianaia, Ilima A., 11
Pineapple, 16, 18, 28, 49–51, 53–54, 57, 60, 68, 71, 78, 82, 144–145, 148
Pitre, John, 159
Plantation Hale, 169
Point Harbor, 32, 124
Pokai, 27
Polynesia, 18, 20, 22, 26–29, 43, 47, 52, 71, 96
Port of Honolulu, 122
Portland, 159
Portugal, 21, 50, 66–67, 127
Powers, Gary, 75
Prince Kuhio Lobby, 169
Princess Bernice Pauahi, 134
Princess Kaiulani, 66
Project Delphis, 169
Propeller Club of Honolulu, 123
Puerto Rico, 28, 67, 166
Puna, 104
Punahou School, 169
Qing Paintings, 135
Queen Emma Liliuokalani, 34, 179, 185
Rama IV Road, 65
Ramsour, Dr. David L., 11, 94
Rarotonga, 116
Reciprocity Treaty, 36, 50–51, 53–54, 66–67
Recycle Hawaii, 158
Red Cross, 115, 135
Reef Hotel, 168
Regency Waikiki, 147
Regimental Combat Team, 69
Rehabilitation Hospital of the Pacific, 177
Retail Merchants of Hawaii, 91, 115
Reuters, 105
Ritz-Carlton Kapalua, 153
Robinson, Robert B., 7, 10
Rome, 116
Ronald McDonald House, 169, 185
Rotary, 161
Royal Hawaiian Agricultural Society, 52
Royal Kunia, 145
Rue St. Honoré, 65
Rural Districts, 55, 99, 186
S. C. Builders Inc., 162
S. C. Ranch Co., 162
S. S. Independence, 35
S. S. Wilhelmina, 34, 85
Saint Andrew's Priory, 185
Saipan, 78, 116, 126–127, 132
Sakamoto, Gordon, 11
Salem, 30
Samsing, 52
Samuel Northrup Castle, 144
San Antonio, 184
San Francisco, 26, 53, 82, 85, 90, 97, 100, 102, 128–129, 139–140, 164
Sand Island, 31, 102–103, 124
Sandalwood Mountains, 52, 67
Sandwich Islands, 61
Sans Souci, 83
Sause, Paul, 122–123
Sause Brothers, Inc., 122–123
Scandinavia, 67
Schuman, Dutch, 162
Schuman Carriage, 162
Scotland, 61, 66, 83
Scott, Archibald, 66
Sea Institute, 11, 38
Seabees, 149
Sears Roebuck, 125
Seaside Avenue, 168
Seaside Hotel, 83, 168
Security Pacific Corporation, 141
Sellon, Priscilla Lydia, 185
Serikawa, Garrett, 115
Seville, 158–159, 162
Shan, Tan Heung, 52, 67
Sheraton Kauai, 146
Sheraton Moana Surfrider Hotel, 150
Shimizu Construction, 153

Singapore, 26, 32, 78, 90, 100, 104
Small Business Administration, 95
Small Business Center, 95
Smith, W. Ross, 11
Society Islands, 18, 51, 116
Sonoda, Bob, 161
South America, 27, 38, 126
South Pacific Commission, 116
South Point, 26
South Seas, 18, 34, 59, 87
Southeast Asia, 28, 38, 71, 94
Southern Methodist University, 184
Southern Oregon Marine, 122
Soviet Union, 38, 94
Spain, 127, 159, 184
Spanish-American War, 53, 70
Special Olympics, 145, 161, 163
Spruce Goose, 123
Sri Lanka, 102
St. Andrew, 185
St. Francis Medical Center, 146
St. Louis School, 184
St. Mary, 184
Stainback, Ingram M., 86
Stanford University, 127
Star Markets, 170–171
State Bar of California, 126
State Department of Business, 41, 90, 92
State Legislature, 55, 96–97, 123
State Senate, 55
Statehood, 22–23, 32, 54–56, 86, 114, 132, 134, 137–138, 161
Steel, 147–148
Stephenson, H. Howard, 132
Stewart, Janet, 159
Straub, Dr. George, 180
Straub Clinic & Hospital, 180–181
Styer, Jennifer, 11
Subaru, 162
Sugar, 11, 18, 21, 28, 34, 36, 49–54, 66, 68, 71, 78, 129, 134
Suh, Sukil, 11
Surfrider Foundation, 158
Sydney, 97
Tabora, Roy, 159
Tahiti, 18, 29, 46, 71, 116
Taiwan, 32, 93, 99–100, 127
Tanigawa, Patrick, 115
Teamsters, 28
Technology, 11, 27, 42, 50, 53, 91–92, 95–96, 100, 102, 105, 120–121, 144–145, 150, 160–161, 174, 176, 181
Telecommunications, 90, 96–97, 99–100, 108
Tennis, 28, 68, 79, 151, 167
Texas, 141, 169, 184
Thailand, 65, 100, 104
Thompson, Myron, 11, 80
Thurston, Lorrin Andrews, 84
Tillamook Bay, 122
Tin Lizzy, 162
Togami, Takao, 147
Tokioka, Masayuki, 139
Tokyo, 78, 90, 97, 129, 140
Tokyu Group, 150–151
Tonga, 29, 116
Toronto, 164
Toyota, 146
Trade Finance Program, 93
Transportation Department, 31–32, 123
Travel-Holiday Award, 167
Treaty of Reciprocity, 36, 50–51, 53–54, 66–67
Triple Crown of Surfing, 158
Tripler Hospital, 147
Tropical USA Rent-A-Car, 118
TRW, 97
Twelfth Federal Reserve District, 135
Ueda, Ester, 11
Ueoka, Paul, 126
United Airlines, 128–129
United Nations, 27
United States Coast Guard, 123

United States Department of Agriculture, 29, 51
United States Department of Business, 11, 41, 90, 92
United States Department of Education, 73, 80, 115, 183
United States Department of Labor, 76
United States Department of Land, 56
United States Department of Transportation, 123
United States Department of Transportation, 31, 123
United States Military, 22, 28, 34–36, 53, 58–60, 69, 76, 85, 94, 102, 114, 123–124, 149, 161, 174, 184
United States Senate, 28, 55
United States Supreme Court, 138
United Way, 65, 114, 129, 145, 161, 165–166
University of Dayton, 184
University of Hawaii, 11, 74–75, 81, 85, 93, 95, 97, 99, 135, 139, 149, 174–176
University of Honolulu, 74, 184
USS Birmingham, 34–35
Uyehara, Letitia N., 11
Varney Airlines, 128
Via Veneto, 65
Vietnam, 71, 94, 102
Wahiawa, 54, 136, 144, 158
Wai Momi, 35
Waialae Shopping Center, 171
Waialeale, 122
Waianae, 59, 151, 185
Waianae Sewage Treatment Plant, 151
Waihee, John, 108
Waihee, Lynn, 161
Waikaloa, 43
Waikele, 145
Waikiki, 20, 34, 37, 56, 61, 83–85, 105, 114, 117, 120, 139, 147, 158, 164–165, 167–169
Waikiki Aquarium, 85
Wailua Falls, 22
Wailuku, 127
Waimalu, 147
Waimanalo, 102
Waimea, 21, 52
Waimea Falls Park, 21
Waipahu, 128, 169
Waipio Acres, 136–137
Waipio Valley, 65
Wall Street, 153
Warm-Hearted Bankers, 135
Warren Commission, 126
Warren House, 82
Washington, 50, 75, 91, 126–127, 141
Waterfront Plaza, 121, 147
Waterfront Row Kona, 158
Western Association of Schools, 186
Western Independent Bankers, 135
Weston, David M., 52
Whalers Village, 158
Whaling Wall, 159
White, Roger, 181
Wiers, Jack, 11
Williams College, 127
Wilson, John H., 86
Windward Mall, 151
Windward Oahu Twin Viaducts, 147
Wong Tze-Chun, 52
World Bank, 27
World War I, 114
World War II, 49, 51, 54, 58, 69, 71, 85, 140, 144, 149, 174, 181
Wright, Lee, 166
Wurzburg, 180
Wyland Galleries Hawaii, 158–159
Wyllie, Robert C., 66
Yadao, Elisa, 11
Yee, Clifford H. N., 136
Yokohama, 140
Young, Alexander, 83
Zakahi, Janet, 11
Zobrist, Ester, 126
Zobrist, Duane, 126
Zurich, 116